Welcome to Canada

Welcome to Canada

David Carpenter

The Porcupine's Quill

Library and Archives Canada Cataloguing in Publication

Carpenter, David, 1941–
    Welcome to Canada / by David Carpenter.

ISBN 978-0-88984-320-2

    I. Title.

PS8555.A76158W45 2009   C813'.54   C2009-903844-7

Copyright © David Carpenter, 2009.
1   2   3   •   11   10   09

Published by The Porcupine's Quill, 68 Main Street, PO Box 160,
Erin, Ontario NOB 1TO. http://porcupinesquill.ca

Readied for the Press by Doris Cowan.

The cover image is after an etching by George Raab entitled 'Lone Tree',
details from which also appear on pages two and thirteen.
http://www.georgeraab.com

All rights reserved. No reproduction without prior written permission of the
publisher except brief passages in reviews. Requests for photocopying or other
reprographic copying must be directed to Access Copyright.

Represented in Canada by the Literary Press Group.
Trade orders are available from University of Toronto Press.

We acknowledge the support of the Ontario Arts Council and the Canada Council
for the Arts for our publishing program. The financial support of the Government
of Canada through the Book Publishing Industry Development Program is also
gratefully acknowledged. Thanks, also, to the Government of Ontario through the
Ontario Media Development Corporation's Ontario Book Initiative.

Canadä

ONTARIO ARTS COUNCIL
CONSEIL DES ARTS DE L'ONTARIO

Canada Council   Conseil des Arts
for the Arts   du Canada

LUTHER COLLEGE LIBRARY
University of Regina

For Bob, Len and Warren,
for Ebie and Pit, for Linda and Nash,
for all those friends who spend time willingly in canoes.

Table of Contents

You Are Now Entering Carpenter Country

Right from the beginning of his fiction-writing career, David Carpenter has been a master of voice and character. Those plucky Jewish footballers in 'Protection', his first published story, have stayed with me ever since I first made their acquaintance more than twenty-five years ago. Theirs was a world I knew virtually nothing about at the time, yet their voices in the story were so vigorous, so pugilistically and poetically authentic, that I believed in them wholeheartedly and wished that I could be welcomed among them, like the story's narrator, Drew. I was just beginning my own experiments with fiction writing at the time (under the extraordinarily patient guidance of one D.C. Carpenter), and I remember reading that story over and over again, trying to understand the trick of how he brought those boys so vibrantly to life in such a short space.

I never did entirely figure out Carpenter's secret, though I knew it had something to do with his remarkable memory for accents, dialects and colloquial turns of phrase. As I've read his many works of fiction in subsequent years, I have never ceased to be amazed at his talent for rendering voices onto the page. His characters don't simply speak; they pronounce themselves into being. He is preternaturally attuned to the poetry of the vernacular and the extraordinary variety of Canadian English, and he is able to place each of his characters in their own particular spots on that lavish linguistic spectrum, so that every phrase they speak contains a compendium of information about where they come from, what they want out of life, their successes and failures. To render dialect in this manner, without it becoming ironic or distracting – without losing the reader's empathy for the characters – is an extremely difficult thing to do. David Carpenter is among that rare company of writers who can seemingly effortlessly transform a few black marks on a page into vital, quirky, utterly memorable people who live on in readers' memories just like the most interesting of their flesh-and-blood counterparts sometimes do. This ability is enough to inspire a twinge of jealousy in even the most saintly of fellow scribes.

I suppose on a fundamental level, David Carpenter's secret is simply that he loves meeting people and he takes great pleasure in learning about lives that are different from his own. He is the rarest type of raconteur: he actually does more listening than talking when he finds himself (as he so often does) in a social situation, and he knows how to encourage the best stories out of the many people he meets. A storytelling enabler, one might call him. A catalyst of volubility. His genuine fascination with other people's points of view is infectious; it empowers people to believe that even their own narratives are worth sharing. And this sensibility is also abundantly visible in the empathy he shows for his characters, even the meanest among them. He is fundamentally a sociable writer, entirely different from the garret-bound recluses and the celebrity-seeking egomaniacs who are much more common in the trade. His stories are conversations with the world, wonderfully vivid attempts to coax us all into the transformative experience of actually listening to one another. In an age that is moving further and further toward the politics of divisiveness and the isolation of individuals, we need Carpenter's kind of sociable fiction more than ever: fiction that reaches out to readers, welcomes us in, and shows us how closely we are connected to those around us.

No one could mistake Carpenterian sociability for mere chit-chat or neighbourly banter, however. His vision of human interactions is fundamentally ethical and political in nature, and this is partly because his work is so finely attuned to nuances of character. Sociability in his fiction extends across the boundaries of class and age and cultural background, so that each story becomes an unstable meeting-place, a zone of unaccustomed interaction. This is also the source of so much drama in his writing. He brings together people from social strata that are usually separated, and he explores what happens when those social boundaries disappear and people are forced, by circumstances, to get to know each other. Thus, in the title story of this volume, he presents us with a rich American tourist awkwardly befriending his Native fishing guide, and in 'Meeting Cute at the Anger Motel' he portrays an unlikely meeting between a middle-class couple and a pair of prodigal drifters. Nearly every story in this collection centres on similarly surprising interactions. In 'The Snow Fence' there is the unusual relationship between the Cree Muskwa family and the narrator's white middle-class family, and in 'Luce' the summer cottage provides a kind of social experiment in which Drew interacts with the tony Bothwell crowd as well as the working-class

Bullmer boys and the Aboriginal fisherman Amos Whitehawk. Sometimes the result of such interactions is comic, but there is always a sense of incipient danger too, because the stakes are magnified in situations like this, where different worlds bump against each other. The friction of such contact breaks open people's lives a little, and sometimes frees them from the bounds they had become accustomed to, but this possibility is always attended by risk and pain as well. And these stories suggest that one of the only reliable solaces for such pain is the company of one another.

Such is the nature of Carpenter's Canada. It's a place where boundaries gradually (or suddenly) break down, until people who have very little in common end up depending on one another for their survival. It's a land of sweet, charming losers and uptight, pitiable winners, a place where adults have no more answers than children do, and where people often play roles in metaphysical struggles far beyond their immediate understanding. In many respects it is a roiling cauldron of contradictions, threatening to boil over into mutiny or anarchy or violent oppression. But something – some tenuous thread – pulls in the other direction, toward a generalized community feeling, a sense that differences need not divide people but might instead provide an opportunity for them to learn from each other. *We've got ourselves into something of a mess here, each story seems to say. Now how are we going to get ourselves out?* 'We' is the operative word in Carpenter country, and not the royal we, either. We as in welcome.

Wilderness is also a crucial part of Carpenter's vision. One might say that the sociability of his fiction extends beyond the human sphere and into the natural world as well, inviting us to examine more deeply the ways in which we are all connected to the ecosystems that surround and support us. The animals in these stories – a mythically huge buck called Appletree, a behemoth northern pike named Adolph, the Coca-Cola-sipping bears of 'The Snow Fence' – are as important and as complexly drawn as their human counterparts, and by their silent presence they raise powerful questions about what humans are doing to the world. Humans are obsessive boundary-makers in these stories, not only drawing lines of social hierarchy among themselves but also repeatedly marking a dividing line between 'civilization' and wilderness, such as the flimsy snow fence that is erected to separate the bears from the tourists in the national park. Animals live by entirely different rules, and often they suffer for crossing human boundaries that make no sense to them, boundaries that exist only to bolster a particular power relationship that legitimizes human

11

exploitation of the earth. However, there are a few human characters in these stories, such as Flora in 'The Ketzer' and Delphine Muskwa in 'The Snow Fence', who recognize that the natural world is not a savage wilderness to be plundered or walled out, but is in fact the dwindling repository of a particular kind of nonhuman wisdom that will some day be needed if we are to have any chance of saving the world from ourselves.

And that is what these stories are ultimately about: the small but lingering possibility of redemption for this tragically messed-up world and its remarkably flawed inhabitants. Carpenter doesn't harbour illusions about the redemptive capacity of his characters, or of the human species in general, but at the same time he refuses to give in to despair or cynicism or empty self-absorption. His stories are beautifully honed acts of generosity. Reading each one is like happening upon an unexpected gift. We return from Carpenter country with a new appreciation for the people and creatures of our own everyday countries, especially the ones we have all too often ignored.

— WARREN CARIOU
Research Chair and Director
Creative Writing and Oral Culture
University of Manitoba

Stories

New & Selected

✩ Welcome to Canada

ONE

At the Amarillo Outdoor Recreation Show a man could choose from over two hundred booths advertising the conquests of the sporting life. He could mill around with thousands of other outdoorsmen on both levels of the Mercantile Pavilion, dreaming and gawking at the spectacle of supersized motor boats, sixty-foot trailers, sonar devices for the location of fish at any depth or coordinate in the lake, all-terrain vehicles built for crashing through the canebrakes in search of big bucks. Aspiring hunters could ogle a wide array of white-tailed deer heads, cougar skins, stuffed razorbacks, or posters that featured dead grizzlies fondled from behind by the men who had brought them down. Anglers might gravitate to the colourful panels of fishing lodges nestled among the pristine forests of the north. A number of posters featured men hefting great northerns and lake trout so big that it was all they could do just to grimace for the camera. And the names, just listen to the names: Winnipeg River, Reindeer Lake, Athapapuskow, Red Earth Creek, Weyakwin, Cree Lake, Lac la Plonge.

A big man in his fifties wearing an elegant white suit was gazing at one of these posters. The Mercantile Pavilion, which he had entered so eagerly, was a glorified Quonset with air conditioning. It was surrounded by strip malls in all directions, a suburb withering in a late April drought. The man had forgotten the milling crowds; he had forgotten entirely where he was. He had become a sleepwalker in a magnetic field, and he was wandering right into the poster: a sumptuous lodge made of logs the colour of dark honey and a green roof surrounded by spruce trees in the background and a calm blue lake with a big wharf and a floatplane and not one single person in sight. He could hear the cool wind blowing through the trees and the wolves howling a lullaby.

'Nice, eh?'

The man blinked, the song of the wolves faded, and he was staring at a woman so blonde, so nordically blonde, with the pale ice-blue eyes and the pale complexion that, as his daddy would have said, *no way that blonde come outa no bottle.*

'Yes'm,' he said. 'Real nice.'

'Seven-hour flight,' she said.

'You must be joshin me.'

'No,' she said. 'One hour Amarillo to Denver –'

'Ah'm from Dallas.'

'Well then,' said she. 'Three hours Dallas to Calgary, one hour Calgary to Saskatoon, one hour to Points North, and one more hour to Medicine Lake. That's six hours' flying time.'

He wagged his hand at the poster. 'You live up there?'

'In the summer I do,' she said with a faint smile.

'Yawl get a big ol jet plane up to Medicine Lake?'

'To Calgary,' she said. 'Then a smaller jet to Saskatoon, and an even smaller jet to Points North, that's just a big airstrip in the forest, then you take a Beaver to our place.'

'Take a beaver?'

'Sometimes a Twin Otter.'

A thousand lovely young women could say that sentence, *Sometimes a Twin Otter,* and all it would sound like was information. But this woman made it sound like love in the bridal suite.

'Nice threads,' she said.

'Why thank you, ma'am.'

'I like a man who can wear a good suit.'

He looked down at his own finery, a white summer suit of raw silk that reminded him of plantations and wealthy colonels and old-fashioned movies. Since his troubles of the past year, he wore this suit on business trips just to feel lucky.

'What's your name?' she said.

'Lester.'

'Well, Lester, by the middle of June you and your wife and family could be up there at the lodge hauling in northern pike four feet long.'

'Don't think so,' he said.

'Why would that be?'

My, but this little girl was persistent.

'Ah don't think so because ah'm wudjacall, ah am one of the newly sangle.'

'Newly sangle?'

'Waff and me, we recently parted company.'

'Sorry to hear that, Lester.'

'Oh, it was bound to happen,' he said, and allowed a deep-ranging sadness to drift into his voice. 'A man has to mand the shop, make his bundle. The waff, she gets to feelin neglected. Currs to me some of us aren't right suited to the married state.'

She did not reply to his analysis. Her face was a mask. Perhaps she too was divorced. She looked to be thirty-five or forty, a fine fryer whatever her age. He squinted at her left hand as she picked through some information on top of her desk and a fountain of blonde hair tumbled off her shoulders. She was not wearing a wedding ring.

'We's a gabbin so friendly I plumb forgot to ask yer name.'

She smiled, lowered her gaze, said, 'Astrid,' and continued to sort through her brochures.

Perhaps Lester was still a captive of that hypnotic state that had drawn him up into the fishing poster. He seemed to swallow Astrid's name, and it tailed down his gullet like an albino salmon and spawned and multiplied and coursed through every vein in his body. *Astrid. Astrid. Astrid. Astrid times Astrid to the seventh power.*

'You a fisherman, Lester?'

'Oh, you bet.'

'What kind of fishing do you like to do?'

'Oh, I've caught my share of bluegill and crappie. Crappie's hard to beat for the fryin pan. Sit under a tree with the cooler and wait for them little critters to bite. Yawl could pass a fine day that way.'

'Ever gone out for anything real big?' she said.

He knew that note. She was trying to get him to rise to the occasion.

'Oh, I've caught me a big ol bass or two.'

'Lester, I mean *big.*'

'Wudja mean *big*?'

'Ever hauled in a forty-pound laker?'

'No'm, but wunst ah caught me a shark off Port Aransas. Musta ben that long. It was just a bitty shark but it put up a hell of a tussle.'

'Sounds like a dogfish to me.'

She opened a brochure and spread it out on the counter in front of him. There was a picture of Astrid in a bathing suit. She was holding a gut-hung grey hog of a fish with a big ugly head.

'Forty-four pounds,' she said. 'Took me an hour to haul it in.'

Lester whistled. 'That there is some heckofa fish.'

She showed him some other photos, as though his shark were of no more significance than a crawdad, as though his fishing experiences in Texas and Louisiana were child's play. But Astrid's photos did not lie. Fish after fish big enough to tow a skiff. Great northerns as big as barracuda.

'Who owns this outfit?' he said.

'Nor-Cor,' she said. 'A man named Thor.' She smiled at him again. 'Thor of Nor-Cor.'

She had a funny way of talking, pronouncing her Rs as though they were somehow important beyond anyone's reckoning. He tried to imitate her voice.

'Tho-werr of No-werr Co-werr?'

'That's the man,' she said.

Lester leaned forward and thumbed back to the first picture, the one of Astrid in her bathing suit with the huge lake trout. Lester's body was a school of minnows singing her name in high frequency.

'You thank that ah could catch me a few of them big ones? Them great northerns and such?'

Her nose was less than one foot away from his.

She said, 'One way to find out, Lester.'

Nearly four months later, when he clambered out of the Twin Otter, Lester Babcock was wearing a brand new camouflage suit with matching hat. He was the last man out of the plane, so he had to wait, and he gazed at the anglers as they clomped down the plank to the pier. There was a group of people from the lodge to greet them and take their baggage, but Astrid was nowhere in sight.

No one else was wearing camouflage.

One fellow on the pier caught Lester's attention, an Indian man. He stood apart from the crew, a big fellow perhaps in his fifties, a man as tall as Lester himself, but bulkier. He looked like he could carry the plane up to Medicine Lodge and empty its contents into the lobby. Lester made his way among the other anglers toward the Indian.

'Heidi,' he said, holding out his hand. 'Ah'm Lester Babcock.'

They shook hands. For such a big man with such a large hand, the man's grip was very gentle.

'Nass spread ygot here. Real quat. Makes a city boy grain with envy.'

The Indian nodded but he looked confused. Perhaps he spoke

another language, French or something like that. Lester had heard that
they spoke a lot of French up in Canada.

A young man hauled Lester's luggage up to his unit. It was a nice clean
woodsy version of a motel room. The walls, the ceiling, the furniture,
everything was done in knotty pine, and mounted here and there was an
assortment of caribou antlers, leather beadwork and framed pictures of
native art.

'Say, young feller.'

The kid paused by the door on his way back to the pier. He looked
like a college boy.

'Ah'm lookin for Astrid.'

The young man just looked at him.

'You never heard tell of Astrid?' he said. 'Blonde? Bowt thirty-five,
forty? Blue eyes?'

The young man seemed at a loss for words.

'Young feller, do you spake Ainglish?'

'I've only been up here for a few days,' he said. 'I haven't met any
Astrid.'

When the young man had left, Lester sat on the bed and wondered
what he had gotten himself into. He was some place nearer to the North
Pole than Dallas. It was well on into the evening and the darkness was
only beginning to fall. What kind of a place is it with hardly any
nighttime? Lester sighed. He could feel the full weight of his travels. He'd
been up since four in the morning to be at the Dallas Airport by six. He'd
waited a long time in the Calgary airport before he could board the plane
for Saskatoon. Then a small noisy jet had puddlejumped from Prince
Albert and La Ronge and Points North all through the hot afternoon. The
vision that had sustained him all the way from Dallas to the Twin Otter
was Astrid's pale blue eyes and her faint little smile and her heavy mane of
blonde hair.

'So,' he said to his favourite white suit hanging in the closet. 'Heidi,
mister. Welcome to Canada.'

TWO

Someone was banging on his door. Someone was also banging on his hangover. Lester asked his hangover real nice to move over so's he could go back to sleep. *You cain't sleep no more, Lester, you got to answer the door.* Lester remembered that he was in Canada and that he was stuck up in the wild north with a bunch of Frenchmen and Indians, for all of which he had paid five thousand dollars, not including the plane fare. He swore at his hangover and told it to get its *sorry ass outen the way.* He waded through pain to the door and squinted at the morning light let in by a man wearing a tractor cap. He said his name was Joe Arsenault, and he was the camp manager.

'Mr Babcock,' he said with a smile, 'you do remember me, don't you?'

Lester did not remember the man.

'At the bar last night? You were asking me if you could have the big guy.'

Lester swayed in the doorway and wondered if he was going to faint.

'Ah axed you for ... for ... the big guy?'

'Yes,' said Arsenault. 'For your guide today. His name is Norbert Lachance. He'll be waiting in the lobby in one hour. You might want to hustle, eh? The weather waits for no man.'

Lester's hangover said something uncharitable to the fellow in the tractor cap, something about what the weather could do with itself, but it seemed to come out strained and garbled. Lester thought maybe he did remember Joe Arsenault after all.

'Ah'm real sorry,' said Lester. 'Feel like ma whalebarrow done tumped over in the night. Mussof fallen outa bed or somethin. Be rat over.'

Joe Arsenault seemed to be an understanding man. Perhaps he was a drinking man himself. And perhaps he had realized in the bar last night that Lester was a kindred spirit. The fellow continued to stare at Lester with a sympathetic look on his face. These Canadians were not a talkative lot.

Arsenault joined Lester for part of the breakfast hour. He talked a great deal about the fish in Medicine Lake. The breakfast was surprisingly good, as good as any morning meal could be without ham, biscuits, red-eyed gravy, and grits and such. By the time he'd slupped down his last cup of coffee, Lester was surprised to discover how keen he was to go fishing. The fishing would be his reward for beating down a mean hangover. He rose from the breakfast table. It was time for action. It was time for his brand new longjohns and camouflage suit. It was time to kick some northern butt.

'No-werr-therrn butt,' he said out loud.

Lester opened the door of his cabin. He stood at the doorway and looked out. The air was chilly. A light wind stirred up the water in smooth waves, and a quiet he had never known enveloped the lake. There were little noises, the chatter of squirrels and whiskyjacks, the smooth humming of a big Honda outboard, and something going on behind Lester. A regular rhythm like someone breathing. He looked back into his room. It was his white suit, swaying on its hanger in the closet as though waiting for Astrid to appear. He clapped a big hand over his eyes and wondered for the briefest moment at his own vanity.

The big Indian fellow, Norbert Lachance, was waiting on the pier. He seemed unnaturally quiet, and Lester wondered once again if he spoke any English. He helped Lester into his fishing duds, a heavy rubberized pair of rain pants with thick suspenders, and a lightweight weatherproof jacket that had northern survival written all over it.

'Yawl got a life jacket for me?' he said to Norbert.

'Don't need one,' said an elderly gent beside him.

The man was wearing a Tilley hat with at least a dozen Master Angler pins from other fishing lodges.

'How come?'

The angler smiled at Lester.

'You go overboard in water this cold, bub, you won't last five minutes.'

Other anglers were zipping up and gabbing merrily on the pier. From what Lester had been told, they had come from all over North America and even Europe. They all roared away together in a loose armada of seven boats, and as they sped out into the lake, the boats peeled off one by one into their separate branches of fishable water. In a matter of fifteen or twenty minutes, as the small rocky islands sped past, Lester and Norbert were all alone on Medicine Lake.

The wind came up. The waves curled quickly into whitecaps, and the guide turned the boat into a cove. He handed Lester a large spinning rod.

'Try over dere,' he said.

Lester cast a yellow spoon into a stretch of pale turquoise water, let his spoon sink, counted to ten, and began his retrieve. In seconds he was fast to a fish. It made some short runs and as soon as it came near the boat it began to thrash more and more frantically. A large fish, Lester could see, about as large as the shark he took off the Texas coast, but this fish seemed to be livelier in the cold water.

'By God, Norbert, this here's like shootin fish in a barrel, wouldn't you say?'

Norbert didn't say anything. He corralled the fish in a big longhandled net and hauled it up to the side of the boat. He grabbed what looked to be a long-handled pair of pliers and began to extract the hook on Lester's spoon. There was a tremendous *whump* and splash, and Norbert grunted. He held up his hand. The great fish had vanished. Norbert's hand was bleeding. It started to rain.

Lester ate supper by himself at the table assigned to him. He was wearing his white suit. He'd had a Maker's Mark or two in his room, so it didn't matter if he looked out of place. If people up here didn't recognize some class when they saw it, well, hell with em. But he was tired of eating all by himself when other folks got to eat with their friends and families. He kept noticing an attractive young couple over by the window, perhaps in their thirties, speaking in little whispers, as though they were engaged in a discussion about national security. The woman had her hair up and legs as long as a pool cue. Lester rose from his table and carried his coffee over towards them.

'You young folks mand if an old guy joins ye?'

They looked up at him as impassive and cool as Astrid had done in her brief conversation with Lester in Amarillo. The man nodded and beckoned towards an empty chair.

'Much obliged,' said Lester. 'A mite lonely over there all by m'seff.'

'How did you do out there in that weather?' said the man.

'Reckon the fish made fools of us all today.'

The young couple had a different story to tell. They had gone deep for lake trout and taken some good ones before the rain set in. They sounded very knowledgeable about this place.

'There goes our guide,' said the woman, pointing to a toothless old man walking slowly past their window. 'He took us right where the action was. Too bad we couldn't continue.'

'Got a question for yawl,' said Lester. 'What if ah was to want a *deffernt* guide? Not that mine's all that bad, yunnerstand. But today he couldn't ketch him a cold in a bucket. He was takin my first fish outen the net and it bit him and he lost the fish.'

'Lost the fish?' said the man.

'He had it in the net,' said Lester, 'right by the boat. And the fish bit him on the hand and plumb ex-caped. It was like he was tryin to let it go.'

'Mr Babcock,' said the young woman, 'we let all our fish go up here. The guide might keep a small one for a shore lunch, but otherwise –'

'Why on earth would you come all the way up here just to let fish go? Don't make no sense.'

'Who's your guide?' said the woman.

'Name's Norbert. Ah thank he speaks French or somethin. If ah talked to the head guy up here, whuzisname, that Joe feller, do yawl think he might gimme another guide?'

'Norbert Lachance?' said the young woman.

'That's his name all right.'

The young woman looked at her husband and turned to Lester. She spoke in a hushed voice.

'Astrid and Joe say that he's the best man up here. People who come here every summer, they ask for Norbert.'

Her husband was nodding.

'Mr Babcock –'

'Lester.'

'Lester, as far as we know, you hit the jackpot with Norbert Lachance. Kelly and I know the man. If I were you, I'd give him another day at least.'

'Just askin.'

Up close, the couple looked not quite so young. Maybe into their forties, but both in real trim shape as though they had personal trainers or something. They had the cut of prosperity about them, even in the way they ate, nibbling their food, nibbling and sipping rather than scarfing it down the way normal folks do. The young woman smiled and waved at someone behind them. Lester turned around in his chair, and there was Norbert, ambling towards their table. He nodded to Lester and to the young couple and stood there a moment, looming silent and bulky like a big bear. There was a bandage on the index finger of his left hand.

'Heidi, Norbert. Hazz yer fanger?' said Lester.

Norbert seemed stumped. Lester cast a meaningful glance at his two dinner companions and shrugged.

'Norbert,' said the fellow, 'Lester wants to know how your finger is doing.'

A light seemed to go on inside Norbert's face.

'I seen da nursh, ah? See gimme dish bannage like.'

It was Lester's turn to look bewildered.

The woman named Kelly placed her hand on Lester's white sleeve.

'Norbert is telling us that he got a bandage on his finger from the nurse. He's good to go for tomorrow.'

She was talking to Lester as though he were a lost little boy. Lester began to wonder just how drunk he really was, when the thousand minnows in his bloodstream swam out of nowhere to sing their name to Lester in unison. He turned to Kelly.

'Yawl know a woman up here name of Astrid?'

The woman explained that Astrid was Thor's right-hand man.

'Woman, actually,' said the husband.

'Yawl can say that again.'

'She'll be up here tomorrow to spell off Joe Arsenault,' said the man.

'Up here t'morra, is that a fact?'

Lester felt his spirits rising, his good humour returning. He rose from the table and slapped his good buddy Norbert (say Norr-berrt) on the back.

'We goan kick some butt t'morra, Norbert?'

The woman named Kelly whispered something to the big man.

'Wedder holds, ah? Sood be puddy good.'

Before the woman could translate, Lester held up his hand.

'Ah do believe ah'm gettin the hang of it, thank you, ma'am.'

'Hang a wut?' said the guide.

'Spakin Canadian, No-werr-berrt.'

THREE

The blonde memory of Astrid had accompanied Lester all through the spring and the lonely summer, all through the last niggling details of his divorce settlement, the boring legalities of selling properties in Louisiana, the endless drought all over Texas. To top things off, some of his friends seemed to side with Lester's ex. That left a scattering of drinking buddies who held cynical views about the married state. All too often he spent his evenings with one or two of them, or in the bar alone with his thoughts. But now and then the memory of Astrid had kept him company. Astrid was there hovering like a butterfly all the way up to Medicine Lake, and now the memory of her nordic pale blue eyes, her lustrous hair and low voice sat beside him in his fishing guide's sixteen-footer.

Norbert Lachance guided the boat over a gentle swell down the central channel of Medicine Lake. The two men (and Astrid's elegant aura) ran with the wind, and the guide steered his open boat between reefs and small islands with great ease. They stopped in a bay with deep blue water that was protected from the wind and began trolling for lake trout. Lester fished in silence for several minutes when a thought flashed before his eyes: Astrid – *God forbid* – in bed with Norbert Lachance, Norbert guiding her to the place of highest glory. At that moment, a lake trout struck.

'I got one,' he said, and Astrid swam away.

The guide cut the engine. He showed no excitement.

'Feels like a big one,' said Lester.

His fish fought frantically in the deeper water, and Lester's spirits began to mount. The guide reached for the landing net, and at last Lester wrestled the fish to the surface.

'Liddle too big for shore lunts,' said the guide.

He netted the fish and let it go.

'Ten pounds?' said Lester.

'Mebbe seven.'

They continued to troll past the rocky slope that protected them from the rising wind on the main channel of the lake. Lester caught some more lake trout, and one was small enough for a two-man lunch, so the guide killed it and threw it into a fish bucket.

Lester's guide brought the boat into a little cove and began to unload for lunch. He let Lester carry the fish in the pail and a sack of food. Norbert took the rest of the gear, including an object rolled up in canvas that he wedged under his armpit. It was roughly the length of a golf club but from its bulk it looked more like a firearm.

The man was just too goddam quiet. Lester wondered if this silence had something to do with him. Perhaps he had made a mistake when he opted to fish alone with this Norbert character. It would have been cheaper if he'd brought a buddy up with him and shared the guide. But not one of his drinking buddies seemed interested in coming all the way up here, not even for a few days. Too bad.

By lunchtime the two men were nestled into the rocks by a big fire and out of the wind. About an hour had passed, Lester noted, in which he hadn't thought about Astrid.

At last the guide spoke: 'You godda real nice wite shoot dere.'

'The git-up I was wearin in the restrunt?'

'Yuh.'

'Ah bought that in New Orleans.'

For a moment, the guide seemed to be weighing Lester's words.

'How mutts you pay for a shoot like dat?'

'Hell, mebbe a thousand,' he said. 'Not much more'n a thousand. That's a thousand dollas American, ah mean.'

There was another long silence, and Lester thought he would outwait Norbert to see how long he would pause before opening his mouth. He checked out the canvas bundle that Norbert had laid on a flat boulder. Lester could see the end of what looked like a wooden stock.

'Yiz know Thor puddy good?'

'Tho-werr? You mean the top guy?'

'Yuh,' said Norbert.

'Never met the man.'

The guide reclined once more into his blanket of silence, and his eyelids started to close. Then he seemed to re-emerge from slumber.

'Dat guy an hizh wife Kelly, ah,' said Norbert at last. 'At da table wit you?'

'Yep.'

'Dat was Thor.'

'You must be joshin me, Norbert. That young feller was the top guy?'

Lester's guide nodded in reply, his expression unreadable.

'No wonder they knew Astrid.' Lester glanced at Norbert to see if he had any reaction to the mention of Astrid's name. 'You know, Thor's assistant? Beautiful long blonde hair?'

'Yuh,' said the guide and continued to stare at the fire.

'That gun you got wrapped up there,' said Lester. 'Can you show me that?'

Norbert unwrapped his bundle and held it for Lester's inspection. It was an old battered shotgun, big and solid like its owner.

'That a ten-gauge?'

Norbert nodded.

'Single shot, right?'

Norbert nodded again.

'A shotgun. Yawl plannin to shoot some geese up here?'

The guide shook his head.

'Dat gun is for bears. Juss in case.'

'You spray it with pellets to send it packin?'

Again Lester's guide shook his head. 'Got a rifle slug in da shell, ah?'

'And you ackshully prefer this to a huntin raffle?'

'Yuh.'

'How come, Norbert?'

'Does a puddy good job.'

Lester had a good guffaw over that one, and when he looked over at his guide, there was the faintest hint of a smile on his lips.

'We get da bears aroun da tent village. Once in a while we have to get da Conservation to soot dem. But da Conservation, ah? He don't always be dere. To soot da bear like. He might be down ta Regina, ah? So don't tell Thor about dish gun,' said the guide. 'Don't tell no one about dish gun.'

'Ma lips are sealed, Norbert.'

The boat nosed its way out of the choppy water and into a long narrow branch of the lake. Here the water by the shore was shallow and lined with weed beds. Lester's guide took them slowly down the middle of the bay. The rocky shores on either side got closer and closer, and at last the guide cut the engine and dropped an anchor into several feet of water. Lester could clearly see some large rocks and logs on the bottom, which might make casting tricky, but he wasn't going to point this out to his guide. Perhaps the man knew what he was doing.

'Go for da weeds,' he said.

Lester held his spinning rod out over the water. A four-inch yellow spoon with red spots dangled from the end of a steel leader. He began to line up a nice passage to the weeds between two groups of logs when one of the logs came to life and began to swim away.

'Holy suffern dawgs.'

'Buntsa big pike,' the guide said. 'Cast over by da weeds an bring it back nice an slow.'

'Then what?'

'Hang on, ah?'

Lester flicked the spoon about one foot short of the weeds and began to reel it towards the school of lunkers idling in the shallows near their boat. Before his lure could reach the first of the basking fish, a great long shadow moved out from the weeds, grabbed the spoon and turned. It all happened too fast for Lester to react, and he felt a jolt from his hand to his shoulder. He tried to raise the tip of his rod, but the tugging at the other end was too great.

All Lester could do was babble.

The big pike turned and charged towards them, yanking Lester's line right under the boat and out the other side.

'This thang muss be long as ma arm,' he cried.

The fish made another run and the guide helped him get his rod around the side of the boat. It took a few more runs before the great fish began to tire, but at last it came spiralling in among the other pike, sending them off in all directions in a great storm of silt.

'He has got to be as long as ma lag.'

'Try ta bring da fiss up,' said the guide.

He was holding the net calmly.

Lester had never seen a fish this big, alive or stuffed. It was bigger than the shark he had caught in Port Aransas. It swam like a gator, slowly to the surface, armoured in a fabric of green and gold and spotted from head to fins. It had long duckbilled jaws like two clamps and teeth like hooks inside. Maybe some of the fish in Astrid's photos might have reached this size, but Lester had his doubts. This one was even bigger than the monster that bit Norbert on the hand. Lester had a vision of his great northern stuffed and hanging over the mantel in his new condo in Dallas. Its jaws would be pried wide open to display the rows of backward-slanting teeth. *I caught that thang way up in Northern Canada. Dang near pulled me in.*

'Norbert,' he said out of the side of his mouth, 'I know we's posed to let fishes go up here, but, um, do you thank we could make us one exception?'

'We can mezzer it,' said the guide. 'Then we can let it go.'

'The regs that strict up here?'

'Yuh.'

'Who would know?'

'Mebbe we jus mezzer it, ah?'

The guide scooped the great fish and dragged it thrashing and thumping to the side of the boat. With his bandaged hand he brought out a tape measure. Lester held the net and the great pike in the water, where it could still work its gills, and Norbert did a quick measure. The guide did it all in metric, but it worked out to fifty-one inches. In seconds the hook was out of the pike's jaws and the fish was free, tailing sluggishly towards the deeper rocks. With a great sweep of the tail it disappeared into the grey billows of silt.

When the motor was roaring again, and they had left the weed beds behind, Lester bellowed out his apology.

'Sorry bout back there,' he shouted. The guide said nothing.

'Back there, with the big pike. I jess got excited, I got carried away. I thought I could take that thang back home with me an, you know, git er stuffed.'

The guide nodded his head and slowed the boat. They were heading into another bay.

'Lodda guys want ta stuff a big fiss. But these big ones, they're like da queen bees, ah?'

'Queen bees?'

'Yuh,' said the guide. 'Da real big ones are females. Dey do da spawnin. Yiz can hook on to em for a wile but yiz can't take em home.'

Lester's guide had taken his boat out into the main channel, and now the wind was up. The waves were much higher than they had been in the morning, and the men were still going with the wind, so the boat moved easily in among the big swells. The guide steered it into a small bay and brought out a long thin rod.

'Can yiz try one a dese here? We got some udder kinds a fiss down dere on da river.'

Norbert had assembled a fly rod with pale green floating line. He presented it to Lester.

'I'll give er a try. By god, thish-ere's the lightest pole ah ever seen.'

'Mosta da guys up here, ah, dey doan know how.'

The two men clambered out of the boat and hopped from rock to rock until they had come to shore. The guide pointed to the place where the stream left the lake.

'Graylings,' he said, holding his hands a foot or more apart. 'Yiz ever seen dem type a fiss?'

Joe Arsenault had told Lester about the grayling that morning. It was a small fish with a big rainbow-tinted dorsal fin, a feisty little troutlike creature that loved to take a fly on the surface. A status fish. Lester liked the idea of catching a status fish. The grayling were getting harder and harder to find, even up north in remote places like Medicine Lake. Most of the guides, Arsenault told Lester, had given up on grayling.

'This bay with the grayling,' said Lester. 'Is it a secret spot of yours?'

The guide looked down at his shoes and shrugged his big shoulders.

'Hey?' said Lester, with a wheedling little smile.

'Me, I juss foun dish place in da spring.'

The guide hauled out a pair of waders and handed them to Lester.

'I was checkin out dish liddle river, ah? An I seen these little ones splassin on a surface.'

The guide was pointing in the direction of the outflowing stream, and this time he really was smiling.

They sorted out their gear and the guide returned to the boat to get his gun. He led the way down a game trail that followed the bends in the creek. The bush was thick near the stream, and the birch and black spruce leaned into the pathway. The leaves of the birch had already begun to turn a pale orange. It was still midsummer in Dallas, but autumn had already begun up here.

Lester stepped past a big pile of dung. His eyes kept darting over the riffles of the creek. Occasionally there was a silver flash and a splash at the surface.

'Didn't know there was moose around these parts.'

'Moosh?'

'Yeah.'

They came to a gravel bar where the creek tumbled into a pale green pool. Fish were rising all over the place. Lester could not believe his luck.

'Furder south.'

'What?'

'Moosh furder south. No moosh up here.'

'That big pile a crap back there on the trail. What was that?'

Lester was almost ready for his first cast. He looked up and saw the guide standing behind him on a small rise, checking out the woods that rose on both sides of the stream. At that moment Lester realized what kind of scat was lying on the trail.

FOUR

The water was fast and cold as it drifted over a bed of pink and green gravel, each pebble and rock magnified with perfect clarity. The grayling drifted like pale ghosts over the creek bottom and raced each other to the surface for tiny midges and damsel flies.

'What kinda bait do we use, Norbert?'

His guide was poking through an aluminum fly box. He handed Lester a bushy-looking fly that was much larger than anything dotting the surface of the clear water.

'This big ol thing?'

'It's got lotsa deer hair,' the guide explained. 'Floats longer, ah?'

Lester was not convinced, but he had trusted the guide so far. He tied on the bushy fly, mounted a dry round boulder, and pulled out his leader and a few yards of fly line. He made a short clumsy cast by flicking the rod just to see if the fly would float. A small explosion erupted around his fly and he was fast to a fish. It leapt clear of the water and bent the small fly rod double. It leapt again amid the merriment of Lester's cussing and laughter. When at last the guide brought the net under the grayling, it was trembling in the sunlight, its great spotted dorsal sparkling bluegreen and magenta. The guide let it go.

'Jeeez Crast,' gasped Lester.

It sounded like a prayer of thanks.

Everywhere Lester waded at the edge of the stream, his guide came along like a sentry, carrying his gun and a small net. In spite of Lester's ineptitude with the fly rod, the fishing was fine. Each time a grayling struck, Lester yelled out *I've got one!* but after the eleventh or twelfth fish, he realized he didn't have to yell so loud or so frequently, and one hour later he wasn't yelling at all. He sat by the side of the stream, listening to the rising wind, and smiled wearily.

When at last he looked up at his guide, the man seemed preoccupied with something. He was looking up at the sky, but all Lester could see were clouds.

'Bears?' he said.

The guide shook his head.

Suddenly the fishing was over. They trudged upstream towards the place where they had put in. When the two men emerged from the trees, Lester could see that the sky was darkening, and the men were greeted with a north wind so strong they had to lean into it to reach the boat.

'Can we go back against this wind?' said Lester.

The guide didn't answer him. They loaded their equipment in, strapped on some life jackets, and the guide poled them out into the deeper water. The bay where they had landed was partially protected from the wind, so the boat was stable enough in the waves as they wove between the rocks and reefs heading for deeper water. Lachance found a long stretch of lake that lay beneath a high rocky ridge, and the wind blew over the ridge without affecting the boat's progress.

Soon, however, they headed out into the main channel of the lake, and the wind and the high curling waves caught them head on. The guide gunned the engine and they slammed into the waves, hammering each one with an up-and-down *whump whump* motion that sent the spume flying into their faces. It took scarcely a minute of this before Lachance eased off the throttle and edged his boat into a small protected bay.

'Lester!' the guide screamed over the roar of the wind and the motor. It was the first time the guide had called him by name. 'We gotta hang up an wait!'

The guide was squinting at him, looking right at him.

'Okay wit you?'

Lester nodded without thinking.

Wait? Wait where? He felt a tightening in his gut. *Wait how long?* He checked his watch. It was just past four o'clock. Soon the other anglers would be gathering around the bar and the fireplace in the lounge overlooking Medicine Lake. They would be watching the storm and watching for the last of the boats to be coming in. They would be drinking whisky.

The guide ran their boat to shore in the lee of the great protecting ridge. They clambered up the rocks and sat down on a couple of sawed-off logs left beside the ashes of an old campfire. Behind them on the ridge, where the wind was coming from, a cliff bulged out and over their heads to protect them, and all around them was a stand of black spruce. The wind screamed over the cliff and bent the trees down by the shore.

A few minutes later, the storm broke and the rain came down. The guide dragged their boat further up on shore. He looked over at the rain and the darkening sky.

'She could be a bit of a wait, ah?'

The rain intensified, so the two men emptied out the boat and dragged it up to the old campsite. At the guide's suggestion, they inverted their boat and propped up one side with the oars so that they could sit down dry and out of the wind. The rain slanted down on them and the wind moaned like the wrath of God.

Under the tilted boat, the guide attempted to start a fire. There seemed to be no method to it. Norbert simply dipped a rag into the gasoline from the spare tank and tossed it into a quickly gathered armful of reindeer moss, slightly wet twigs and pine boughs. Someone had stowed some sawed-off logs, perhaps the guide himself, so he brought back several armloads of these logs, tossed a few onto the pine boughs, and piled the rest of them around the pit where they could dry from the heat of the fire.

The guide extracted a box of wooden matches. Lester caught himself shivering, mesmerized, holding his breath. The first match fizzled. The second one caught, and gingerly the guide held it to the gasoline-soaked rag. There was a sudden flare, the men leaned back, and the pine boughs caught and began to crackle.

'Injun fire,' Lachance muttered.

The rain was mixed with hail, and it pelted the lake like an avalanche of gravel. The air grew chilly, and as the rain and hail struck the water, a white mist boiled up around the shore. Smoke from the pine boughs blew into their eyes and their nostrils, drifted away, came back like the spirit of something wild, checking them out, making them hack and cough. The rain continued and the wind howled, and Lester could only imagine the height and ferocity of the waves out on the open lake.

Lachance was rarely still. He had dragged in all kinds of bags and boxes from the rain and stacked them under the boat so that they surrounded the two men. This wall of gear and provisions had the effect of cutting down on the cold air drifting under the boat and hovering around their shoulders.

'If da win goes down,' said Lachance, 'we mebbe trow dish boat inna water an load er up real quick. Get home inna daylight, ah?'

'Yeah?'

'Doan wanna drive dish boat inna dark.'

'Right.'

'Too many reefs.'

'Right.'

Lester was trying to remember what he had learned in boot camp about wilderness survival. Due to a severe case of pneumonia, he had missed out on a good deal of military service, so he'd never had a chance to put his survival skills into action. Still, Lester Babcock was thinking about alternatives. They booted up before his gaze like company strategies on-screen, commanding his complete attention.

Plan #1: go back to lodge right now;

Plan #2: head for lodge after dark as soon as wind dies;

Plan #3: head for lodge next morning.

Disadvantages of plan #1: might take in rainwater,
   drown in waves caused by high wind;

Disadvantages of plan #2: bad visibility and too many reefs,
  probably drown in the dark;
Disadvantages of plan #3: might have to sleep under boat with guide,
  might die of hypothermia, might drown anyway next morning if
  wind persists, might be eaten by bear during night or by pack of –

'We got some food inna sack, ah?'

'Yeah. Real good, Norbert.'

'Make some tea, ah?'

'Ratto.'

The hail had all but stopped but the rain fell steadily and the wind continued to moan and bend the trees above and around them. From time to time a black spruce would crack at the trunk and crash down into the forest.

'So, Norbert,' said Lester, 'them waves would still be purty bad out there on the main part of the lake?'

'Mm.'

Lester glanced at his watch. It was seven minutes after five. By now the other anglers would have their first glow on, and the smells from the kitchen would be drifting into their nostrils. Astrid would be there, and all the guys would be buzzing around her, waiting their turn to impress the hell out of her. Would anyone at the lodge be thinking about Lester Babcock and his guide? The light around them was dull and growing darker, but it was impossible to tell if this waning effect was because of the lateness of the day or because of the mist around them and the heavy layer of clouds above.

'Will they, you know, come a-lookin for us?'

Lachance looked up at the sky.

'Inna mornin.'

FIVE

Lester had sunk into a deep wooze of dread. He was reviewing his fantasies of death in the wilderness. It was like looking at the movie channels on Hallowe'en, one horror after another. A wolf sniffs them out and howls for its pack to come down for a feed. Cold seeps up from the rocky ground and both men freeze like granite. Lachance turns Windigo and butchers Lester for his flesh. A big old black bear, the same one that dumped that immense pile of crap on the game trail by the stream, yes: that would be their final end. The bear would drag the guide out from under the boat, there would be a terrible struggle, and then silence. After a pause, it would come for Lester, wheezing musky breath from its labours.

'Norbert,' he said, 'where's that gun of yours at?'

Lachance was pouring tea into a couple of fireblackened tin cups. He handed one of them to Lester.

'Can't finda damn sugar. You want sugar?'

'No. Thank you, no. That lil ol shotgun. Do you have it handy?'

'Back dere,' said Lachance, jerking his head to the left. 'Unner da tarp.'

Lachance rooted through an old duffel bag and came up with some peanut butter, a box of crackers and a small tin of sardines. He drew his knife, pulled out the blade, and poked it into the peanut butter.

'I was just a thinkin,' said Lester. 'You know. In case of, you know.'

'Bears,' said Lachance.

'Yeah.'

'Up here, dey doan mutts bodder ya.'

'Right.'

'Wanna biscuit?'

'Thanks.'

The guide handed him a small soda cracker. Lester nibbled on it, blew on his tea, sipped a little and sighed. It tasted surprisingly like hot tea. The smell of sardines drifted up into his nostrils, he laid a few on a soda cracker, and they too tasted surprisingly good. But wouldn't the ...

'Norbert, wouldn't the smell of these ol sardines tend to, you know.'

'Bring da bears?'

'Well, ah was jest –'

'Bess way to bring a bear is to clean some fiss here, ah? Wait a day or two till the guts start ta smell.'

'Right.'

The men were chewing on their biscuits when a tree blew down behind them with an enormous crash.

Some nights are darker than others, and this night, without a moon or stars, was as dark as Lester had ever seen. All the scenarios of doom that Lachance had been holding at bay with his food and his tea and his nonchalance, began to creep closer to the fire. Were they far enough from the edge of the trees to be safe from windfalls? How did one distinguish between noises caused by the wind and noises caused by large animals rushing towards their campsite in the dark?

Strategies of Survival in the Short Term:

#1) Get out and measure distance of campsite from edge of forest.
Determine height of trees by measuring and comparing shadows.
Subtract height of trees from distance between trees and campsite. If result
is a negative figure, move site farther from trees.

#2) Determine whether the damn shotgun is loaded, and if not, where
shells are located.

#3) Determine where to perform bodily functions, and especially how far
from campsite such activities are feasible.

#4) If storm persists, develop Plan B strategy for –

'Me, I wunner if dat Thor, does he wear a wite shoot?'

'Wouldn't surprise me none.'

'He go to a club, Thor.'

'Huh?'

'Da club for genius guys.'

Lester had heard about that club.

'It's called Mensa. You got to have a IQ pretty much sky high to join up with that bunch.'

'Whadda guys do in dat club?'

'Well,' Lester began, and then realized he had wondered the same thing himself. 'They meet, you know.'

'Yuh?'

'They meet like once a month and discuss things. Idears.'

'Talk about da ideas.'

'Yeah, you know. Sa-ance and flossophy and such things. Books. Ah reckon they must all read the same books so they can, you know …'

Lachance was chuckling deep down in his throat.

'So dey can bullsit wit udder real smart guys, ah?'

'Guess so.'

'Me, I seen a real genius only once mebbe.'

'You did?'

'At da lodge. Some time ago. He was dish famous guy who knew about the conomy, ah, the conomy like everywhere in da entire worl. He was even smarter den Thor. I was his guide en he say to Arsenault, your prices are too high up here. En Arsenault, he say why are my prices too high? En dis guy he say New Zealand, ah? En Arsenault, he say what about New Zealand? En dis guy who knows the conomy, he say New Zealand like she's all tits up now. In da Mexico too, ah? En Arsenault, he don't know dat New Zealand. He don't know dat it's all tits up in dat conomy, so he says what dat got to do wit my prices are too high. En dis guy, he tell us a long story wit all da numbers why she's like all connected. Soun like a genius to me.'

'He did?'

'Couldn fiss wort a damn but he soun like a real genius.'

Lester laughed. It was the first time he had laughed in quite a while.

'Lost a good rod in two hunnert feet a water dish genius guy.'

The evening light was all but gone now, and still, Lester could not tell whether it was the onset of night or just the effect of such a thick blanket of mist and clouds. The fire helped to cheer him up, but he couldn't help thinking that some female companionship would be even more comforting.

'Yawl talk much with Astrid?'

'Dat blon lady.'

'Yessir.'

Lester hadn't thought of Astrid for hours. It was hard to imagine that soon she would be up there at the Lodge. He wondered how she would receive his news of being stranded on the shores of Medicine Lake. He would lay on the southern charm, leaning lightly but not absurdly on the virtues of toughness and practicality in northern survival. He began to form his narrative for her. *The day began with a strong wind from the west. I warned our guide that the weather looked a mite unsettled, but he only grunted. We didn't mind the wind at first because we was a-runnin with it. Not many clouds, but on our way back, that wind turned into a screamin banshee, and it was all we could do to keep to keep to keep …*

The thought returned, Norbert Lachance mounting Astrid from behind, the sound of her panting, crying out like a banshee herself beneath the throbbing pillars of the aurora borealis. It occurred to Lester that he didn't know what a banshee sounded like. What was a banshee anyway? He couldn't remember if it was a type of airplane or a warsher-woman.

'See like to let her hair down, dat one.'

'Astrid?'

'Yuh. See like to go after da guys.'

'You mean after Thor?'

'No, not Thor. But dat blon one, see get a nidear in her head, see go for it.'

'She went for you, right?'

'Once or twice.'

'You had sex with Astrid?'

'Nop, nop.'

'You turned her down, you mean?'

'Yuh.'

'How come you turned her down, Norbert?'

'Eulalie, dat my wife, ah?'

'Yes?'

'Go for a fas one wit dat blon lady, Eulalie, see have my balls for lunts meat.'

Lester roared. So did Norbert. They couldn't stop. They laughed like big men do after boilermakers in the bar, they outroared the wind and when they stopped laughing, Lester wondered what he had been so afraid of.

The rain fell, the wind moaned and the temperature dropped. Lachance roused Lester to help him set about their preparations for the night. The guide pulled out a machete for himself and gave Lester a hatchet, and the two of them went out into the woods to get some pine boughs. They hauled out several armfuls and laid them under the boat. On top of the pine boughs they spread out some life jackets and on top of those, a thick sheet of poly and then a ground sheet. The men huddled as close to the fire as they could, and they talked well into the night. Lester told Norbert all about acquiring properties for a song, improving them, then turning them around for a fine profit. He told his guide all about the failure of his marriage, how his rise in the financial world and his fall from marital grace seemed to coincide. Norbert told Lester about his own business ventures: more than ten years on a trapline and a recent attempt to harvest wild rice. Lousy prices shut down the first venture and unfair competition killed the second. His wife Eulalie never seemed to mind how badly he did or how poor they got. They always ate well.

'Da women,' said Norbert, 'dey doan mind you lose your money. Dey jus wan you at home in da bed at night. I believe on dat.' Every so often, one of the men would stir the fire and pile on a log or two. Lester told Norbert about where the high rollers in Dallas did their drinking, a bar in a highrise known as the Tower of Power. Beautiful view of the city lights. He went on about hunting doves and mallards down in Louisiana, and Norbert countered with hunting stories about caribou and wolves, moose and bear. By the time they made it back to women, they were almost too tired for any more man talk.

All night long, the wind came and went capriciously. Each time it shifted, the acrid smoke would change directions and sometimes drift into their faces and make them cough themselves awake. Their clothes reeked of smoke, pine sap and sardines, but they stayed dry and the fire kept them just barely warm enough. Lester fell asleep sitting up and found himself at first light collapsed around a seat cushion, ass to ass with Norbert, who snored softly like a great sleeping dog.

SIX

A low ceiling of clouds drifted above them as Norbert's boat roared up the lake. The wind was down. A light drizzle was falling, little more than a faint spray, but it beaded on their raincoats and caused Lester to shiver. Several other motor boats joined with theirs along the way home. The boats emerged one at a time from coves along the main channel, and at first Lester thought that they too must have passed their stormy night under a boat. *This is it*, he thought. *What an end to the story.* But Lester was wrong. As the boats came closer and the men began to wave at Norbert's boat, he realized that they had all been searching for Norbert and himself since early in the morning.

Just as the wind began to rise and the rain began to fall again, the fishing boats arrived at the dock, and Arsenault was there with his staff to greet them. There was no sign of Astrid, but perhaps she would be arriving on a plane later in the day. A few young men helped Norbert and Lester unload, and they lugged Norbert's gear up to the lodge. It was seven-thirty in the morning.

Later, when Lester had showered and shaved, donned his brand new camouflage outfit, he strolled into the dining room for breakfast. Anglers converged on him and wanted to know what it had been like to spend the night in a storm without a roof over his head. They swarmed around his table to hear him tell of his adventure. They seemed to envy him the experience. They laughed a lot and went all quiet when Lester spoke glowingly of his guide. A fellow from Colorado wondered out loud how one might reward a guide who had kept his head in such a crisis.

'I'd maybe bring him down to Denver, show him around, take him to a Broncos game, that's what I'd do.'

'I'd pay the man a thousand dollars,' said another man. 'No questions asked.'

'Yawl got a point there,' said Lester. 'The man saved my damn life.'

The man saved my damn life. This became Lester's mantra and he kept repeating it to anyone he talked to. He wasn't sure how Norbert was going to cash it, but he was determined to make out a cheque for a thousand dollars American, and hand it over to the man. The rain came down and fishing was forgotten. Men played poker, flirted with Arsenault's waitresses, and hopped from table to table as though they were all golfing buddies from the same small town, and Lester was their very best buddy. More than once the name of Astrid came up.

'Looks like the rain's a goin south,' Lester said to the man from Colorado. 'Ain't you goan try for a big one?'

'Oh, maybe,' the man said. 'If it stops completely. I just want to be here when Astrid arrives.'

'You know Astrid too?' said Lester.

'Hell,' the man said. 'Everyone knows Astrid.'

And that was that, the end of the story. The joke was on Lester. He had been lured north by a *good ol northern si-reen.* He ought to be a mite downhearted, but he felt too good for that. Too good and too tired to be brokenhearted. Perhaps the heartache would follow later, but he had his doubts.

Lester could not stop yawning. He roamed the dining room and the trophy lounge, talking to men from all over North America. He was determined to keep awake at least until after lunch, when he would allow himself a nap. And after that, perhaps the wind would be down and the sky would clear. He gazed out at the lake and mouthed a prayer of thanks that he was in here and not out there. The camaraderie was so intense, he forgot to go outside and look for Norbert Lachance. By the time he remembered, it was late afternoon, he was sleepy, and he made his way back to his room for a nap.

Lester woke up around the Happy Hour and went to the lodge for some Canadian whisky. They called it rye up here, but most of the Canadian anglers seemed to prefer Scotch. Astrid was nowhere in sight. That didn't bother Lester. He was a hero and he was alive and he deserved a drink. The more he drank, the more Texan he became, which meant the louder he became. More than once he cursed the perfidy of women, extolled his

Indian guide, and praised America.

The man from Colorado joined him for a last belt before turning in. He wanted to know how the fishing was down at the far end of Medicine.

'Great,' said Lester. 'We got into some a them graylings. Had to use a damn fly rod.'

'I don't believe it. You found some grayling?'

'Hunnerds of em. Couldn't keep the buggers off ma line. What about you?'

'We did okay, but we didn't find no grayling,' the man said. 'No one's catching grayling as far as I know. Except for you, Lester, you lucky ol son of a bitch.'

With a good glow on, Lester made his way downhill on the wet path to the tents that had been erected in the lee of the lodge inside a high barbed-wire fence. A precaution against marauding bears, he had been told. Each guide had a tent for himself and his family. There were more than a dozen of them, great white canvas structures, smudged black and grey with the wear of many summers, each one with the black stack of a wood stove poking through the roof. In the centre of this smoky clutter of tents was a summer kitchen area and a log frame with caribou meat hanging to dry from strung-out ropes. With the wind up and the rain pelting the tents and the trees, the afternoon was chilly, very cold for late August. But the tents looked pretty cozy to Lester. There was something oldfashioned and exotic about them. He might have been drifting down into the Kasbah on the other side of the world, this compound was that foreign to him.

He asked a woman where he could find Norbert.

'Nor-bare?' she said, giving his name a funny pronunciation. It seemed to Lester that he was being corrected.

'Lachance,' he said. 'Where's he at?'

She pointed to a tent cabin somewhat larger than most of the canvas ones in the community. It had walls made of long planks, a real wooden door and a roof of canvas. As he walked over to the tent cabin, he could still feel the exuberance in him of a man brought back from the brink of death. He was full of life's boundless possibilities, full of Canadian whisky and mischief.

He knocked on the door of the tent cabin. There was no answer. A man walked by. Lester recognized him as the toothless old guide that Thor and his wife had been extolling the day before at the dinner table.

'Say, feller,' he said. 'Thish-ere Norbert's cabin?'

'Yuh,' the man said.

'Is he here?'

'Mebbe Norbert he's a little busy.'

'You mean sleepin?' said Lester.

The old man grinned at Lester, showing him some nicely weathered gums. The grin had a hint of innuendo to it.

'Oh, you mean ...'

The man said, *Yuh,* and toddled off.

Lester grinned back at the man. He knew what he had to do. In his pocket he had the cheque made out to Norbert Lachance. He fingered it there and glared at the door.

'Norbert?' he called. 'You in there?'

No answer.

'Norbert, ol buddy, I know yawl're in there. Now you come on out. I got a little somethin for you.'

No answer.

'Norbert? This is Lester Babcock, and ah got me a nice little gift for you! Comeon, now. Outta the sack, Norbert. Time's a-wastin. Besides,' he continued, 'I'm bout half froze to death out here.'

No answer.

Lester could not suppress the onrush of devilment that continued to well up inside of him, this Texan within, and now he had an even better idea.

'Norbert?' he roared. 'Yawl don't come out-cheer and talk to me, y'know what ah'm goan to do? Ah'm goan stand here and sang until you open the door. And Norbert, I have the worst sangin voice you have ever heard. Ah kin scare little children juss by sangin to them.'

Lester knocked one more time on the door. He banged it with his big fist until it rattled.

'Okay, Norbert, you done axt for it.'

Lester turned away from the door and smiled at some Native people walking by. They regarded him from the corner of their eyes and kept going. Lester planted his boots a few feet from Lachance's door and took a deep breath.

> *O, say can yew see, baaa the dawn's early light,*
> *What so prowdly we hailed at the twa-light's last gleamin,*
> *Whose broad stripes an brat stars ...*

Lester Babcock's voice very much exceeded his opinion of it. It was solemn and thunderous by turns, as sonorous as any voice ever heard in all the tent village. Raising the volume for all to hear, Lester belted out the anthem in a baritone that made the glass vibrate on Norbert Lachance's flimsy door. Lester had never felt less inhibited in all his life.

> An the rockets' red glare
> The bombs burstin in ay-er
> Gave proof thew the nat
> That ar flag was still there.

Lester stopped for a moment. Ear to the door, he heard what might have been the sound of someone groaning, and then perhaps the sound of a body bumping into a chair. *What the hell.* He turned his back to the door to enable him to serenade the entire tent village.

> O say does the Star Spangled banner yet wave
> O'er the land of the fray
> An the home of the brave.

When he turned around to check the door, he was face to face with Norbert Lachance. The man had no shirt on. His chest was massive, fleshy, hairless. A purple scar lay diagonally from the man's right shoulder to his left breast. There was no expression whatsoever on his face. He looked on Lester as though he were a whiskyjack or a pine cone.

A voice from inside the tent cabin cried out, 'Doan ask him ta come inside.'

'Eulalie,' Norbert began.

'Ah git the picture, mah friend. She don't want no drunken buddies ta spole her little love nest.'

Lester reached inside his pants pocket and fingered the cheque.

'Look, Norbert, ah'm sorry to bring a good man out of the sack on such a cold evening, but hell, ah might not see yawl before the plane comes in tomorra, and … well …'

He brought out the cheque.

'I just wanna say thanks for takin care of me in that awful storm.'

Lester handed Norbert the cheque, and the guide put it in his pocket without looking at it.

'Whoa now,' said Lester. 'You should read the amount. That's a thousand dollars, Norbert, and them's American dollars.'

Lester had a sudden moment of doubt, and the doubt became a certainty: he had done the wrong thing.

'Look,' he began falteringly, 'money's jess money, and it don't go very far in sayin, in tellin you people, in … you know, tellin yawl …'

A woman was now peeking out of the doorway, squinting up at Lester somewhat the way horsetraders look at nags at the end of a long week of trading. She was neither young nor beautiful, but compelling to look at, and Lester could only stare.

'You wanna come in?' she said.

'Oh, I don't want to bother you folks.'

'Come in,' she said in a neutral voice, more an order than an invitation, and she opened the door. A warm swell from the wood stove enveloped Lester, and he realized that he was shivering.

The tent cabin had a floor of rough planks nailed to a frame. There was no electricity, and two squat candles were burning on an improvised table at the far end next to the stove. There were two beds, one covered with gear and clothing and the other for sleeping in, and a larger table in the centre of the tent with aluminum plates and cups and cutlery. Norbert's shotgun was leaning up against the wall next to the stove.

Eulalie poured some boiling water into a teapot.

'You want some?' she said.

'Thanks.'

Lester straddled a chair and Lachance sat on his bed. The three of them sipped their tea before anyone spoke.

'Dere ya go,' said Norbert, 'lookin at my sotgun again.'

The guide was looking at Eulalie.

'All night long, dish man, he wanna know where da sotgun is. He wanna be ready to soot da bear, ah?'

'Oh, no, Norbert, that was your job,' said Lester. 'But I did wonder if you'd remembered to load that thang.'

Eulalie almost laughed.

'Oh no,' said Norbert. 'Why would I do dat?'

'He doan soot da bear,' said Eulalie. 'He juss wack it on da head.'

It seemed all right between them, and Lester thought that maybe they would forgive him for his intrusion into their home and for the cheque he had thrust so haplessly at his guide.

'Norbert,' he said, 'could I see that ol gun?'

Lachance got up from the bed and grabbed his shotgun by the barrel. He broke open the gun as though to show Lester that now, at least, it was not loaded. He handed the gun to Lester.

'How long have you owned this baby?' he said.

'It was her dad's gun. He give it to me a long time ago.'

'He give it to you when we got married,' said Eulalie.

'No,' said Norbert.

'Yes,' she said. 'Because you help him all winter, ah? Jesus, man, you forget everything.'

'I remember,' said Norbert.

'A sotgun marriage, ah?' said Eulalie, and they all laughed.

'Wanna trade?' Norbert said to Lester.

'What? You wanna trade this here gun?'

'Yuh,' said Norbert, and Lester saw that he was serious. 'I'm not shuppose to have it up here. Thor fire me if I have it up here at da lodge.'

'I'd love to own this ol gun,' said Lester.

He was stunned. The gun had to be at least sixty years old, the stock was battered, but Lester could see that it was made of walnut, and the gun was still in good working order. A genuine old-fashioned ten-gauge, a goose gun, and because Lester was a big man, the gun's heavy recoil would not throw him off. A man could look for a long time in half the pawn shops and gun shops in Texas, but he wouldn't find a gun like this. He could take it hunting with his buddies from Dallas, who shot with newer, more expensive guns. Smaller guns, mere twelve- and sixteen-gauges. One of their shotguns would be worth more than Norbert's entire yearly income. But Lester could bring out this gun, this worthy old-timer, yes, he could hide it inside the case he used for his Browning twelve-gauge. And when they headed for the wetlands, one of his buddies would notice it, and he could tell them of how he traded for it away up north.

'Wait a minute,' he said to Norbert. 'What do I got to trade with?'

He stood up from his chair, snapped the gun closed, and handed it back to Norbert.

'You got dat wite shoot, ah?'

They were checking each other out. They were both big men, of similar height and girth. Norbert was bulkier around the chest, but the white suit would fit with alterations. Maybe even Eulalie would be able to do the work. Lester rubbed his chin for a moment. This was his lucky suit they were talking about. He'd bought it off the rack in New Orleans for a small fortune. His ex had loved him to death in this suit, told him it reminded her of a time when men used to dress up and look dignified. Other women had admired it as well. Including Astrid, who had an eye for such commodities. The suit was more than twenty years old but it wore like iron.

Definitely, Lester did not want to trade his suit away. But he was caught in something he could not understand; nor did he want to understand.

'Let's see that gun again.'

Lachance handed him the gun and he held it up to his shoulder. He turned away from Norbert and Eulalie, and he pointed the gun at their door. The gun smelled of a hundred campfires and gunpowder and the grease of animals. It smelled of Norbert's hands. It allowed Norbert to take his boat farther down the lake to the stream where the grayling were. Because with a gun like this, he wouldn't have to be afraid of bears. No wonder the other guides never took their clients after grayling. The grayling took them ashore into bear country up the lake, and they weren't allowed to have guns in case of emergencies.

Lester raised the weapon one more time to his shoulder and squinted down the barrel, and for one brief flash of vanity or insight or perhaps the faintest pulse of ancient maleness, he felt a tremor of transformation, and he said, 'Norbert ol buddy, you got yourself a deal.'

SEVEN

Lester went to bed with his window open. A breeze from the lake made the empty hangers chime faintly in the wardrobe where his fine white suit was no longer hanging. Norbert's shotgun now leaned at the back of the wardrobe, with a plastic shopping bag containing a handful of ten-gauge shells next to the battered walnut stock. The shells were surprisingly heavy. Getting the shells down across the border could be a little tricky.

And so the story ends.

Grinning at the vast dimensions of all he had lived through in the past day and a half, Lester fell sound asleep.

It would take a wiser man than Lester to know when the story really ended, that it was over and done with only when you began at last to tell it. And so he slept deeply until the moment when Astrid arrived naked at his door, naked and love-fraught, murmuring, *mount me, big guy, I'm your queen bee.* He tried to speak but she placed a forefinger on his lips. *Send your minnows up my stream, Lester. Fill me with your spawn.* Norbert was there as well, but only to advise on erotic matters. *Yiz can hook on to em for a while, but yiz can't take em home.* Lester did not care, he just wanted Astrid any way he could get her. *Then open up the goddam door!* she cried, and he sat up in bed, his forehead glistening with sweat.

Someone was pounding at his door.

He got up and yawned. He opened the door a few inches so that the person outside would not see his erection. It was Eulalie.

'Get da gun, you. Bring da gun!'

'Wha?'

'And doan forget ta bring da shells.'

He didn't even have to ask. He knew by looking at Eulalie that Norbert was in trouble. He pulled on a pair of runners, loaded the gun with one of Norbert's slugs, eased the hammer down, grabbed the shopping bag with the other shells, and lurched outside in his pyjamas and bedroom slippers. Eulalie stayed ahead of him holding the beam of her flashlight on the path. A bright half moon picked out the humps and deadwood branches that jutted from the shadows. Lester ran on rubber legs like people do in nightmares, heaving one leg in front of the other, struggling for breath, stumbling on stumps and roots towards the sound of high and frantic voices.

When they entered the tent compound, there were two men circling in front of the summer kitchen. One man was all white and glowed like snow under the yardlight, and one man was all black, and as they feinted forward and backwards the one looked like the shadow of the other. Children and their parents were yelling and darting both ways past the tents. It had the flavour of an Old West shootout, but neither man, it seemed, had a gun. One of the combatants was doing all the shouting. He held a sturdy length of wood, ready to strike as the two sparred back and forth on the rocky ground. The man with the chunk of wood was Norbert, and he was wearing Lester's beautiful white suit.

Eulalie was shouting at her husband in Cree. She shone her light at Norbert's adversary and he ran on all fours between two tents, not a man at all, but a large bear that had blundered into the compound for a quick meal and could not find its way out. A child began to scream. The bear reappeared at the cook shack and when Norbert approached, shouting again, the bear was panting heavily. It ambled towards Norbert, veered suddenly to the side, and began slapping its paws on the path and huffing and snorting. This was almost a circus act, it was almost funny.

Lester edged closer. Norbert muttered to the bear in Cree. The man and the bear glared at one another.

'Get over der behind da bear,' Eulalie said to Lester, pulling on his arm. 'Drive out da bear da way he come in. You might not have ta soot him.'

Shoot him? Lester moved around behind the bear and Norbert Lachance. The bear opened and closed its mouth rapidly, sending forth a series of popping sounds. The fur rose high on the back and shoulders.

'Hey, Muskwa!' cried Norbert. 'Dat way! Dat way! Get da hell outa here!'

The bear licked its lips and panted one more time and then he charged. Norbert clubbed downwards with his chunk of wood and they grappled like heavyweights in a clinch. The great paws and their terrible claws were doing their work. Someone screamed, it could have been Norbert, it could have been Eulalie, but the bear seemed to let go, or Norbert let go, and once more they circled. Norbert had lost his big chunk of wood.

'Get outa here!' Norbert yelled, and this time there was desperation in his voice. Perhaps the bear sensed an advantage, or perhaps it was simply acting like any cornered bear. It made a gurgling sound and seemed to be gathering itself to charge again.

'Yiz only got one chance,' said Eulalie, pushing Lester from behind. 'Aim for da chess.'

'Ah cain't shoot that critter,' he cried. 'Ah might hit Norbert.'

Eulalie yanked the gun away from Lester and leapt over to the cook shack. Lester loped along beside her. He stumbled on a low pile of uncut firewood, grabbed a longish piece and held it in both hands like a baseball bat and kept running. He was scarcely fifteen feet from the bear when it turned to face the two of them, then back at Norbert, then back at Eulalie. She yelled something to her husband that had the word *shotgun* in it. Using both hands, as though she held a basketball, she threw the gun sideways to Norbert and he snatched it out of the air. In one motion Norbert cocked and pointed the gun. He moved right in on the bear and it launched itself at him. He squeezed the trigger and the night exploded into its own bright myth.

EIGHT

When Lester went for breakfast, Astrid came up to him and said, 'A reporter wants to see you.'

'And a fine good mornin to you too.'

Astrid heaved an enormous sigh, sat down next to Lester and seemed to drift by slow increments back into character. She smelled of cigarette smoke. In the time since they had met in Amarillo, she had acquired a fine tan. She was dressed like a mountain guide in a brilliant orange fleece pullover and stretch pants. Her fingers were clutching the edge of the table.

'Lester Babcock, good morning. Long time no see.'

She put out her hand and he shook it.

'Was it you who shot that damn bear last night?' she said.

'Me?'

'What happened down there? I can't get a straight answer from anyone.'

'Didn't you talk to Norbert?'

'He's still under. They had to give him something for the pain.'

'Did you talk to Eulalie?'

'Eulalie,' said Astrid in a tired low voice. She buried her face in her hands. 'Hah.'

My my, Lester almost said. *Now why would that lady not wanna be a talkin to ye?* Instead he said, 'They was children down there, and all kinds a hell broke loose. Your man Norbert, he stood up to that bear –'

Up came Astrid's lovely face from the refuge of her lovely hands.

'Was he drunk?'

'He was sober as a judge.'

'Then what on earth was he doing in a suit wrestling with a bear?'

Her beauty had, at least temporarily, lost its hold on Lester. She was sounding like some –

'Astrid, you are beginnin to sound like some gulldang dee-vorce lawyer. Now relax. Ain't no bear gonna sue yawl for cruelty to animals. Norbert ain't goan sue no one. They was little kids there. Norbert was a headin him, that's all. Ain't no one in ten thousand mile goan stand up to a bear that big, but Norbert done it. He had to send it out the way it come in. And it plumb would not move its ass outa there.'

She looked away.

She said, 'They're flying him out this morning. He's lost some blood.

He's –'

'He's goan be fine.'

'Lester, fess up. I have to know.'

She took his hand in both of hers, as though somehow she were begging for his love. He met her gaze, and in a moment of yearning, he almost fell into it.

'Was it Norbert who shot that bear?'

Astrid's pale blue eyes sent out a beam of intimate light so strong, so all-encompassing, he could not seem to escape. At this moment it was like he was dancing a slow waltz with her. Everyone else in the restaurant faded into nothing because Lester Babcock was dancing with Astrid.

'No,' he said at last.

'They said he *fought* with the bear. Was it Eulalie? Lester, a reporter is going to be on that plane. Do you know what that means?'

'For the record, ah shot the goddam bear. Me, Lester Babcock. And don't let nobody think otherwise or Norbert will get the sack and probably a big hefty fine. Ah shot im. Bang. And that is how the story ends. Look, ah'll tell that reporter that Medicine Lodge is safe as six hunnerd dollars and the fishin is great. What are you so damn worried about?'

She looked nervously down at her empty plate and shook her head.

'I get this way when things get out of control.'

'Well then,' said Lester, in a hushed voice, 'there you are.'

The woman from the radio station was comely enough, Lester reckoned, to make Astrid jealous. She brought a tiny tape recorder and placed it on the table in front of him and he told his tale. Astrid was there, and Thor and his wife Kelly, and some of their guests. They gathered around and listened while Lester told his story. He skipped the part about his trade with Norbert for the gun. He skipped the part about the allnighter in the storm. He went directly to the confrontation in the tent compound, where he had been summoned. *Ah had this ol blunderbuss, see, an suddenly there was the bear and it was a big one....*

Lester told his yarn, earnestly playing down his role as hero and giving Norbert and his stick of firewood centre stage. He even pronounced the man's name in the Canadian way, *No-werr-berrt La Shonz,* for the Canadian listening audience. The more he tried to play down his role as mere facilitator, however, the more it seemed to Lester that he was coming off as quite the hero. Perhaps Astrid's presence was to blame, because she had a way of bringing out the man in a man.

'Ah went up to that ol bear till all ah could see was bear an nothin but bear, and blammo! One dead bear. He jess went down like a tree in the – '

The woman was waving to him.

'Ma'am?'

'Mr Babcock – '

'Lester.'

'Lester, how did you happen to have what you refer to as an old blunderbuss? Was this your gun?'

'Why yes, ma'am, ah brung it down to show some guides. They's right intersted in that ol piece of mine. They was a passin it around. When the bear come, why, some Indian lady, she grabbed it offen someone else and she jess up an thode it to me.'

'Thode it to you?'

'Yez'm. It was jess like a forward pass, and damn, if ah didn't catch that gun an shot that ol bear dead.'

Lester sat on his bed and stared out the window and down at the lake. It was raining heavily, and a mist was coming off the water as though the lake were coming to a boil. He could barely make out the shore less than a mile away on the far side of the bay. He could almost hear the sound of the waves exploding against the shores of Medicine Lake, the sound of trees crashing in the forest, the sound of the wind lashing over their upturned boat, the sound of Norbert's voice. *Go for a fas one wit dat blon lady, Eulalie, see have my balls for lunts meat.*

Norbert had stood up to the bear with a long piece of firewood in his hand. But why was he wearing the white suit? Did Norbert throw the suit on when the bear arrived because he thought it might contain some powerful medicine? Power dressing, like they say in Dallas? Or was Norbert simply wearing that suit to do some strutting? Maybe impress the hell out of Eulalie.

Norbert was a hero. He did what Lester could only dream of doing. Little wonder Astrid had gone after Norbert. She would have sensed that thing in him. She would have come right up to him and looked nose to nose at him, reeling him in with her pale blue eyes. Lester had the feeling, however, that Astrid might be dropping in on him, Lester Babcock, this evening. There had been some vibes. Hell, stranger things had happened.

It was ten minutes after five. Lester stood up and took off his camouflage pants and shirt. That was somehow wrong for the occasion. He went to his closet and automatically reached in for his lovely white suit, but of course that suit was probably in tatters in some hospital south of Medicine Lake. Lester was nervous, flustered. He threw on a pair of jeans and a western shirt with pearl studs for buttons. He was about to pour himself the last of his Maker's Mark when someone knocked on his door. *Oh, heidi, Astrid, what a pleasant surprise.*

Eulalie stood frowning in the doorway, or was she frowning? Perhaps she was just tired. She was holding Lester's suit. He asked her in out of the rain.

'Too bad about da blood,' she said.

He couldn't tell if it was bear blood or Norbert's. She had stitched up the biggest rips in the fabric using some very strong black thread. It gave his lovely white suit an entirely different look.

'You tell dat lady reporter?'

Lester grinned sheepishly.

'Ah didn't snitch on Norbert, if that's what ye mean. No, Eulalie. Ah told a little fib. Told that little girl with the tape recorder that ah shot the bear.'

'Brave hunter, ah?'

They stood there grinning.

'Eulalie, you're a batchin it tonight. Why don't you join me for dinner?'

She shook her head.

'Me, I don't go in dere.'

'Well, how about you come as ma date.'

She barked out a laugh and her eyes disappeared.

'No no no.'

'Ah don't care if yawl come as my seamstress, Eulalie, I ain't goin in without ye. It's lonely in there.'

They came through the main entrance and past the bar, which was overflowing with anglers who had taken the day off. Lester and Eulalie had to weave through the crowd to get to the dining room. Thor and his wife were standing by the entrance, blocking the way and gabbing happily with some guests. Lester came up on them from behind.

'Oh, they do like their guns down there,' Thor's wife Kelly was saying.

'It figures,' said the gent beside her.

'Next time he asks me to go hunting in Texas, remind me to say no,' said Thor.

They all laughed.

'Ah doubt that's goan happen,' said Lester to Thor.

Thor's expression changed ever so slightly.

'We were talking about your vice president,' said Thor.

'Ah believe he's from Wyoming,' said Lester. 'Don't go a-tarrin us all with the same brush.'

'Well,' said Kelly, 'you're the one who brings his guns up here. If we'd known you were bringing guns up here we might have had to cancel your reservation.'

'Missus,' said Eulalie, in a voice devoid of emotion, 'dat wasn't his gun dere.'

'Aw dang it, Eulalie,' said Lester, 'yawl don't have to lie on my behalf. Ah brung up that gun and ah'm goan take it back. Ah'd be lost without that ol gat.'

When they sat down to supper, Lester asked Eulalie where she had hidden the ten-gauge.

'In a good spot,' she said.

When Lester arrived at his condo in Dallas, he was very tired. He bought a paper, ascended in the elevator, and shovelled in some cold cereal in front of the television set. He found the article on the third page, *Dallas Angler Ties into a Big One.* The story was eleven lines long. Lester peeled off his clothes, had a hot shower and pulled on his pyjamas. He went to get his dressing gown from the clothes closet. He slid open the door and beheld his lucky white suit, blooded and stitched, swaying from the rack. He didn't have the heart to throw it out.

'Heidi, mister,' he said to his suit. 'Welcome home.'

☆ Turkle

A long time ago there was a great storm, a blizzard that pummelled the prairie for one night and one day and one long night. Oldtimers from the district will use it as a benchmark for other memories. One of the hardest hit was a farmer who owned more than a section of land along the North Saskatchewan River. On the morning of the great storm this man awakened before dark, walked out into the yard, and noticed that even on the path he took to the barn the snow was up to his knees. In the midst of doing his chores he discovered that during the night his cow had wandered away through an open gate. He was fairly sure that, unless something had driven it off, the cow was not going to wander far. The cow's name was Turkle, but the farmer never used that name. This was just the family cow as far as he was concerned, and it didn't pay to get sentimental about animals.

On the morning of the storm, his wife and children got up as though nothing were different. The immense snowfall was exciting, perhaps almost a novelty for them. And so the children dressed for school.

It was a three-mile walk. The farmer announced that he would take his almost new 1924 Model T out of the shed, put on the chains, and drive them all to school. This would give him a chance on the way back to check for the missing cow because someone had left the gate open. He knew every pebble on the road, he was proud of what his new car could do with chains on the wheels, and he was too stubborn to let a snowstorm divert anyone in his family from their daily routine.

Apparently his wife protested. She felt that the children should be allowed to miss school, stay home, and do their lessons in the kitchen next to the wood stove. It was twenty-five degrees below zero that morning and dropping. But the farmer must have brushed aside her protests with his usual admonition, that only babies are meant to stay home in bad weather, and the children aren't babies any more, so why baby them?

He went outside and cranked up his new Model T, and in a minute they were gone. They were gone long before it was light.

For some reason, perhaps a small act of rebellion, the youngest daughter, the one who they say left the gate open, smuggled her cat from the barn into the car beneath the folds of her winter coat. The cat was a tabby named Albert. The names of the children were Clarence, who was ten; Eleanor, who was nine; and Berta, the girl with the cat, who was six.

The farm was less than one hour's drive north of Saskatoon, a section of grainland with a large coulee that flows into the river southwest of Hepburn. The road the farmer drove runs through this coulee, and so in a tough blizzard it would be sheltered from a north or a west wind. Away down in the coulee, you could underestimate even the severest storm, which explains why the farmer thought he could negotiate the road in his car. But when you climb up out of the coulee and onto the flat land, these prevailing winds can catch you very suddenly with a wall of driving snow.

And that's what must have happened to the farmer, whose name was Elmer Foster, as he wheeled the Model T out of his coulee so many decades ago. Still more than a mile southeast of the schoolhouse, he drove into a massive whiteout, and before he could stop or turn back into the coulee, he was off the trail and spinning his tires in snow up beyond the running board. The farmer tried to extract his car from the snow bank, but when he spun his wheels, something seemed to blow its top (my grandmother's words), and the car's engine went dead. He tried to crank it up again, but to no avail.

The farmer waded all around the car. He was almost blinded by the driving snow which by now was propelled by a barn-crushing wind that greeted the first rays of daylight with one long demented howl. As the story is told, the farmer was a fearless man, and less unnerved by the storm than angered by this turn of events.

Elmer Foster was a tall man. Ducking his head back into the car, he must have had to hunch over to deliver his speech to his three children. He was by reputation a man of few words, so this speech must have seemed something of an occasion to the children. 'Better stay put,' he is reported to have said. 'I don't care how much yiz want to go out there or how long yiz have to sit in the car, do not I repeat do not leave for so much as a minute in this storm. If it gets cold, huddle up, light this here candle, sing songs, nibble away at your lunches, and keep the blanket over top, but don't try to make it to that school or yiz won't last three gulldam minutes.'

One of the children asked him where he was going.

'I'm going to get the horses.'

With his coat flapping like the wings of a great stricken bird, he staggered back towards the coulee and disappeared into the driving wind.

The three children and the cat arranged themselves together in the back seat, and their voices were almost silenced by the terrible wind. They sat so that little Berta was in the middle between the bodies of the two older children. In return for this favour, Berta allowed them to hold her cat inside their coats, and all day long they passed Albert back and forth beneath the blanket.

As I write this down (in a warm house in the city), I'm sitting merely one room away from the same blanket. It is a faded and worn but still red Hudson's Bay blanket with black stripes. In one corner are four parallel black bars woven into the wool. These indicate the heaviest gauge, a fourstar, as they used to say. The four bars are there for native trappers who could count but not read. This family heirloom is probably about ninety years old.

But as I was saying, the children lit the small candle offered to them by their father and nibbled away at their lunches until the last crumb was gone.

The farmhouse was sheltered from the storm at the lower end of the coulee. The children's mother could hear the wind rising, she could see the snowfall increase, and for half an hour or so, she went about her chores half distraught and half denying the peril that had enveloped her children and husband. When at last she went outside to the henhouse, she had to catch her breath in the cold. Instead of feeding the chickens, she plunged a short way up the road to see if she could spot her husband's car coming back. But there was no sign of the car, and the tracks the car had left had already filled in with snow and disappeared. Elsie Foster retreated to the house, filled the stove with firewood, and waited by the kitchen window. Even down in the protected coulee, she could now assume that this was one of the worst storms she had ever seen.

The window she waited by looks out onto the trail her husband took to drive the children. On all but the foulest days the view from this window conjures a remarkable illusion. The viewer is closer to the river bank and to the cottonwoods and willows that line the river than to the vast prairie up above, and so from the Foster house, the table land that constitutes this prairie looks more like the top of a ridge of hills or a plateau – anything but a prairie. If you had to live away out there, my grandmother used to say, that was the place to be.

There was no telephone, so Elsie Foster waited. The wind got worse and worse, and the temperature sank to thirty below. Several times during the day, in moments when the wind seemed to taper off, she left the warm house and tried to break trail up the road through the ravine that led to the schoolhouse. Each time, the driving snow forced her back inside. Sometimes she imagined her husband and her little ones safe inside the schoolhouse and merely unable to return home in the storm. But these short respites of desperate hope soon gave way to agonized mourning for each one of them. She never slept that night.

When she got up in the morning long before daybreak, the storm had passed, the wind had fallen, and the temperature had risen dramatically. When she left the house the temperature was still rising. In Alberta, this sudden warming after a cold spell is called a chinook, but in Saskatchewan, this phenomenon was so rare that back then, it didn't even have a name.

The farmer's wife harnessed two horses to the cutter and grabbed a scoop shovel. She sat in the driver's seat beside a supply of blankets and a large rounded rock heated on the stove that she had wrapped in cloth. She urged the horses all the way up the coulee to the place where the car had gone into the deeper snow. It looked like a huge humped animal asleep in the ditch. She could not scrape the snow off the new Model T; she had to shovel it off in great scoops. It was some time before she managed to yank open the door on the driver's side.

The first thing she discovered was that her husband was gone. The second thing she saw, as a waft of candlewax and urine passed through her nostrils, was her three little ones still as death beneath the blanket, and then, nosing its way out from where they lay, the tabby named Albert. She cried out the names of her children, Clarence! Eleanor! Berta!

Slowly, one by one, they opened their eyes as though called back from the dead. Their candle had burned to a stub.

She carried the children from the Model T to the cutter and bundled them in with the cat and the hot bound stone. Then she led the horses back on foot and carried the children into her own bed. She massaged their limbs and fed them tea and soups and anything else they would take down, and though the two eldest turned feverish, she could see that her children had a good chance of making it back from their long sleep. One of them told her that their father had gone for the horses, so she realized he must have fallen somewhere between the Model T and the barn.

Berta, the small one, seemed strangely unaffected by the ordeal in the Model T. Her mother spent more time tending to the needs of the two older children while little Berta slept between them in her parents' large bed. When Berta woke up, she said that she would come with her mother to find their father. But her mother made Berta stay home to care for Clarence and Eleanor if they should wake.

Elsie Foster knew she had to hurry. Once more she climbed into the cutter, though this time without the heated stone and the blankets, and urged the horses up out of the coulee and toward the schoolhouse. The snow was whipped and banked in bluewhite folds beneath a clearing sky, yielding not a sign of her husband. Perhaps he had gone in the other direction and found his way to the schoolhouse. If not ... and she prayed all the way to the sound of the wheezing horses and the hissing runners.

There was a jubilant crowd of survivors at the schoolhouse. Some of her neighbours had kept their children home; others had accompanied them to school and spent the entire day and night in the teacherage. When Elsie Foster burst into the schoolhouse, the happy mood gave way to one of great urgency. Elsie's neighbours set out at once to find her lost husband. All day long they kept arriving with food and fresh horses for the search.

A team of horses managed to tow the Model T back to the Fosters' yard. The men waded back and forth over the trail poking and kicking at anything that might have fallen in the deep snow. But no one found a trace of Elmer Foster, the children's tall, strong, fearless father. Their indestructible father.

Elmer Foster, people said, would sooner have taken a horse or a car than walk a hundred feet. When he left the Model T, he half sailed, half stumbled down the trail back through the coulee, but even there, the wind was almost unbearable. It drove him along like a tumbleweed, sliced through his winter coat, and every time he drew breath, the air sank like a cold thin blade into his lungs. He managed to walk for half a mile, and then the trail turned west so that he had to face almost directly into the wind for a painful stretch. At this point on the trail, he must have seen very quickly that he wasn't going to make it. As the story goes, he ran into something huge and motionless somewhere near the trail. It was Turkle, the missing cow. She was still alive, in fact still standing and covered with a deep layer of snow, but the storm had been so intense the poor animal was played out, her breath coming in short feverish whistles. When he kicked the unfortunate creature, she scarcely even moved.

Foster always carried a big jackknife in his pants pocket. Perhaps the knife was in his hand before any clear messages had reached his half-frozen cranium. He had no sledge, of course, with which to stun the animal before he stuck it, so with the cow standing there in a state of frozen immobility, he probed the dewlap for the hole that cows have at the front of their brisket, and drove the long blade into the lower part of the cow's throat. As he had always done at the smokehouse, he twisted the blade, severing Turkle's jugular. The blood fountained out, the cow shuddered in the man's arms, and her old legs buckled.

Away from his ropes and pulleys outside the smokehouse door, Elmer Foster had never slaughtered a cow, so the work was clumsy and rushed. At first he could scarcely feel the knife in his hands, but when the warm blood covered them, the hands seemed to revive on their own. He opened up the cow, pulled out her intestines, and with them a sizeable calf fetus, and slowly wedged himself inside. Caught in a lesser storm, he might have chosen to fight his way down the coulee, but something must have told him that this was absolutely his only chance. He went into the foul steaming carcass feet first so that his head and nostrils would remain closest to the opening, and like the womb's former inhabitant, Elmer Foster closed his eyes to the awful storm. It howled over his head all that day and all the following night.

I have always wondered what Elmer Foster thought about in his moments of consciousness. Did he fret about his children in the car or his wife, alone in the house? Did he hear his own words to his wife that same morning? Only babies are meant to stay home in bad weather, and the children aren't babies, so why baby them?

During the warmest part of the day, the search continued up and down the trail from the point where the car had foundered to the Fosters' yard. Clarence and Eleanor, the two oldest children, slept and woke throughout the day in a state of feverish recovery. Their mother left them in the care of her sister and joined in the search. As the afternoon wore on, a neighbour boy brought little Berta out on the trail so that she too could search for her father. She had been told that either they would find him and take him home, or that God would find him and take him to Heaven. This seemed a reasonable explanation, so the little girl, bundled up and drawn by her older companion on a toboggan, remained calm all through the waning afternoon. The boy left her and went to help the men search through some snow-drifts a short way off the trail.

Sitting on her sled, Berta thought she heard a noise. She made her way over to the sound and discovered after some vigorous digging that she was standing on a massive object beneath the snow. She began to dig down, singing and talking to herself. From time to time, the men would walk by, and perhaps note with some surprise that the girl was helping in her own way. As the light began to fade, she had uncovered the head of her beloved Turkle.

The name, I'm told, had come from Berta herself, a mispronunciation of turtle, and was applied to the big cow for her painstakingly slow movements around the farm. Apparently the name had stuck for everyone in the family except Elmer.

'Moo,' Berta said to Turkle, and the cow seemed to moo back.

'What are you doing in the snow?' said the little girl.

Turkle grunted a faint reply.

'Are you deaded?' said the girl. This time there was no reply. 'Turkle, you should go home and get warm.'

The cow seemed to agree. It even growled her name, or seemed to. Turkle had spoken many times to Berta, but never in a voice so strange and anguished. The girl stood up and began to back off.

When her mother came to take her home, she found Berta hitting the massive head of the cow with her mittened hand. She explained to her mother that Turkle was a bad cow, but that was because she was sick and cranky, and maybe they should take her home too.

'It's too late for Turkle,' her mother said. 'Turkle is dead, Berta.'

'No, she's not,' said the little girl. 'Are you, Turkle.'

Without so much as the flicker of an eyelash, Turkle stared like a mother, sadly, and perhaps a little bit offended, up at the rising moon. I know what I know, she seemed to say.

'Come over here,' said Elsie Foster. 'Mummy wants to have a word with ...' She never finished her sentence.

Much of this story, perhaps too much, was told to me by my grandmother. She signs her name Mrs Judson Gerald Steward, but back then she was a girl named Eleanor Foster. She has a small flair for the dramatic, and I find I have pared her story back some. For example, she swears that the coyotes had already gotten to Turkle and her precious cargo, which is highly unlikely. She has little Berta standing triumphant upon the head of Turkle signalling to the searchers in a gesture made all the more dramatic by the setting sun and the rising moon. If this were such a big moment for little Berta, why does she still avoid talking about the day they found her father? My grandmother simply shrugs. This is an older sister's gesture. In her rendition, brother Clarence is holding Albert the cat and openly weeps to a reporter as he tells the story his mother cannot bring herself to tell. This description doesn't quite square with my old taciturn Uncle Clarence, a solitary alcoholic whose memory of his father seems pretty shaky.

But the story survives in an even more pared down version in the *Saskatoon Star-Phoenix,* and from there it was carried all across the nation. It is typical of my family that the only national fame they ever attained was entirely unsought.

But one dramatic detail of Eleanor's that I cannot bring myself to leave out is the moment in the smokehouse when all six feet of Elmer Foster's body were finally pried free of the great carapace of Turkle's body like a thawing T-bone, and oh, she moans, oh, the sight of his clotted head when he first smelled the air of the barn and he opened his mouth to howl and cry in mother's arms.

ONE

I used to tell this story during my drinking days down at the Athabasca. It was a good test of people's sobriety. The moderate drinkers would give me that Oh-sure-Barney look, and the drunks would grow wide-eyed with belief and make me feel for a while like a shaman. I've told two people this story when I was completely sober: my wife, Molly, and my younger brother Darryl. Molly took the diplomatic approach and said there were certainly parts of it that rang true, but Darryl looked at me as if to say, *So that's where three years of university and all that reading got you.*

'You were always the one with the imagination,' he told me.

Spiritless little prig.

I too have had problems with believing things. It's a family trait. Before my mother met my father, she believed in salvation through Jesus Christ and he believed in oblivion through Johnnie Walker. She agreed to lay off the religion if he agreed to lay off the bottle, and they got married in 1944. I was the fruit of their brief armistice. I've tried Mom's church and Dad's boozing, and as far as I'm concerned neither one inspires belief in anything worthwhile. I'm on the wagon from both, and Molly says that's just fine with her.

So I've decided to write this story down and send it somewhere, a magazine maybe, the kind that will print things that most magazines won't; the kind that will print a story in which a guy can call his little brother a prig, for instance. And if a magazine or newspaper won't take it, I'll send it to the Jasper archives and let someone else live with this thing for a while.

It began with the death of Annette Muskwa in a TB hospital around 1948. Her husband, Noel Muskwa, was left without anyone to take care of their youngest child, so Nokom (everyone's name for Annette's mother) came and lived with them. The child was Delphine Muskwa, an afterthought, you might say. She was my only real playmate until I was eight or nine years old. She had long black hair, a mouth that reminded me of cartoon frogs; and when she smiled, her eyes disappeared. Delphine Muskwa. Sometimes just saying her name makes me feel sentimental.

Delphine's dad Noel was a trapper and a hunter. Due to pressure from Annette, and because of his own love of solitude, Noel always kept his distance from the reserve. Today we would probably call Noel and his family non-Status or non-Treaty, but in those days Father called them bush people, and around there that explained everything. Mother thought Noel was a difficult man. No one could ever get him to do anything he didn't feel like doing.

We must have been very dependent on them: Father on Noel because (in spite of his intractability) he knew so much about the bush, he was handy, and liked my father; Mother on Annette for several years before her death, because she was someone to visit with; I on Delphine because she was good to play with; and all of us on Nokom because she knew things about sickness and babies and the like.

Every summer after the Indian Days Rodeo, Noel's people would pay him a visit. These were reservation Indians (what my grandmother Sharples called 'real Red Indians'): uncles, aunts, Noel's older children, and dozens of his children's children, and some very old people who spoke Cree with a little sprinkling of French. They came in wagons, some of the young men on ponies. All hell broke loose in a nice sort of way for me and in a fretful sort of way for my parents. Delphine would grab hold of me and we'd run off with all the other kids and go fishing or play games. Once I'd been given the okay from Delphine, I was accepted; that's all there was to it. My parents would worry that we'd run into a bear, which we sometimes did on the upper meadow, but nothing ever happened, except later of course, and that's something I'll get to.

For the most part the Muskwa men were a peace-loving lot, but one or two of them would sometimes get drunk. That meant climbing my father's tower, which usually meant falling off, which in turn meant the clown in question would have to get taken to town because Nokom, for all her medicinal know-how, was never much good at setting bones. Once one of the uncles, Clayton Muskwa, an obnoxious fellow drunk or sober, took Father's half-ton and drove it into the Muskwas' backhouse. Trying to pull out, he high-centred the truck on a stump. It took a team of horses to pull it off and my father lost his muffler. He got awful mad.

He must have made a compromise with himself. Like most reformed drinkers, he disapproved of drinking and carrying on, but he knew how much we all depended on the Muskwas; so he tolerated their occasional summer excesses and counted the days till the uncles and their families would pack up the wagons and head back down the trail. Which they did whenever Nokom had had enough of what she called 'Injun's people'. She often called her son-in-law 'Injun'. I'm not sure why. Maybe she associated Noel with his former reserve. The reserve was anathema to her. After Annette's death, Noel used to swear he'd go back to it, but he never did go back. I think he just missed his wife.

Trapping and hunting inside Jasper Park were and still are illegal, so Noel did his trapping and hunting just outside the park boundary. He claimed the boundary was exactly one quarter of a mile from the east end of his and Dad's corral. He may have been telling the truth here, because when the school district was surveyed, Noel seemed to know to within a few yards where the line came. I think he had a shrewd sense for that sort of thing.

Before their kids grew up and left them, in fact before Delphine was born, Noel and Annette tried living in a shack at the edge of town. His idea then was to live near town but not in it, because if he was within the town limits his children would have to go to the residential school. He absolutely refused to let his kids go to any school, least of all the one where he'd lose them for most of the year.

When the school district was formed, he built another shack in the bush. He claimed this new shack was just a bit outside the new line. He eyeballed it, as they say. When a school official came to his door and said the kids had to obey the law and go to school, he simply pointed to where the line was and said as long as he was outside that line, no child of his would ever set foot in that damned school. So they surveyed the line, putting in stakes, and sure enough, Noel's cabin was outside by several yards.

The town grew. With its collective eye on more tax dollars, the school district expanded. Once more, Noel and family abandoned their shack and threw up a cabin back in the bush. Once more the authorities drove out to claim the children and once more they discovered that Noel's new cabin was just a few feet on the other side of the boundary. He told them what they could do with their 'residentzel scole'. The first year our cabins sat side by side on Celestine Lake, Noel had moved his family half a dozen times. This time he was so far from the school line he could feel safe for years. He and the last of his family lived winter and summer in that last cabin of theirs. It always smelled richly of hides, moose meat, dogs, bannock, berries and tobacco, many of the things I couldn't smell in my own home.

Around the time I was born my father manned the forestry tower every spring and summer at Celestine Lake, which is just inside the eastern boundary of Jasper Park among the hoodoos and gravelly ridges too high to be called hills and too low to be called mountains. Nokom attended at my birth. I was supposed to be born in the Jasper hospital but I came several weeks early, and old Nokom was there. My mother preferred her to the doctor in town who, according to Mother, was a whisky-soaked old coot. She liked to stress that fact in Father's presence, which was always good for a tirade from him on the subject of Bible-thumpers.

For half a dozen years or so Delphine was the only permanent kid up there my age. My parents would tease me and call her my girlfriend, but I think they were grateful for Delphine because she, and occasionally her cousins, gave me something to do and somewhere to go in those endlessly long days from June to September when time seemed to crawl along like a garden slug.

Comic books were the key. We acted them out even when there was just the two of us. We got to be animals and other people. Absolutely the best one for acting things out was *Tarzan*. If you got to be Tarzan himself, you could give great war whoops and swing on the rope that hung from the Douglas fir in front of the corral. Or if you were Tantor, you got to lumber through the forest on your hands and knees with Tarzan or Boy or Jane on your back and everyone ran from you. They had to. You were the elephant and that was the game. And if you were one of the apes or one of the natives you got to yell things like, *Kree-gah Gomangani! Bundolo, kill!*

Delphine did animals real well. When she became Tantor and crashed through the trees, you never doubted that she was Tantor. And when she was a monkey (I taught her monkeys; I'd seen some at the fair in Edson) she hopped around all hunched over, gibbering, arms dangling. By God she was a monkey. And when she did a bear, she'd walk on her hind legs, beat the air with her front paws, scrunch up her face and look fierce. Boy, let me tell you, she was a bear. She could scare me sometimes.

I have a photograph of her and me at Celestine Lake. I think Mother took it. We're holding hands and squinting at the person with the camera.

We're both eight or nine years old, skinny and very brown. My smile is a bit shy; Delphine's is smug, like she has a secret and she's not telling.

Two or three times between the first of May and the Labour Day weekend, we had to drive to town. My father would go about his business at the warden's office, my mother would get provisions in the truck, and Delphine and I would go down to the CN station. It had to be timed just right. The bears would arrive as the train came in and leave minutes later after it left. Their timing was never off.

When you heard the chugging of the Edmonton train just after 10 a.m., all you needed to do was look west on Connaught Drive and there they'd be, ambling toward you: mamas and cubs, uncles and aunts, old boars with chewed-up ears, cinnamon bears, dark brown ones, but mostly black with a white star on the chest, and mostly ragged-looking, like gypsies. They'd come down the main street in twos and threes, slowly at first, stop and sway their heads, smelling the air, listening like old blind men. Then the older ones would pick up the pace, look a bit bolder, the cubs would tussle a bit, get behind, scamper back; until finally they'd all be gathered on the grass beneath the totem pole where the passengers debarked. The bears were never pushy about their panhandling. They just waited there pretending not to be hungry and stayed out of the redcaps' way until the show began.

After the shock wore off from seeing this army of bears out there, the tourists would grab their cameras and any junk food they could get their hands on. They'd pay the redcaps large sums of money to have their pictures taken with the bears. Occasionally a man would try to find a docile one and place his hat on the bear or induce it to stand up so he could put his arm around the bear or clap it on the back. These games of course proved worrisome for the park wardens because sometimes a tourist would pick the wrong bear to get familiar with. This must have been before the time when fear of lawsuits governed all social behaviour, because (knowing bears were good for the tourist business) all Thurmon Butters, the superintendent, did was put up a snow fence on the grassy area with a ten-foot opening for the bears. No people were allowed inside the fenced area. The tourists would gather on one side of the fence; the bears, on their hind legs, would rest their front paws on top of the fence and sort of sway back and forth with the give and take of it. These fences are insidious things. They have their own logic, like slinkies.

Word got around that the best way to feed a bear was to put your hands on the fence and gently lean towards the animal. The tourist didn't want the bear falling onto his side of the fence, and he sure as hell didn't want to fall onto the bears' side, so both bear and tourist tended to respect that fence. Coca-Cola seemed to be the preference among the younger bears. The tourist would invert a six-cent bottle of Coke, baby bottle fashion, into the bear's mouth and watch the bear slobber Coke till it was all gone. It was considered particularly touching if the young bear in question would rest its paws on the wrist of the tourist long enough for other tourists to say awww and click their shutters.

Up on the alpine meadow north of Celestine we had *real* bears, grizzlies. They were big, and they weren't garbage bears. Once in a while a family of these grizzlies would amble down from the high country to the west of us and into our meadow. I have very good eyes, so I usually spotted them before Delphine did. We'd watch them for hours, downwind of course, and in the trees, so we could scamper up one if they got our scent and charged. But none ever charged us.

I can still see those bears. The sun brought out the pale gold in their fur and the wind made dark ripples through it. Their humps were like dry grassy hills. I remember grizzlies not as *Ursus horribilis,* killers or brutes, but creatures of golden light, otherworldly, bigbellied like sumo wrestlers.

One morning I came early to breakfast. Mom looked worried. I think that's when she was pregnant with my brother. Dad was talking on the radio, yelling rather, and swearing. With him that was a bad sign.

'Fine, Thurmon, I'll just abandon my tower and hightail it down there like I've got nothing better to do....' And, 'Fine, Thurmon, I'll just toady to the tourists. That's what we're paid to do, right? Toady to the goddam tourists?'

Like I said, Thurmon Butters was the superintendent. He was a big man with a soft paunch. He always wore sunglasses and his hair combed straight back like a gangster's, and he always had a toothpick in his mouth. His best friend was a sergeant in the Mounties, Orly Cobey. Orly and Thurmon had far more authority in Jasper Park than they could handle. They hunted together, played poker together, drank together, and because neither one could make a decision about anything, they consulted together, a perpetual committee of two. I think they must have seen the whole world through each other's eyes, having so little to see with on their own.

'Oh, sure, Noel be just smilin' ear to ear. He's got nothin' better to do,' my father continued in a high voice, bold and craven both. Maybe only once a year did my father get this mad now that he was sober. 'Why bring Noel in on this? Why not tell him.... You tell him yourself, Thurmon. This is your baby. I'm not paid to go around –'

My mother stood by the sink, finger to her lips even though I was quiet, listening to the buzz and crackle of radio static and the thunderous lisping retorts of Thurmon Butters, who was out of bed earlier than he liked to be and obviously still without his teeth.

You can live in a cabin miles from anywhere but you can never really get away from the likes of Thurmon Butters. Maybe that's what Mother was thinking when Father finally agreed to Thurmon's orders. He and Noel were off in the truck without any breakfast. I asked Mother where they were going and she told me to mind my own business. Go and play with Delphine.

Dad and Noel had their rifles.

Nokom responded to this event with a grim smile, or what might have passed for a smile among white people. 'Kuh!' she grunted. 'Injun gonna soot a bear. Thinks he's gonna be a man, ah? Join up wit da posse.'

'Noel and my dad?'

Delphine said nothing. For a moment all I could hear was the blowing of the kettle.

'*Mikoskateyihtamowin,*' Nokom muttered, not really to me or anyone in the dark kitchen. '*Mikoskateyihtamowin.*' Trouble.

No one spoke, the kettle whispered, the dogs lay on the floor, heads on their paws, eyes rolling up red and mournful to watch us: Nokom whispering like the kettle, Delphine picking up her food, me shrugging to no one.

'*Maskwa,*' muttered Nokom. 'You better run.'

For the longest time, I thought she meant Noel, until I learned that *maskwa* in Cree meant bear.

There had been a mauling down at the CN station. Not a bad one either. A boy had gone and leaned on the snow fence at feeding time while he was snapping a picture. He fell head first into the bear welcoming committee, camera flying. The camera struck a cub on the nose, the cub set up a yowl, the nearest sow gave the boy a swat, and he screamed. I guess that boy must have put the panic into all those bears: a kicking screaming human-thing in their midst, one that hurts cubs when he's supposed to be feeding them. The sow took him by the shoulder, gave him a good shaking, and let him go, then lit off for the woods with a dozen other bears. The boy took ten stitches.

I've seen some people in my time, but let me tell you, this boy's father was something else. According to my dad, who got the story second-hand, this man was a grand pooh-bah with the civil service. He had some pretty strong opinions about bears. They travelled in 'packs' and this 'pack' probably had rabies, every one of them; and if not, then they were still dangerous, and why didn't somebody do something before someone got killed?

Thurmon Butters asked the man what he had in mind. It's easy to imagine their conversation.

'How about shooting that bear before I have the lot of you fired for endangering people's lives?' says the man from Ottawa.

'Which one?' says Cobey. He always has an eagerness about him when it comes to hunting bears.

Well, they sort of thought it was a sow, because around cubs the sows get the most skittish. But Cobey himself claimed it was a big boar. No doubt Cobey was dreaming of bear hides. And of course Thurmon had some plans of his own. With his job on the line and that man from Ottawa looking over his shoulder taking down names, Thurmon Butters, with the help of his perpetual committee, made an administrative decision. 'We'll get up a posse,' he would say to the man from Ottawa. 'We'll get a posse, and you come in at the end of the week when the Injun's done his work, and by garsh,' he says with a toothpicky smile, 'you can have your pick of the hides.'

Noel should never have gone into town that day. This is what happened. Thurmon Butters was very nervous about shooting what in all probability would be quite a few bears, though at the same time, very eager to do it. He just didn't want any screw-ups. Wounded bears, that is. If, after the first barrage, one or two of these wounded bears remained, he wanted to be sure there was someone present who was a good enough shot to finish them off before they made it into the trees; or who, if one or two bears actually made it into the trees, would have the nerve and the know-how to track them down and shoot them. Sergeant Cobey wasn't the least bit nervous. Likely he saw the whole thing as a glorious counter-attack against the dark forces of nature. The more firepower the better. And they both needed someone to skin out the animals because when would there be another opportunity to get their hands on so many bear hides?

Noel Muskwa was the answer to their prayers. But he had to be lured in. After all, he had little love for the town that was forever attempting to take his kids away, and he had no quarrel with the bears. So my father was the key. Under threat of dismissal, he agreed finally to ask Noel to come along as a personal favour.

But why did Noel agree to participate in this supreme folly? He never did Father favours unless he felt like doing them, and he could not have felt much like doing this job: slaughtering a bunch of innocent animals and skinning them out. Who knows? The body of an ancestor? Up north lots of Cree elders still refuse to kill bears.

I think Noel wanted recognition. Here was his chance to show these people who were in constant pursuit of his children that what he and his family did in the bush was important: the hunting, the skinning, the horsemanship, the bush lore that he taught his kids. His services for the town's respect. And when he arrived in Jasper with the tools of his trade, skinning knife and rifle, they'd see him as he really was. And they'd see he came in Joe Hetherington's half-ton. While my father was in his sober period, a lot of people respected him, so doing Father this favour might serve to kill two bears with one stone.

My God, what an awful way of putting that. But maybe in ways I can only begin to understand, that's just how it went.

Dad and Noel only just managed to make it into town before the road went all greasy from rain. There on the station platform were sixteen men with rifles. Several were Mounties and wardens but most were made into what Thurmon Butters called special deputies, and some of them pretty unhappy about getting roped into this caper. Roadblocks were set up to keep people away. Several horses stood patiently in the rain, one for Noel and the rest for the men who were to ride with Noel after the 'stragglers', as Butters called them.

An hour or so before the Edmonton train was due in, several out-of-town photographers showed up. Thurmon Butters and Orly Cobey had discouraged this, but some people reckoned that Ottawa should know of their determination to keep the park safe for tourists, and they might as well read about it in the newspapers. The reporters raced out beyond the platform to where Noel was stationed, rifle in hand, on a borrowed horse, looking very dubious; looking, I imagine, as though by some mistake he had found himself fighting for the wrong side.

One of the photographers asked Noel if he didn't mind posing for some pictures in someone's borrowed buckskin jacket. The bears weren't due in for at least another half hour. Noel told them if they didn't get out of the line of fire it would be their hides he'd be nailing to the barn that night.

When the train pulled in that day, only seven bears showed up. Some people said it was the rain. I doubt that very much. My dad claimed it was the smell: desperation, fear, something like that. All those men with guns in the midst of a huge complicity bigger than the callousness of Orly Cobey, the dumb authority of Thurmon Butters, and the sheer sissiness of the man from Ottawa. You give a man a horse and gun and orders to kill, you line him up with a bunch of men with the same orders, I think you bring out something ugly that's been buried in all of them. I think the bears, even the ones imprudent enough to show up that day, could smell the smell of all that. They never reached their patch of grass and all that sweet Coca-Cola. They got past Noel Muskwa sitting quietly on his borrowed horse (perhaps he smelled just fine), they got past the mounted 'deputies', and about halfway between Noel and the snow fence before they began to hesitate and sniff from side to side.

Noel was supposed to give the signal for the men on foot to fire, but he never got his chance. When Cobey saw the bears hesitate, he jumped the gun and yelled, 'Now or never, boys!' and fired. About a dozen more rifles went off all at the same time. Noel's horse shied and he fell on the tracks with his boot in the stirrup. The men around him on horseback had to worry about their own horses. Some were thrown. There were bears in all directions, some of them injured, men firing wildly, bullets ricocheting, and for a minute they had too much in their sights to worry about Noel, whose horse was dragging him across the tracks, slamming him into cattle cars, whipping him around like a teddy bear. Finally someone looked up and just shot his horse. I'm glad I wasn't there.

When Butters and Cobey called on their men to stop firing, there were four dead bears (three had escaped down Connaught Drive), one dead horse, and some injured men (two from being bucked off, one from a ricochet). Noel Muskwa was found half covered by his horse, cursing and coughing blood, his body utterly broken. Father stayed with him in the Jasper hospital for two days until Noel died. He wasn't really my father after that. He sort of fell apart.

I can't begin to imagine the impact of this tragedy on Nokom, Delphine, and all their kin. When you come right down to it, I only know how it hit me. The changes in Mother, Father, Delphine and Nokom, for me, were like being told one day that the rules of the world had changed; nothing would be allowed to remain the same.

My mother took up with religion again, and Father went back to his bottle. He quit his job under Butters (who was fired soon after, along with Cobey) and returned to work in Jasper for the CNR (which he'd always hated and continued to hate). When my brother was born I had to 'take care of mother' by spending a lot of time around the house as a babysitter, for which I was bribed with Dinky toys. Anyway, I'm getting ahead of myself.

Some people from town brought Noel home to Nokom's cabin. Dozens of his own people came in wagons to say goodbye to him. They threw up teepees and old grey canvas tents and stayed for several days. They laid him out in the cabin in a big wooden box on a couple of saw-horses. A priest sent Delphine and her cousins into the woods to hunt for paintbrushes. They gathered armloads of them and laid them on the floor of the cabin.

I was too disturbed by Noel's death to be of much help, and so frightened that I even refused to go in and look. My mother said it was their way of saying goodbye to Uncle Noel, as she called him, and that I should go over there as our ambassador and pay my respects.

Later Delphine came over to fetch me. It was her job to keep the flies off her dad and lay the flowers on him, and she wanted me to help. I hid in the backhouse. Delphine planted herself outside and said she wouldn't move until I came out.

'I'm busy. Can't you see I'm busy?'

'Doin' what?' she asked in a listless voice.

'None of your business.'

'You've got to help, Barney. Nokom says.'

'She's your grandmother, not mine.'

'Your ma says too. You got to help me.'

'I'm busy in here. Go way.'

'You're just ascared. You don't have to be ascared.'

'I'm not scared.'

'C'mon, Barney.'

I refused to speak. My mother came out and said that if I didn't unlock the door she'd go and get my father. No answer. She got him and he said if I didn't come out he'd tear the door off its hinges. I came out. Delphine took me by the hand and we walked that immense hundred yards from our backhouse to Nokom's place.

Noel was dressed in everyday clothes: fresh cowboy shirt, jeans and boots, skinning knife and sheath on a wampum belt of moose hide and a big silver buckle lying on his chest. He looked smaller than life, shorter than his five foot seven inches, much lighter than his hundred and seventy-five pounds, the great chest somehow deflated and the cheeks sunken. There were horrible gashes on his head, I don't remember where exactly. I remember how much, in spite of death, he still looked like Uncle Noel, and that his face retained that look of a man cursing. The same sparse black moustache, the same thrust-up lower jaw, the same deep lines around eyes and brow that you see on the faces of so many old hunters. But now the jaw, the lines, the moustache, everything ordinary about his face, even the stained-log pigment of his skin, conspired to look fierce.

I returned later and his body was covered with paintbrushes. Only that fervid face was showing, the red of the flowers reflecting like new life on his cheeks. He was gathering his strength to spring out of his box and do battle.

We kept the flies off his face and out of his ears, Delphine and I and one of her cousins, while all about us his people mourned in Cree and bits of French and English. Even the men wept and wailed openly.

Delphine developed a daydreaming look about her and bit her nails day after day until her fingers bled. On the last day of mourning, when Noel was getting pretty high, I found piles of faded paintbrushes on the floor of Nokom's cabin. Someone had come in and taken Noel's beautiful belt, but left his skinning knife behind.

I don't remember much else. They took him away in a wagon and buried him somewhere north of Grand Cache. I don't think I saw much of Delphine that July. I spent my time reading war comic books. I have a sharp memory of one of them. A sergeant, who'd lost his entire platoon, stormed a big nest of Korean or Chinese soldiers and mowed them all down with a machine gun. He was unshaven and had extremely white teeth. He yelled things like, 'Take that, ya lousy gooks!' and the lousy gooks all went 'Aieee!' and died.

Someone from town gave Nokom a bear rug as an expression of the town's appreciation or bereavement or something.

A week or so later Mother found Nokom alone in her cabin, obviously distraught. Delphine was gone.

'Where is she?' asked my mother.

'Nowhere,' said Nokom.

'Who took her?' Mom asked.

'No one,' she said. 'He had a car.'

TWO

I don't recall hearing of a bear getting shot anywhere in the park before that
rainy day, except in the old days before I was born, when no one rode
through that country without a rifle and hunters came from the ends of the
earth just to kill something big.

A few days after his bear ordeal was over I found Father staring at an old
photograph, one that now hangs framed in my house. This photo says a lot
to me about those early times in the park. It was taken by an unknown
photographer near Jasper, a picture of four men who are leaning against a
flat-car, circa 1910. Three of the men have big floppy Stetsons with the rims
folded up at various rakish angles. These three also have bushy moustaches,
the kind that collect food from every meal. They do not smile and they're all
cradling rifles in their arms. The rifles are important somehow.

The fourth man holds a big revolver. He is unshaven, his whiskers light-
brown or blond. He has a small moustache, wears a monocle, dirty tweeds
and a deerstalker. He's the only one smiling. He looks unhinged, nervous. If
I were to guess, I'd say he was the boss out there, a remittance man who'd
been cut off and fallen into a bottle, and retained some sort of deranged
authority by flashing that six-shooter of his. This guess at least fits with the
skimpy bits of information I have on him.

Behind the four men is a straggle of shacks and tents. The encampment
looks scarcely more permanent than a bivouac, like they would stay there
for some time, but like they were none too fond of their place in the woods.

At the edge of the photograph sits a fifth man, young, unarmed, an
Indian. He has a child in his lap. It seems that this man was not intended to
be in the photo. He's only half interested in this show of arms. Perhaps he's
disgusted with it, hiding his disgust. This is not apparent in the picture; this
is me moralizing. But perhaps it's also the truth.

The man with the child on his lap is dressed in a shirt, trousers and
boots that conform to those of his fellow workers. The only difference is
that he is wearing no hat while they are all wearing hats. I can't imagine

these four men without their floppy hats or the deerstalker, their whiskers, or their various guns. And I can't imagine the man with the child on his lap growing whiskers, wearing a hat or flashing a gun. My father claimed that these hunters were a railway crew on a siding just west of Jasper.

The clothes on the man with the child on his lap bother me. They don't sit right on his body. I'm tempted to offer the usual theory: he's an Indian imprisoned in the white man's ways. I know, I'm moralizing again. But I do have some inside information. The man holding the child is Etienne Muskwa, born during one of the last skirmishes of the Métis resistance in Saskatchewan, what people around here call the Riel Rebellion. They say he was descended from Big Bear's people. Etienne was a fine hunter, famous for it, and yet here he is unarmed with a kid on his lap. The child is Noel Muskwa.

When I look away from the photo, I retain an impression that the four men, especially the boss with the revolver and the monocle, are scared, or at least very nervous. Perhaps they're bushed or something, the woods leaning in on them, sasquatches chasing them in their dreams. I think the crazy Englishman blew off most of Etienne Muskwa's hand with that gun of his. (I think so. Father told me that, shortly after the bear episode when he'd taken out the photo. He was in his cups and very gloomy.) The crazy Englishman was my grandfather.

One night in bed, a week or two before we moved away from Celestine Lake forever, I found someone's hand in bed with me. It touched my face, plucked my ears, pulled my nose, brushed my eyelids, all this as light as a moth. I clenched and unclenched my right fist and I could feel it, so it wasn't my right hand. I drew my left hand out from beneath my leg, waved it around and felt it. I lay there with my hands in the air, opening and closing them as though milking an invisible cow. Neither hand was asleep. So what in God's name was this third one? A mouse? A dream? Etienne Muskwa's severed hand?

I opened my eyes and slowly sat up. I could make out the wooden Coke cases Father had nailed together for my dresser, a small stack of comic books on top, my fishing rod leaning against the window, my baseball glove hanging on the wall.

Someone snickered.

It was him, I knew it, he'd come back for his hand. He was hissing, he smelled like a bear. 'Sssss!' he went. And giggled.

Delphine stood behind my bed. (She always did have trouble with the 'sh' sound.) I was wild with joy. She pounced on me and we rolled around the bed shushing each other and giggling in whispers.

'How long you bin standin' there?'

'Bout a mont' or two.'

'How'd you get in?'

'By there,' she gasped, pointing to my open window. 'I ran away. I'm not never goin' back.'

'What if they find you?'

'Nokom's got me hid in the daytime. Don't tell your mom and dad.'

I stared and stared at her. She smelled rank. They'd cut her hair short, but otherwise she was the same old Delphine, the frog-faced grin, the eyes disappearing, the way she pulled her head in like a turtle when she laughed. We lay on the bed and whispered for a long time. She had walked the thirty-five miles from Jasper to Celestine the previous couple of days. She claimed some of the sisters of the convent were trying to 'get' her, whatever that meant. So each day Delphine slept on a shelf rolled up inside the bear hide the townspeople had given to Nokom. A man from social services and a church woman came to find her the next day. Nokom let them look around, pretending to speak only Cree. They went away empty-handed.

Each day Delphine slept inside the bear hide and breathed in the musky smell of fresh bear. After a while this smell must have become normal to her. In fact, each night, when she snuck into my bedroom, she smelled overwhelmingly of bear. I'd have had nightmares, perhaps in dreams become that *maskwa* so dreaded by campers.

Each night Delphine was awake and frisky. When Nokom nodded off to sleep she stole over to our cabin, crawled in my window and woke me up. We were so quiet. It amazes me how quiet we must have been. We devised an animal game where words were unnecessary. We were a mama and papa bear. We arranged my blankets under the bed. This was our den. Inside the den we were safe. Outside it, however, collecting fish and coconuts and things, we had to be careful. Zulu warriors were everywhere. They'd spear you and eat you and make you stand all day memorizing things till you got them right. They had a witch doctor who spoke a funny language.

There were dangerous snakes beyond the den. Socks were poisonous snakes and Delphine's bluejeans were a python. Baseballs and rubber balls were coconuts and other fruit; shoes were fish. We always fed each other; we never fed ourselves. Zulus could come in through the bedroom door but they couldn't come in through the window. I kept wanting to shoot the snakes with my cap gun (unloaded, of course). I remember that. But Delphine would not allow this. We had to swat them with our paws. Delphine must have known that even the click of the hammer could have awakened my parents.

The Zulus had wiped out our tribe of bears, all except for some cubs. There were a few out there in the jungle and we had to find them and bring them home. My Bambi was one, my pillow another.

We would always fall asleep in the den, and if I woke up first I would rouse Delphine, help her to throw her clothes on, and pack her out the window before Nokom discovered our secret arrangement. Usually, though, I'd be the one to fall asleep first and wake up last beneath my bed, and in the morning Delphine would be gone and back inside her skin. Around that time I decided that when I was a little older I'd ask her to marry me. We'd go and live in Africa or somewhere, because Africa would have adventures, and we would refuse to wear clothes or speak words, and we would never come back. I wonder if I ever told her that. I don't think so. It bothers me that I may never have told her that. Sometimes you wish things could have been different.

One day when Mother and Father were packing boxes for our big move and I was picking berries with Nokom, the man and the woman came back. They searched Nokom's shelves. Maybe they spotted Delphine's foot sticking out of the bearskin or something like that. At any rate, they hauled her off in her sleep. Probably she didn't even wake up till she got down to Jasper. I came back with Nokom, and Delphine was gone.

I had never felt so alone in all my life. I moped around for days and weeks. I would refuse to sleep in my bed, only under it, and when my mother insisted that I sleep in it, I would do so only if I could sleep with Nokom's bear hide. I spent hours in silent communion with Nokom. I began to follow her around each day, imitating her, asking her questions. She wasn't very responsive. One night I overheard Mother talking to Father near the corral when I was supposed to be asleep: 'He's spending too much time over there. He's beginning to smell like them.'

That September it was hot and dry, the fire hazard up, and they got Father to stay on at Celestine for a little longer. Some nights I heard Nokom moaning and muttering things in Cree. This went on through the late summer and early autumn. Sometimes I awoke to her monologues at four or five in the morning when it was still dark, which meant she'd been talking to thin air all night long. Her voice would drift across the clearing in a high monotonous lament.

Father got very tense. He had spotted a grizzly near the corral at twilight. Nokom's dogs chased it off, it was a big one. So he would sit around drinking whisky and listening. I was not allowed out after dark. Father's rifle would lean against the door, and as he sat there, he would roll a thirty/thirty shell around and around in his hand, staring and listening. He reminded me of the men in my grandfather's picture, the one he had shown me a few days after Noel died. In spite of the dark and Father's bear vigil, Mother would occasionally put down her Bible and go over to visit with Nokom, but Nokom would just go silent. When Mother left, Nokom would start up her monologue again and go all night long.

One night I heard her muttering outside my window. *'Tanewa, tanewa ... napao?'* Then, *'Tanewa, tanewa ... iskwasis?'* These were the words, or some of them. *Where is he, the man? Where is the girl?* Then softly, *'Tanu? Tanu?'* She said other things but I couldn't make them out, or if I could, I've forgotten them.

I looked out the window and saw her small figure heading slowly past the corral. A horse whickered. She went up past the horses and into the trees. Another horse whickered, and another. From inside Nokom's cabin the dogs began to bark. In a minute or two there was an awful uproar. Father ran out in his longjohns. He had his rifle and he was mad as hell. He hopped over to Nokom's cabin, opened the door, and all the dogs flowed out. They raced into the trees the way Nokom had gone and raised a terrible racket.

None of us could figure out why Nokom had chosen to lock the dogs inside. In the daytime, they could come in and out as they pleased, but at night they had always slept outside.

The next night I woke up once more to Nokom's voice: *'Tanewa, tanewa?'* She went up back of our cabin and I threw on my clothes. I had this idea that maybe Delphine had come back. I'm sure I'd been praying for such a thing.

Nokom stood in the clearing, facing uphill toward the ridge, swinging this thing in her hand. All I could see on the ridge were some very big tree stumps, burnt-out Douglas firs, and a big boulder. In the dark, though, the tree stumps looked alive and massive, with stubby arms and legs. They looked like totem poles. I started to think about maybe going home. Under my bed or on it, there were always certain guarantees of safety.

Nokom's voice changed, it wailed high and cracked, a child-voice singing and weeping at the same time. I remember some of the words too, partly because I'd learned them from Delphine and her people, partly because they reminded me of other words.

Soskwats, she said, which means 'for no reason'; *wanitipis-kipayiw,* which means 'it becomes dark'. Noel's name was mentioned, and her daughter Annette's name, and *awasis,* meaning 'the child'.

It's funny, I don't remember many of the words any more, but I have dreams about her up there, wailing and swinging that thing at the tree stumps. In my dream she's on the ridge with her back to me, but at an angle. I'm in the trees. The top of the ridge is about thirty feet away. There's the big burnt-out tree stump, then a boulder, then another tree stump and that's about all. And Nokom waving this thing like a plumb bob at those objects. There must have been some moonlight too, because otherwise I wouldn't have seen the boulder move, which is exactly what it did. A big head sort of grew out of that boulder, and as Christ is my witness, it just stood up as huge as those two tree stumps. Right then Nokom gave a final cry and heaved her thing at the boulder with all her might. The boulder caught it, ate it, and I fainted dead away on the spot.

Some of this can be explained. I've done some thinking about that night. Nokom likely went up that hill with what must have been a chunk of meat in her hand, a chicken maybe, or a dead rabbit. There's no boulder on that ridge between the two burnt-out stumps, so it doesn't take a genius to figure out that my boulder was a large grizzly. I mean old Nokom *knew what she was looking for.* That's why she kept shutting the dogs up in the cabin. She was out hunting up that big old bear. She found him and she fed him. When he ate the rabbit or whatever, there wasn't ten yards between them.

Why she sought out this bear is another question. Bears are sacred to those people. You take it from there. I am not one to speculate about religion, much less someone else's religion. My mother spent the last half of her life in the arms of Jesus and scarcely ever got out of bed except to go to church. My little brother Darryl was born in the midst of her voyage back to Jesus and he still hasn't recovered from it. All I have to do is swear a few times or criticize our parents for their ostrich-like tendencies and Darryl gives me this look of his, as if to say, *I feel sorry for you, Barney. I really do.* So endeth the lesson.

I've kept a souvenir from that night, my jean jacket, made by Great Western Garments. The cloth is very tough, wears like leather. Right now it's hanging on my hiking stick just next to my typewriter. I was wearing that jacket when I got dragged down the hill. It was like a dream. Either I couldn't move out of fear, or I was still half into a faint. But I got dragged down that hill, face downwards, by the collar of my jean jacket. Dragged down the hill and dropped on the steps of Nokom's cabin. You take it from there. I don't want to give the impression that some child-loving bear, fresh from an engagement with Walt Disney Studios, just picked me up and took me home. That's roughly what I used to think when I was a boy. (What can I say? I read *Tarzan* comics like scripture.) In fact, if some altruistic bear did bring me down and drop me on the steps, why didn't the horses in the corral and the dogs in the cabin make a sound? But they didn't. If they had, my father would have been over there in a second.

But if it was Nokom who dragged me down the hill (assuming for a moment that a one-hundred-pound granny could do such a thing), why would she drag me past our cabin and drop me on the steps of her own? You can't get down to Nokom's cabin from the slope without passing ours.

I remember several things about my trip down the slope: the snuffling sound of laboured breathing right in my ear, a musky stink of warm breath on the back of my head and neck, the feeling of being half-strangled by the collar of my jean jacket, and the sensation of being borne along by a lumbering, powerful force through the brush and up the steps.

I wonder, of course, how much of this is my own invention. I pick up my jacket and hold it to the light. In the collar are two holes, at least five inches apart. I stick my thumb and a finger through these holes and wiggle them.

You see my problem here: I don't know what to make of this event. To write it down like this, as I remember it, makes me feel as though I've crossed some kind of line.

Nokom's people took her up north of Cache Creek and we never saw her again. Apparently she died not long after leaving Celestine Lake. We moved and Darryl was born. The rest of this story can be read in summary in the *Jasper Herald*. The back issues are in the Jasper archives. This one is September 30, 1954, one year after my bizarre trip down the mountainside.

GIRL CARRIED OFF BY GRIZZLY

RCMP and armed parks employees are combing the bush around Willow Creek in search of Delphine Muskwa, ten years old, of St. Theresa Residential School.

According to a playmate, Barney Hetherington, also ten years old, young Delphine was grabbed by a marauding grizzly.

The two were playing in the Hetheringtons' back yard when the attack occurred. Little hope is held out that the girl will be found alive.

The bear was seen entering town by several children in a nearby playground. They ran immediately to the nearest building, the Athabasca Hotel, and reported their sighting to patrons there. Some men investigated but failed to spot the bear.

It was seen leaving town by a group of girls who were returning from a hike near Patricia Lake. One girl, Amy Cobey, told reporters that the bear dragged the screaming victim across the Patricia Lake Road and into the bushes by the Willow Creek culvert.

Parents are advised to keep a close watch on their children. According to the former Superintendent, Mr Thurmon Butters, 'a killer bear may strike again'. He claims what the Park needs is a 'new policy on bears'.

The victim is the daughter of Noel and Annette Muskwa, both deceased, native Indians who resided for many years near this town.

You can talk to reporters till you're blue in the face, but they rarely get it down right. I object to words like 'marauding', 'screaming victim' and 'dragged'. That's not how it happened. I know, I was there.

To understand what happened when the bear came you need to know what led up to it. With Delphine, I mean. Nokom was gone and my parents had applied to become Delphine's foster parents. The minister of Mother's church thought it would be a good idea, part of a program to get Father off the bottle and Mother out of her stupor: a daughter for my mother, who had once expressed a preference for daughters. The Sisters of St. Theresa didn't seem to mind either, even though Mother and Father weren't Roman Catholics. A series of visits was set up.

One day, it must have been on the weekend, two sisters showed up and told Mother that Delphine was out in the car. 'Give her time to come around,' one of them cautioned. I was delegated to play with Delphine. Apparently the sisters and my mother had gotten together on this. I was to play with Delphine all day and never once let her out of my sight. Very solemnly I agreed to this arrangement and Delphine was led in by both the sisters.

She was wearing new jeans, a new shirt, and runners, but what caught my eye was an oversized belt tied to her waist, one too thick for the loops on her jeans. It had a big silver buckle, and I could tell right away that it was Noel's belt. There she stood between the two nuns, hanging from their hands, looking distracted and perhaps, too, a bit sulky, gazing back over her shoulder into the distance. This is how a prisoner might have looked who was coming to trial in a police van. The nuns looked nothing like cops, though. I mean they were just doing their job and with Delphine it couldn't have been easy. Stand up, Delphine. Say hello to Mrs Hetherington. Don't slouch. That sort of thing. She rolled her eyes upward at her bangs and stood, choosing not to focus on us or anyone else. She made a silly frog-face at no one in particular.

'You wanna see my trucks?' I said to her.

'Wanna see my twucks?' she said in a baby voice to the ceiling.

I led her to the sandbox. Her hand was limp with indifference. We knelt in the sand and I gave her a car. She put it on her head, bowed, and it fell to the sand.

'Kreegah!' I cried. 'Bundolo!'

She picked up my car and threw it backwards over her head. It landed next to the snow fence Father had recently erected.

In that same wilful baby voice she said, 'I'm too little to play with you.'

They brought her a week or two later and she seemed to have changed. She wore a dress and a pink barrette in her hair, but once more Noel's belt was around her waist. This time she looked us all in the eye, stood up straight, refused the sister's hands. When we greeted her at the door she bobbed stiffly and walked right in.

'How come you got all this stuff?' she asked when we were alone.

'What stuff?'

'All this stuff,' she said, waving a hand nowhere in particular. I think we were in the front room. Our home was a very modest war-vintage pre-fab, sparsely furnished, owned by my Grandmother Sharples. I think Delphine was referring to the things in our front room, pictures painted by my grandmother, framed photographs of birds, Indians and mountains, the brass lamp next to Father's easy chair, an old couch Granny Sharples had re-covered, an old radio in a wooden casing, a box of my Dinky toys.

'You should give it all to Jesus,' she said.

'What for?'

'Because He's comin' back.'

'Let's go outside,' I said. I figured maybe we could play a little catch. Delphine was good at catch; she threw like a boy. She looked at the implements in our shed (Father's tools, his old horse gear, Mother's gardening stuff).

'You got so much stuff. You should give it away. You should give it to the Doukhobors.'

'Let's play catch,' I said.

She looked around the shed for a moment, then came out and stood in the centre of the sandbox.

'Jesus ever talk to you?' she asked.

'Nope.'

'He talked to me. Once when we was singin' and once in my dorm.'

I'd had it up to here with religion, even then. As far as I was concerned it was about as beneficial as Father's imbibing, just another source of embarrassment for me at school. Why couldn't they be like other people's parents?

I told her that that was a load of horseshit.

'What's that supposed to mean?' she said, spoiling for a fight. I guess I was too.

'I got better things to do than go into a church and pray to a guy hanging there with his guts spilling out.' I was of course referring to crucifixes and pictures of saints with bleeding hearts. I'd seen them in the chapel where Delphine went. They were awful. They made me think of Noel oozing blood beneath his horse. At least at Mother's church there was no blood and guts, only pictures of Jesus in the prime of life. He looked like someone out of Prince Valiant comics, except of course he had no armour. I think I mentioned that to Delphine.

'We got holy water,' she said.

'What's that?'

'The Pope blesses it and then God blesses it. There's a bunch of it in our chapel. I could drink some if I wanted to.'

'So why don't you then?'

When you come right down to it, I was being as obnoxious as I could possibly be.

'Maybe I will. Maybe I'll be ready when He comes. It's plain as day that you won't, so never mind. He's comin' and it could be real soon. Any day, so there.'

It never occurred to me that she might have been trying to tell me something else: that if I did prepare myself, she and I would go to the same place, that we belonged together, like being back in Africa, or

84

whatever she imagined Paradise to be. But she was talking to me as though I were *her* foundling, abandoned like someone's bastard on her doorstep.

The last time Delphine got brought over, I was in my room stalling. Father had to drag me out and haul me down to the sandbox, mad as hell at both of us. At least he was sober, but it was like having to view the body of Noel again, except this time I had to contend with a live Muskwa.

She was down on her knees in the sandbox. I think that it was beginning to rain. She was praying. Off in the distance I could hear some kids yelling things. I remember thinking, Jesus, I don't want those kids to find me here with this Bible-thumping Indian kid. It sounded like they were coming my way. They'd probably be from my school and here was Delphine mumbling to God in the sandbox.

'There,' she said, took off Noel's big belt, and stood up. She held the belt like a snake by the tail and began swinging it. 'This is what the priest does with his therble,' she said. She meant the censer they use, the thing that holds the incense. It reminded me of Nokom with her dead rabbit, or whatever it was, up on the slope that strange night. It gave me the creeps. The kids were getting closer; I could hear them yelling.

'Delphine?' I cried. 'Don't do that. Delphine?'

She kept swinging her belt, the big silver buckle downward, and humming a weird Indian chant. I got scared and yelled at her, and the kids I kept hearing got closer and closer.

'It's going down the lane!' one of them shouted.

'Stop it!' I cried. 'Stop it! Stop it! Stop it!'

She stopped and fastened the belt around her waist. There was a noise.

We both looked up at the snow fence and the garbage cans beyond: a huge frosted hump loomed up, then a pale yellow head, flat like a big spade, pig snout and unseeing eyes that seemed to burn. It didn't actually hit the snow fence, it just sort of moved and the entire fence came down like cardboard in a gust of wind. The animal came up with a woofing sound, sniffing, an immense bear.

I remember screaming but not *us* screaming. Just screaming, as if everything in our yard, the ruined fence and the house included, were screaming out at this creature that walked through things we thought belonged there; and Delphine and I performed in slow motion our last act together: I in the sandbox reaching out to her, she by the shed falling towards me with her arms out – reaching for me? I don't honestly know. It came down over her gently, and with the delicacy of a great regent nibbling on a grape, closed its mouth on the belt and hauled Delphine into the air. Her expression was that of a kid tobogganing down a mountain slope with an avalanche behind her. The bear swung back toward the ruined fence and lumbered down the lane.

'A grizzly!' cried one of the kids nearby. 'It's a grizzly bear!'

Note: it never dragged her, it carried her. And from that moment on, she never screamed. And they only found her clothes. You can ask those Mounties and wardens. Ask them if they found one piece of flesh or even a drop of blood.

The last time I really tied one on was a pretty sobering experience. Darryl and his wife were over. He is blond, fat, successful and pious, a mama's boy who made me feel in those days too much like Papa's boy. He kept staring at the photograph of the four bewhiskered hunters and their guns.

'Here's to our dear grandfather,' I said, and wanting to shake out some of the complacency from Darryl's face, I added, 'He blew Etienne Muskwa's hand off with that six-gun of his.'

'I know,' said Darryl. 'Mom told me.'

'Blew the man's hand to kingdom come. Thought he was a bear,' I added morosely.

'Like father, like son,' Darryl said.

'What's that supposed to mean?'

I must have sounded surly. The wives started looking pretty nervous.

Darryl didn't even blink. He said, 'Come on, Barney. You mean to tell me you never knew?'

'Knew what?'

'It was Dad who shot that other Indian's horse from under him. That's what did him in, what's his name, Noel. Didn't he ever –'

'How do you know?'

'Mom told me.'

'Jesus Christ,' I said.

'Amen,' he said.

I knew he was telling the truth. It would've been just like our mother to tell Darryl and not tell me. Maybe in some way I'd known this fact all along. But Darryl's little revelation went through me like a bolt from the other side of the universe. Another look at the photograph confirmed it for me. It. Something connecting all three generations of us. A look we Hetheringtons get when we've learned something we didn't want to know.

Something about the bush. One night a group of men are sleeping around a campfire. A paw reaches out from the wilderness, crossing the line between the Vast Other and you, fumbles for your shoulder, you grab the revolver and fire again and again. Men leap from their bedrolls, a whole tribe of bears roars out in brute pain: *Mamuskach! Uy! Uy! Uyiwakekin!* and there it lies by the campfire, spurting blood. Clenching like a dying spider. Maybe he only wanted to cover your shoulder with your blanket, but you shot his hand off. You repeat this act again and again in a film that winds through your head until you die. Or maybe your film is the one where you shoot your friend's horse and it falls on him. Or maybe, in the most recent version, you repudiate the only friend you had, send her back into her own solitude with such finality that (after your brother has gone, leaving you alone with your very last drink) when you play it back, the whole wilderness rears up to rebuke you.

☆ The Ketzer

Und niemand weiss

Indessen lass mich wandeln
Und wilde Beeren pflücken,
Zu löschen die Liebe zu dir
An deinen Pfaden, o Erd.

       – Friedrich Hölderlin, 'Heimat', ca. 1805

ONE

1.

Steve Schuyler met Head Kreutzer and his friend in an unusual way. Steve was doing bench presses in the weight room of the Saskatoon YMCA and overheard the following conversation.

'… shoulda been there, Neville says. Mrs Potts, she goes out an lops the head off this young rooster, eh? Well instead of runnin around an bleedin to death, this rooster – an this is no bullshit – it *conserves its energy* an doesn't die. I mean, for days on end it keeps walkin around, I swear to God.'

'I'd say you been reamin too many toilets lately.'

Still on his back, Steve eased the barbells off the stand. He began to count: one, two, three, four. Each press took a four count, two per breath. Each time between rests he would do eight presses. He had worked his way up to one hundred and fifty pounds. One of the guys at the store had told him this was where the bulk was. Steve liked the results but he found the process boring. He switched from counting to words. De-cap-i-tate … de-cap-i-tate…. He tried to think of the word for what happened when you got your balls cut off, but he couldn't remember. It had four beats. It was right on the tip of his tongue.

'Neville told me himself,' the young plumber said. 'We had this weird conversation.'

Still pressing, Steve checked out the two fellows. The plumber was tall, built like a diver or a swimmer, had an abundance of sandy brown hair, a hawk nose, and an amiable twist to his grin. The grin never seemed to disappear. That was Head.

'An get this,' Head continued. 'Neville says Mrs Potts has taken to feedin this rooster with a eyedropper down his ...'

Puffing now, Steve thought e-soph-a-gus, e-soph-a-gus. He had two more to go, one more to go. At last he eased the barbells onto the stand.

'An this friggin bird is still walkin around.'

'Lemme get this straight. Mernie Potts is still feedin this thing?'

'Neville says she uses this eyedropper down his ...'

'Esophagus,' said Steve.

They both turned Steve's way, one with annoyance, the stockier of the two. He was good-looking, wore his hair long like some hockey players Steve had known, and shot Steve a bumptious look as though Steve had somehow wandered into the wrong dressing room.

The plumber didn't seem to mind. 'Yeah,' he said to Steve. 'She feeds him an he don't know his head's missin type thing.'

'Amazing,' Steve said.

Head carried on. 'I guess they bleed to death, eh, when their heads are chopped off, but Mrs Potts, she didn't get the jugular or somethin, so this bird he don't know the difference. He flaps his wings, he preens his feathers ... well, sort of.'

When the two country fellows had left and Steve was back on the bench, he started to wonder about them. They were transplanted, that was obvious. He had the impression that they had more fun than he did, got a bigger kick out of things.

Off came the barbells. Eight more and he could quit. Bench presses. That's where the bulk was. De-cap-i-tate ... de-cap-i-tate ... e-vis-cer-ate ... e-rad-i-cate ... e-lim-i-nate ... e ... e ... e-mas-cu-late.

Steve was bored with work, where he sold skis and sportswear; bored with weightlifting, which he found even more boring than jogging; bored with Saskatoon, which seemed to have lost some of its shine since his girlfriend Cora had gotten on as a fitness counsellor for some company in Toronto. He was bored with everything, but when he thought about it some, it always came down to Cora's absence. He would probably see her at Christmas, and, knowing Cora, she would re-introduce the subject of marriage, so that thing was in the bag, but in the meantime he was simply wishing time away. He needed some adventure. He needed precisely a three-day adventure, because that's the longest he could get off work before Christmas.

It was September. Steve not only missed Cora, he missed the feeling he'd had each September when they were in university. Perhaps that was it. The old student life was irretrievably lost, the old times gone, the parties not so crazy any more. And Cora, by her phone calls at least, seemed to take this all in stride. She loved her work. She gushed about it.

Steve had liked doing zoo labs, anthropology seminars, travelling with the ski team. He had liked all those coffee breaks and beer breaks and clandestine parties at his parents' cabin.

That was another thing. When Steve got his job at the Ski Shack, his parents announced the day had finally come when they could move out permanently to B.C. Soon after this piece of news, they sold the cabin and that was that. He missed the cabin. He missed the speedboat. He missed the hunting trips out there, or the annual bash he'd throw each fall under the pretence of closing the place down for his parents. Now it was gone. He felt like an orphan. Some of his friends had, like Cora, already left for jobs or schooling elsewhere. Two of them had even gotten married.

Orphaned. At twenty-four.

'I need a new scene,' Steve explained to Head Kreutzer in the bar. The beer was starting to work, breeding enthusiasm. 'A new scene,' he said again.

The two of them had begun to go for beers on Friday afternoons after work. They chose a large beer hall where Head wouldn't feel self-conscious about his smell. Occasionally it got bad. Head would take off his coveralls, wash his hands and face, and hit the beer parlour by five-thirty. Steve would dress down for the occasion, leaving his tie and sports jacket in the car.

'Huntin?' Head inquired. 'Fishin? Booze?'

'Keep going.'

'What else is there?'

Steve thought for a moment. The standard reply was sex and drugs. Instead, he said, 'There is adventure. Spectacle.'

'Come again?'

Steve smiled and belched simultaneously. 'For example,' he said, 'there's that chicken at the Potts place.'

'You wanna see that thing?'

'Why not?' said Steve. It was September. A new season, a whole nother ball game, as Head would say.

Head pointed his finger at Steve. 'You bring that twenty-gauge of yours and we'll hunt up some grouse along the way.'

So they drove halfway across Saskatchewan to an old cabin on the Assiniboine River. Head and his friends often hunted from this cabin. It was hallowed ground, wild on all sides, half encircled by the river valley below.

The Potts ranch, on the other hand, was a big spread. At the end of the driveway in an aspen grove was a large pre-fab bungalow. Head and Steve were greeted by two big yellow and grey mongrels. The largest one came at Steve when he leapt from Head's pickup, and Head had to come over and drive it off.

Neville Potts answered the door. He was a stocky man of about fifty-five years with a vigorous look about him. 'What's up, Kreutzer?' he said.

'Yo, Neville.'

'How's plumbin in the big city?'

'Can't complain. How's the cows?'

'Gettin fatter an meaner.'

'See any bucks?'

'Not like there used to be.'

Out came Goober, Neville's oldest son. He was tall, balding, looked shy, and he had a methodical manner about him. 'Yo, Head,' he said.

'Yo, Goober.'

'Off yer beat some?' Neville said.

'Fartin around,' Head replied.

Goober and Neville nodded almost imperceptibly at Steve but there were no introductions. Neville's gaze fell on Head's Toyota pickup.

'When you gunna getcher self some proper wheels?'

'Does the job.'

'So does walkin,' said Neville, grinning at Goober.

Head looked in Steve's direction. 'Steve here, he heard about that rooster.'

'Head, you didn't come all this way t'see no rooster,' said Neville.

Goober said, 'Yiz wanna see it?'

Steve said, 'Yeah.'

He noticed Neville and Goober exchange a look. The four of them went to the henhouse followed by the dogs. The smaller mongrel cowered behind the big one, as though it were just recovering from a recent attack.

Mernie Potts was at the henhouse. She welcomed Head and Steve. 'You lookin for Flora?' she said to Head.

'No. Is she lookin for me?'

'Don't you wish it,' said Mernie.

She wore coveralls, a tractor cap, and had a face that was tanned, handsome. Her brown eyes blazed out of her face with a look that could dart either way to anger or delight.

Head looked down at his boots, but as usual his grin never quite disappeared.

'Head, he come in a toy truck,' said Goober, laughing.

Mernie led them to a row of square enclosures on the south side of the henhouse, each pen next to a window. On the floor of every pen was a square of feeble sunlight where the chicks stood, squared off, as though in regiment. A number of mature birds were in the fourth pen. Mernie pointed to an object fastened above the pen. 'There's his rack,' she said.

His rack? Steve squinted at the object. It took him a moment to realize that it was the head of a rooster. Goober had nailed it like a religious icon beneath the archway of the ceiling beams. Mernie plucked it off and stuffed it into Head's jacket pocket.

'Add this to your collection,' she said.

Neville pointed to something in the shadows beneath the window of the fourth pen. It looked like a dishrag.

'There's your miracle bird,' he said to Steve.

'God,' said Steve. He was referring to the smell.

Mernie climbed into the pen and picked it up. The headless rooster had been dead for some time. She said, 'I guess he was gettin henpecked.' She knelt in the square of sunlight, scattering the chickens, and examined the dead rooster. 'Others done him in,' she murmured.

Goober said, 'Yiz shoulda heard im crow, eh?'

Steve tried to read his face, which was as bland as a dirt road. Was this a friendly smile or a smirk? He assumed the latter: let's show this guy from the city where the bear shat in the buckwheat.

'I bet he could talk too, eh?' Steve said.

'No,' said Goober, 'but he could crow excellent. I'm not shittin ya.'

Neville said, 'He sort of croaked like.'

'Without his head,' said Steve.

'Yep,' said Goober.

Mernie held the tattered rooster to her coveralls, smoothing down the feathers, kneeling on the straw, and looked down – it seemed tenderly – on the bird. Some roosters nearby began to crow.

'He could do lotsa things,' said Mernie, 'but he was none too slick with them hens.'

'You'da bin out here when you shoulda,' said Neville, 'we could of sold im. Or at least we could of et im.'

She looked up at her husband. 'No tellin what might of happened. You and the boys eat this bird, Neville, his condition might be catchin.'

2.

Flora, alias Harry, was the Potts' only daughter. Unlike her brothers, she had made her escape from the farm. She had only made it as far as Melville, but from there, she and the baby could come back for visits and free baby-sitting several times a year. A month after Head and that friend of his had visited the family ranch, she and little Carey came home for the weekend. It was a gritty day in late October. Flora was clearing the table when her younger brother Clyde made a suggestion to the men of the household.

'Head come up for the weekend. He's at the cabin right now. Let's tool over there an get pissed.'

Her mother was in the kitchen changing the baby. Not one to be left out of the action, especially on a visit home, Flora called into the front room where the men sat: 'Fine with me.'

So all but Mernie Potts, who did not enjoy drinking, tied one on at Head's hunting cabin.

While her brothers talked hunting at the far end of the table, Flora, getting drunk with unaccustomed speed, began to clamour for her father's attention. He would not even look her way. Then they began to refer to her in the third person and this she could never stand.

'Hey, Dad? It's my turn now. Dad? You gotta listen, Dad.'

She tried her youngest brother. 'Clyde! Hey, Clyde!' He looked her way as though a fly were buzzing too close. 'Clyde, it's my turn to say something. Tell Dad.'

Clyde gave her a blank look and the men talked on. Their conversation had reached a level where words began to stick together and get replaced by guffaws, yawps, and growls.

'May as well give up, Harry,' said the friend from the city. He had soon picked up on Flora's nickname. In fact, he had remembered everybody's name after only one evening's drinking.

'What, Harry give up?' Head mumbled.

'Why do they call her Harry?' asked the new man.

Head shrugged.

The city guy turned at last to Flora. 'Why do they call you Harry?'

'Everybody's got a nickname around here,' she said. 'What's yours?'

'Folks in these parts call me ... Steve.'

'Steve don't cut it.'

'Best I can do. Maybe I should get one.' Steve turned to his friend. 'Why do they call you Head?'

'Because I collect em,' Head replied, when the laughter had died down. Head gestured at his trophies, a moose head mounted on one side, a buck's on the other, some hides nailed to two of the walls.

'Collect em or ream em out?' said Clyde.

'I don't see that rooster's head,' said Steve.

Head smiled as though he had a private joke. 'It's bound to show up somewheres.'

Flora looked away. She did not feel inclined to join in on the laughter. 'Dad!' she yelled, but Goober just picked up where he had left off. Flora was in this story. It was being told primarily for the benefit of the guy from the city. Flora had heard this tale so many times, she could mouth some of Goober's words as they were being spoken. She wondered if she just cussed a blue streak, could she then get her father's attention. Or maybe, she thought, I might just get the back of his hand.

Goober spoke slowly and methodically. 'So me an Clyde here, an th'ol man,' he said, nodding to Neville, 'we split up. I go up the east side, th'ol man he goes up the west side, Clyde, he's the dog this time, see, because Harry's too tired. He goes real slow through the bush. *Nothin* could get by him. I mean, that bush is never more'n fifty yards wide at the besta times. Well me, I'm waitin, th'ol man's waitin, we hear Clyde barkin like a dog, see?'

The guy from the city stopped Goober. 'You mean so those bucks will think they're being chased by a dog?'

Clyde turned to him. 'You're walkin through a bush surrounded by a buncha bozos with their fingers on the trigger, by Christ you want them to know where you are, an that you don't wear no antlers for a livin.'

Goober cut back in. 'Anyways. Clyde found the tracks in the snow. He never seen tracks like this one.'

'Fresh, you mean?' asked the guy from the city. Steve, that was his name. She couldn't be that drunk, if she could remember the new guy's name.

'Fresh?' Neville grunted. 'Big!'

'Huge,' said Clyde. He formed the shape of a heart with his big hands. 'These tracks was the size of a elk, no shit. They was that big, we all seen em.'

'I get to say somethin after you're finished, Goober,' said Flora.

'Wait,' said Goober. With his tractor cap on, his skinny neck and squawky voice, he sometimes reminded Flora of a cartoon duck. He seemed to be gathering in his memories; this was his story. 'So Clyde keeps bustin through the bush, barkin as loud as he can, Head shows up, me an th'ol man we're on point just awaitin....'

Looking at Steve, Goober jerked a thumb in Flora's direction, and said, 'Here comes Harry outa nowheres, she's got th'ol man's bush gun, as she just stands on the east end of the bush where Clyde come in. She's just standin there, she doesn't wanta be dog no more, she's tired, she's just standin there, I'm ready, th'ol man's ready, an we know – we goddam *know* – there's no way this dinosaur of a buck is gonna get past any one of us. I mean, mister, this is the biggest buck I ever seen in my whole life, rack like a apple tree? Fawwwk, wouldn't you know it, somehow he sneaks past Clyde –'

'How?' asked Steve. 'How could he?'

'You tell me,' Clyde cut in. 'No way in hell that buck coulda gotten by.'

Goober resumed his story. 'Anways, there we all are. Out comes ol Appletree – the back way. I yells to Harry, "Shoot," I says. Th'ol man he yells out, "Shoot the bugger!" We're all of us yellin at Harry!'

'What's so new about that?' said Flora.

The guy from the city laughed.

'An what does Harry do?' said Goober. He was looking directly at Steve. 'What do you think she did?'

The city guy gave Flora what amounted to a sympathetic smile. 'Shot the buck?'

'Shot the buck, fawwwk.' Goober paused for effect. 'She stands there an watches it trot on by. Come any closer, she could of bit off his ear.'

'You always tell it wrong,' said Flora, her voice sliding downhill. 'You an Clyde, you never get it right. Dad, have they ever gotten it right?'

Neville Potts turned at last to his daughter. His broad nose, his cheeks, his massive neck had reddened unevenly throughout the course of the evening. These glowing beacons on his face were almost the same colour as his old hunting cap. 'They got it right, by the Jesus. They got it right. You just stood there with my thirty/thirty like you was usin it for a umber-ella.'

'It's my turn now,' she said. 'I got a question.'

'She can shoot a whisky bottle at seventy-five yards with that ol gun,' Neville went on. 'Y'think she can hit a buck the size'a Goober's half-ton at ten yards?'

Eventually the laughter died down and Flora asked her question, directed at her father. 'Do you think if you was the dog an I was on point I wouldn't some day shoot a buck? Is that what you think?'

Neville looked at his daughter and glared red at her.

'A buck, I mean. Not a fawn, not a doe. Just one of them horny ones. D'you think I couldn't pull the trigger?'

Neville looked away. Gone was the anger of the afternoon when the power generator had broken down, the fans had stopped turning, and all the lights in the henhouse had gone out. All she'd done was deliver the bad news and he yelled at her. He wouldn't yell at Clyde that way, not even at Goober that way. As though a broken-down generator were her fault. Or as though by visiting the farm she had brought them bad luck.

The whisky had mellowed him, it seemed.

'Bullshit,' said Flora. 'I'd do it. I'd pull the trigger. You don't think I'd some day drop a buck? There's nothin to pullin the trigger.'

'I don't know, honey,' said Neville, his voice unaccountably soft.

3.

As he worked a last lump of coal into the cookstove for the night, Steve said, 'So, you figure she doesn't go with anyone at all?'

'Got your sights on er?'

'Just wondered.'

'She used to see this warden, after her marriage bust up. But the warden, he wasn't what you'd call too popular around here type a thing.' Head paused as though weighing how much he could reveal and resumed stoking the Franklin at the far end of the cabin. 'Way I see it, she works all day at the bank, curls weekends for the women's league, and whatever time's left over, she spends with the kid. She doesn't have no time for no social life. She says she can't *afford* one.'

Steve watched the fire in the cook stove. He would need to stoke it and the Franklin one more time during the night. Head tended to drag his feet at such tasks. Once asleep, Head was always out for the count.

'Why do they call her Harry?'

Head dropped an empty forty of vodka into the garbage pail and held up a nearly empty forty of rye, mumbling, 'Jesus.' He put the second bottle on a shelf near the stove between a bag of all-purpose flour and a box of Minute Rice. He grinned at Steve.

'I think Neville give her that name because he wanted a third son, but this time maybe a son with some *brains.*'

'Doesn't he like her much?'

'He *likes* her, as far as that goes,' Head replied. 'He just doesn't know what to *do* with her type thing. He wants her married again an outa the way.'

'She should stand up to the old man.'

'Tell me about it.'

'What happened to the guy she married?'

Head yawned, stretched, and carried the candle to the centre of the room. He began to arrange his sleeping bag on the bunk next to the Franklin. 'Mate's okay. He still hunts with me sometimes. Them two just didn't get along.'

'Does she ever laugh?'

His friend shook his head. 'Serious.'

Slowly Steve unrolled his bag, sniffing the mildewed scents of a dozen outings, remembering the feel of every fall when his dad had the cabin and they went hunting. This place was good, too. It would do just fine. He could imagine coming here for years and years. He was down to his long-johns and he wondered if he'd be too warm at first. He turned to Head, by now curled up on the bunk.

'You ever ... you know...?'

'I thought about it a few times,' Head replied. 'Most guys from around here have looked her over. She's real prime rib, that one.'

'But you never actually...?'

'Nah,' said Head and blew out the candle.

4.

Neville drove home drunk with Clyde, Goober, and Flora, all squeezed together in the cab of the truck. He had driven this road drunk from Head's cabin before. He knew all the trails around here; he owned half of them.

Neville still had his temper. Clyde still thought he was God's gift to women. Goober, like Clyde, was also unmarried, and he still plodded around the barn like an old farmer. And Flora's mom still spent every night alone in front of the television.

'We're all too big for the cab,' said Flora.

'You up the stump again?' said Clyde.

'No,' she replied, 'an I don't have no spare tire like someone else in this cab neither.'

She gave Clyde an almost affectionate elbow. She felt the full weight of her father on the left and Clyde on the right. Had it been Goober on the immediate right, she would not have felt this constrictive weight on both sides, like being between two steers in a crowded stall. In his shy way, Goober would have leaned into Clyde's body and away from hers. As it was, she had become a sack of feed.

'Think them buggers'll be up at six?'

'Head'll be up.'

'They'll be up an rollin.'

'Who's the guy from Saskatoon?'

'Buddy a Head's.'

'Seems okay.'

'They're up for this one.'

'Think we should do the top road first?'

'I think we should walk the river valley.'

'Couldn't do the river with a hundred dogs an two hundred guys on point. Too much cover.'

'I think we should walk the river valley.'

'Fawwwk.'

'Slow down. There's some new tracks in the snow.'

Neville slowed the truck, shifting down to second, and just as Flora said, 'C'mon, Dad, it's late,' a large animal vaulted from the ditch into their headlights, its nose high in the air. It was a white-tail, a big buck. Neville slammed on the brakes and the buck squared to face their vehicle.

'Holy Jesus,' Neville whispered.

The truck had stalled but Neville made no move to start it up again. The buck stood perfectly still and glared at their headlights. His rack was huge. A tourist could have mistaken him for an elk.

'Appletree,' whispered Flora.

'Sure as Christ,' said Goober.

The four of them stared at the animal and he peered at them with a wavering attention. Then his nose went back into the air as though he were sniffing the galaxies. As though this truck full of people was, after all, only the second most important thing out there in the snow, and then he launched himself out of the truck's beams, off the road, and up into the woods above the ravine.

'Is Carey okay?' Flora asked her mother.

Mernie Potts sat in her dressing gown close to the television so that she could hear the program and not disturb the baby's sleep. This was how she had listened to the radio at nights when Flora was a child.

'I just changed him last ad,' she said, without turning to face her daughter.

Flora tiptoed behind her mother and into the room she used to occupy as a girl. She didn't turn on the bedroom lamp. The yard light cast a bluish glow over the baby's crib and Flora bent low over Carey's head to hear his breathing. He lay on his belly with his head turned away from the light. There was a raspy sound down in the throat from a cough the baby couldn't seem to lose. But he slept. She went silently out to her mother again. A movie was on, an old one. The women wore full-length gowns, crinolines, and petticoats that made them look like flowers turned upside down. The men wore tight-fitting uniforms and swords at their sides.

'Mom, we seen Appletree.'

Flora's mother turned slightly. 'You smell like a distillery. You smell like them.'

'Mom, I'm goin out early with Dad an the boys.'

Mernie nodded and turned back to her movie. A love scene was in progress, one of the flowers wilting.

'Carey'll be fine.'

'Thanks, Mom.'

Flora tiptoed back to her bedroom. She stood in the glow from the yard light, swaying slightly. Her boy's breathing came regularly between long pauses. That always amazed her, that he could pause so long between breaths. Sometimes she caught herself waiting to see if he'd make it to the next one. She touched his head lightly and his left arm came up to his mouth in a fist.

5.

Neville slept the same way, fist at his mouth, with very slow breaths. He was dreaming about the cattle when the bawling started. But it didn't sound like a cow. It sounded more like a sheep. Why would it sound like a sheep?

Mernie was sitting up in bed. 'It's that cough,' she said.

'What cough?'

'Carey. He coughs himself awake and then he cries.'

The baby kept crying for a minute or more. It was almost four o'clock. The alarm would ring in a couple of hours. Mernie put her feet on the floor but just before she could rise, the baby's voice dropped and made a mewling sound to the softer sound of Harry's voice. Neville thought, that's how Harry used to cry when she was a calf. They never sound like people at that age, they sound more like sheep. But it wasn't sheep exactly, it was something else. Neville fell asleep before he could figure what it was. He would figure it out before the coming day had passed.

6.

Steve held his flashlight up to the snout of a large whitetail buck. Cradled in one of the forks of its rack was a box of wooden matches. As he reached up into the antlers, he felt as though the animal's eyes were real, and at any second he would lower his head and charge.

Shivering, Steve stoked up the stove. The kindling caught at once from the embers so he dropped in some larger chunks of wood and then some coal. The fire crackled. The sound was very satisfying. He took the matches over to Head's end of the big room. It was chilly there but Head snored away in the warm depths of his bag. Steve opened the door of the old Franklin. A few coals blinked among the ashes so he started from scratch with newspaper, twigs and bark from the wood box. Head snored on. Steve could find no larger chunks of wood, so while the paper and twigs smoked, he went into the store-room. It was even colder in there than around Head's bunk. A tarpaulin lay over a large pile in the middle of the room. He threw back the tarp and grabbed at what he thought was

the dried branch of an old log. It was hard as stone and he let go. The way
it clattered with the others on the pile, he knew it was antlers. He held
the flashlight on them. There were dozens on the stack, some from small
bucks but most from bigger animals, enough here to decorate a dozen
hunting lodges.

He found the woodpile in the corner and grabbed an armful. As he
kicked the door and turned to the Franklin, he heard the paper catch and
a *whoosh* from the mouth of the heater. In the orange flare he spotted yet
another rack above Head's bunk, that of the bull moose. He looked as
though he had just arrived and stuck his head through the wall. He
seemed somehow opposed to the presence of these men with their guns
and their liquor. A look of stupefied disapproval hung on his long lips.

Head snored on.

Steve stoked up the old Franklin and waited until there was a good roar
before he returned to bed. He looked back and forth at the buck, the moose,
and then at a lynx hide nailed to the near wall. He thought about the big
stack of antlers in the anteroom and wondered how these men could have
even the slightest doubt of success this weekend. The woods were
seething with life. It was just a question of finding a bunch of fresh tracks,
setting up a drive and picking off the best bucks to come out of the bush.

He checked his watch. It was a little past four in the morning. He had
to get some sleep, so he tried to think of one object that would hold his
attention so that his thoughts would stop flying around the room. He
settled at last on Flora.

TWO

1.

Growing up small among bigger kids and older brothers, Flora learned to
look up at the world. Sometimes her long brown hair got in the way so
she would toss it back and look up sideways just to see the faces of those
she walked with. This adjustment would produce a look of elfin
bemusement, so all sorts of people would call her cute.

She was quiet. She learned secrets. If you were small and quiet there
was security in whispered secrets, and of course power in being thought
cute. Her nose and chin were fine and pointed, almost witch-like, her eyes
a mossy hazel. One assumed she had many more secrets than she did and

that various enchantments lay behind her smallest gestures.

She played a game that was a secret from everyone but her mother. She would pretend she was invisible. When the feeling came over her, she would shrink from sight behind a curtain, a bale of straw or a bush, and watch. If someone spotted her, brothers being the usual offenders, the perfect feeling would be destroyed. But if she remained undiscovered for as long as she wanted to be invisible, the game was fine.

Humans did not always co-operate, but animals did. She would sit perfectly still in one of her spots. A favourite place for this game was a large copse in the middle of the lower meadow, Flora's Bush. It had a pond in the centre and the deer would feed around her unperturbed. Sometimes they would graze the alfalfa within a few yards of her hiding place. On some occasions they seemed to know she was there, but also seemed willing to *pretend* that she was invisible. Once she touched a moose calf on the haunch while the cow across the pond looked off in the other direction. More than once she was surrounded by a brood of ruffed grouse chicks while the hen pecked away at the swath on the edge of the copse. She had memories, too (which she didn't trust), of talking to bears.

When Flora began to fill out and lose her desire for solitude, and stopped being a tomboy, and (in his typically contrary way) her father started calling her Harry, the disappearing game was forgotten. At nineteen she married Maitland O'Donnell, a man's man who was like a brother to Flora's brothers, a lazy handsome popular boy, a dreamer who failed at almost everything and came to feel tremendously sorry for himself. He and Flora began to fight, he took to drink and bullying, and in the summer when he left to find work on the oil rigs, she had an affair.

She told her mother her marriage was on the rocks. She even told her a censored version of the affair, how it had ended, how the man in question was now in Europe.

'Men want to be like them bucks,' was Mernie Potts's response. 'Off with the other bucks an no women please, we got better things to do. Except in rut, an then look out. They get their noses in the air an next thing you know, you're all they ever wanted.'

'Well, there's some truth to that, I suppose,' Flora said, putting her hand on her belly.

'Oh, my God,' said Mernie.

Oh, my God, Flora said a year later to herself as she remembered this conversation. She remembered it with some bitterness, because there was so much she couldn't tell her mother, so much more she couldn't tell Neville and the boys or Head Kreutzer or the guy from the city. And Goober, who always meant well, how could he have known what was really going through her head the day they ran into old Appletree? How could he have known, for instance, that she was pregnant? That she had been fraternizing with the enemy, so to speak.

Oh, my God, Mernie had said, *was it Head Kreutzer?* Flora shook her head, put a finger to her lips and clammed up.

It was just then that the men came in for dinner. They had been trying all morning to get a buck. There seemed to be fewer legal deer each season, a fact Goober always left out of his Flora vs. Appletree story. They were all in a bad mood. Neville blamed the road construction crews, the grain farmers, the wardens and the government. There were fewer places for the deer to hide and soon they'd all be driven down into the river valley, most of which would soon become a federal sanctuary with no hunting allowed.

Neville said to Flora, 'Harry, you know that river valley. Them lower meadows, eh?'

Flora looked away.

'Why not come along this afternoon? You can have my bush gun.'

'I dunno.'

'Do you good,' he said. 'Besides, you know every one of them bucks by name.'

Clyde asked her where Mate was.

'Where he always is. Gettin pissed with his friends from Alberta.'

'Never mind Maitland,' Neville said. 'Harry, you find us old Appletree an we'll all get pissed like one big happy family.' He smiled at Goober and Clyde. He knew his daughter and her friends in the bush. Last year she'd spent more of her holiday time down by the river than she had on the ranch.

'I bet you'd rather be a buck than a rancher,' she said to Neville. Mernie's theory about men was still playing over in her mind.

'Be a bit lonely,' he said. 'Them other bucks, they know what I'm like. They wouldn't trust me.'

Neville had begun using a new .270 with a scope. He figured it would change his luck. He hadn't brought down a white-tail in several years. He handed Flora his old bush gun and seven shells and offered to show her how to stuff them in, but she gave him an impatient look which meant *Do not underestimate me,* so they all shuffled off to Goober's half-ton, Head Kreutzer in the box, and made their way in silence toward the lower meadows. She had been the one to take them there, a fact Goober always forgot when he told the story. Sure enough, the tracks were everywhere; among them, a half-dozen does and one big buck.

'You an Head be the dogs for the first bit, hey?' said Neville, and Flora went off into the bush, she and Head barking and howling back and forth till she was hoarse and exhausted. Head went forward and managed to put up some does, but the men on point held their fire. They moved up through the hills of the narrow meadow, Flora dragging behind, thinking about her last fight with Maitland. (He had accused her of making him feel like two cents in front of her friends from the bank. She had countered that all he cared about was fixing his goddam snowmobile for hunting, and she wouldn't mind him looking like a grease monkey half the time if at least he got paid for it.)

And then the part that Goober liked to tell: As she topped a big rise where the meadow narrowed and then widened, the river down to her right, the wooded hills rising to the ranchland on her left, still replaying her fight with Maitland, she came to a stop. Something was wrong. The big copse in the centre of the meadow, surrounded now by the men, was hers, Flora's Bush. Head was ambling up to it as though this bush wasn't special in any way. And down toward the river with its thick fringe of bush and trees rose the knoll she had dubbed Gopher Mountain. With the recent sifting of snow it reminded her of the head of a bald man. She had given the knoll its name on a hot afternoon less than three months earlier – something seemed to move in her belly.

She whispered, 'I am the Ketzer.'

She walked on in Head's tracks and prayed there would be no buck in the centre. When she reached the edge of the copse the only sound was Clyde's barking and she thought her prayer had been answered. She slumped away from the wind and wished she were back at their apartment in Melville, lying on the couch where the sun came in, with a cup of tea, and her mom in the easy chair, just relaxing, gossiping, planning what they would eat for supper. Then she realized she was holding a loaded rifle on her shoulder. A desolate little laugh shook out of her chest.

And there was Appletree. One second he hadn't been there; the next, he was out of the bush walking toward her.

Clyde's voice boomed out of the woods: 'Hey, you guys, there's some big tracks in here!'

Goober was looking her way, several hundred yards up the meadow, and Head doing the same on the other side of the bush. And they were yelling at her, even Neville, who she still could not see: *Shoooot the sonofabitch!*

The great animal walked her way, head low, as though he had just played a trick on someone and was trying to sneak past. She wondered if she'd known him as a fawn. He looked directly at her. She wished she could be invisible again. And then, for a few seconds, she was invisible, and she knew it, because old Appletree was looking right through her, or pretending to. *Yes*, he would say if he could, *I know you brought these turkeys out here, but I will forgive you and play along with this old game of yours.*

As he passed by she smelled the warmth of him.

The men began to run toward her, their voices getting louder and angrier. His tail went up like a rabbit popping from a burrow, his head came up, and he bounded into the woods toward the river. A few seconds and she couldn't even hear his progress through the trees.

Goober was more aghast than angry. 'What in the name of Jesus,' he cried.

Thank you, God, she whispered.

She and Goober exchanged a quick brother and sister look.

She would never be able to tell Goober her side of it, because he would never listen long enough. She would likely never be able to tell the guy from the city either. Steve, that was his name.

2.

'You got a hangover?' Steve asked Flora, handing her an extra pair of gloves he discovered in his pocket. Ordinarily he would have said, *Do you have a hangover.*

She put on the gloves and said, 'You mean you don't?'

'Nope, I never go to bed after drinking without taking an aspirin and a glass of water. Never fails me.'

She stood on the trail with her hands in the pockets of her parka and clamped her limbs to her body, shivering, staring at nothing. Her dad's old thirty/thirty was leaning against a fence post.

'You know what Head has in the storeroom?' he said.

'No.'

'A stack of antlers this high,' he said, exaggerating slightly.

'Wouldn't surprise me,' she said, and shivered.

'Where does he get all those antlers?'

'He gets some from Dad an the boys. He gets some from his other friends. He shoots the rest himself. Mostly after huntin season's over.'

'What's he going to do with all those antlers?'

'He's your friend.'

He didn't want to sound as though he were quizzing her, so Steve waited for a moment. 'My friend the poacher.'

'Your friend the trophy head dealer,' she said. 'Real good rack'll sell for five, ten thousand in the States.'

'Is it legal?'

'About as legal as poachin.'

He gave her a grin. 'You seem to know a lot about this racket.'

She executed a bleak little dance, shivering out loud, her arms at her sides, turning and bobbing in a small circle like a puppet, and all the features of her face, the fine pointed nose and chin, the hazel eyes, the pursed lips holding back (it seemed) on dozens of things to be unimpressed with, endeared themselves to him. Perfectly. He wanted to ask if she ever considered laughing once in a while. Instead, he said, 'How much would you get for Appletree's rack?'

'About a year's suspended an a three-thousand-dollar fine.'

Steve laughed but Flora looked grave. 'Guys keep killin the trophy deer, the whole breed suffers. The gene pool, it gets ...'

'Impoverished?' he offered, and wondered where she would learn such things.

She looked at him. 'Yeah.'

'So what are we doing out here?' Steve asked, holding his rifle with both hands out in front of him.

'I go out now an then, with Dad an the boys. But *legal*. I'm not makin war with bucks an I'm not makin money.'

'Sounds okay by me,' he said. After a while he asked, 'You ever get to Saskatoon?'

'Not since I had the kid.'

'Just wondering.'

'I better stand at the other side of the bush,' she said, yawned, and stumped off slowly up the trail that cut through the woods.

'You might want that,' he said, pointing to her father's gun.

'Oh,' she said. 'I might just.'

3.

The snow began to fall around noon. They put up a doe and a fawn that morning, but saw no sign of a buck. For dinner, they went off to Head's cabin and had some stew. Flora told Neville that maybe she should pack up Carey and head for Melville.

'Not if you want some wild meat for the winter,' Neville said.

'Magpie or gopher?' she said.

'Just never you mind,' said Neville. He almost grinned at Flora and she almost grinned back. So she stayed.

THREE

1.

In the last year of Flora's marriage, but before her pregnancy, her husband Mate went to Alberta to look for work on the rigs, and Flora took her two weeks off from the bank and went home at haying time. It was dry and hot, and she spent most her time down by the river picking berries.

One day Head went by, trolling upstream from his motorboat. She spotted him first and hailed him from the shore. He wore a bathing suit and a striped towel over his head that looked vaguely Egyptian.

'Catch anything?'

'Na.'

He was hunched over in the stern, squinting at her. The sun had reddened him all over.

'Excellent hat y'got there,' she said.

He asked what was in the pails.

'Saskatoons.'

'Bit late for saskatoons.'

'Yep.'

'You gettin any competition down here?'

'Haven't seen any yet.'

'They're around,' he warned. 'I'd bring a rifle if I was you.'

'Well, you ain't.'

He had always had a thing about bears. As Head and Flora talked, she caught him giving the bush a circumspect look with his watchful grey eyes.

'I hear you been plumbin in the city.'

'Yeah.'

They sat on the clover by the riverbank. It was like being in high school again, one of those days for playing hooky and talking about what you'd do as soon as you left this dump behind. One of those days when anything had seemed possible.

'That's good,' she said finally. 'You guys earn good money.'

'Tell me about it,' he muttered.

When he could find no tracks, he seemed to forget about bears, so he helped her pick the saskatoons. He towered above most of the bushes and got quickly to the best berries, eating about a third of his take. After a silence, he said, 'Know what? We're like frickin doctors. No one wants nothin to do with us till there's a major disaster type thing, then it's *Oh, Mr Kreutzer, we thought you'd never show up.*'

'I read where you guys get the same as teachers an cops.'

Head didn't seem to hear. 'You come home on the bus, people look at you like you got the clap. You tell people what you do for a livin an they have this way of lookin at you. Like you was dirt?'

'I'm sorry I asked,' said Flora. Her day was beginning to sag.

'You're dirt,' he went on, 'until their sewer lines are blocked, an zappo, you're a goddam saviour. You know what I have t'do sometimes t'get ridda the stink?'

'Look,' she said, 'I'm not your social worker. Besides, you're not the only one with troubles, okay?'

He looked at her then in a way more personal than resentful, and she always wondered what he saw, with the bushes between them and something dawning on his hawknosed reddened face, his perpetual grin faltering, because from then on, from time to time, he seemed to look at her differently. She told him about Maitland, the temper tantrums, the long brooding silences, the drinking bouts and blackouts, and that silenced him.

Then the grin returned. He said he might be back the next day, if it was nice, and went down to his motorboat. As it chugged into the slow current and disappeared around the first bend, Flora was left with the impression of his almost perpetually grinning face. Their conversation came back to her and she began to enjoy it. It was the only complete conversation she'd had with him in years, just him and her, with no brothers to interrupt, no father to drag him away with man talk. And that

personal look he'd given her when she'd told him about her own troubles
– as if in the vacancy of this place by the river, a true friendship could
begin, love could begin, her whole life could begin again … because for
the first time he was seeing her as – not a noise exactly, more like a
presence on the path behind her. The edge of a smell. Rotten, musky.

She turned slowly. It was a scruffy male, black except for the beige
nose, down on all fours, watching, moving his head myopically from side
to side, sniffing her, as though Head Kreutzer had conjured him out of his
own fears and left him there.

The river lay fifty yards to her right, and the path up the hill to the
grazing land was blocked by the bear. At her back were the saskatoon
bushes, impenetrable to her, irresistible to the bear. At her feet were two
pails half full of saskatoons. The idea, she saw, was to get over to the
riverbank and all that open space, and to let the bear into the saskatoons,
but not into *her* saskatoons. He seemed to wait proprietorially, as if to
remind her that it was, after all, his land she was on.

She began to wish for invisibility, and when that didn't work, she
talked to the bear. Not words exactly, but an old language of crooning
syllables, slow rises and falls in a voice that seemed to come back to her
from somewhere.

The bear stopped moving his head.

Later, she would wonder where this monologue had come from, the
bear words or whatever they were, but at the time, bending to pick up her
pails, and moving slowly to her right, and crooning in her woodsy
Esperanto, she did not wonder in the slightest.

The bear watched as she backed towards the river.

'Per-heps you could put the berries on the ground,' someone said
behind her.

She stiffened. The bear bolted and crashed through the trees out of
earshot.

Beside a beached canoe stood a man, smiling. He was very tall and
thin, his skin and hair so fair, his teeth so large and white he seemed to
have been bleached like linen in the sun. She had never seen a man so
blond, a face so homely in quite that way: the bulging teeth, the shy
delight, the cotton whiteness of his skin, the frolic in his eyes. And he was
clapping. It was a formal clap, his long fingers faintly, nervously tapping
the palm of his left hand reminding her of words she never used, like
virtuoso, concerto.

'That was wary good,' he said.

She stared at the man in search of a category: clown, giant child, albino. All those strange words (*Lederhosen?*) had nowhere to go.

'What were you saying to him?' the man asked.

'Who are you?'

He told her his name.

'I am the warden's assistant,' he added. 'The bears are my clients.'

He wore the regulation shirt and badge, the government logo was on the prow of his canoe, the rifle stowed beneath the seat beside a battered guitar. She tried to recall his name. Not a syllable would come.

'Were you anxious?' he said.

For a moment, perhaps, Head's stupid prowling fear had become her own. 'No,' she said.

He laughed nervously, foolishly.

'What did you say your name was?'

Again he told her. It sounded like someone rutching up food and spitting it out. She'd never heard the guys talk about this one, he had to be new.

'Would you do me the extreme plesher of having tea with me?'

She squinted up at him and shrugged.

'Your name?'

'Flora.'

'Flora!' he whispered, as though she had given him a password. He laughed again, a nervous knee-slapping whinny of a laugh accompanied by much shaking of the head. 'Anyway,' he said, hunkering down with his thermos in one hand, some cookies in a small bag in the other, 'you are amazing, your name is amazing, your friend the bear is amazing, the day is … I have had an amazing day,' he said, his face at last restored to its pensive cast.

She asked him where he was from.

'I am chust three months here from Germany,' he said and smiled. 'I have studied for a while at Heidelberg, my father has a small chalet in the Schwarzwald, my hair is blond, my eyes are blue, I am good at science, I love to climb and hike in Bavaria. I am the perfect German cliché. They should make me into a sign and hang me on a hotel in the Rhine for all the tourists to behold.' Again, the nervous chuckle, the gasping for air.

He offered her a cookie and a mug of tea and she offered him some berries.

'You moved to Canada so's you could get to be a warden? Did I get that right?'

'Not exactly. This chob is my research. I am exchange student in environmental studies. I am doing total immersion in all things Canadian, then I write my see-zus. I want to go beck with a Canadian accent. I want to blow them away. I'm learning Country and Vesten. I'm telling you, Flora, Canada is a fantastic place.'

'Write a see-zus?'

'Ya, a long research paper,' he said, and leaned back on his elbows in the sand.

She got the impression that if a bird were to call, he would worship it; if a fish were to break the surface, he would worship that, too; and if she spoke anything at all, he would worship her voice and immortalize her words in song. That was their first day together; she would remember it from all the others as the day they met the bear. That night she dreamed she met the warden's assistant in the dark by the river and he glowed like a light bulb.

2.

On the second day she woke up early and took a walk even before Neville and the boys were up. She watched the stars fade and the sky light up clear as the wind blew across the ranchland. The sky was ripe with … what? Premonition, was that it? Either she would meet the bear or she would continue her conversation with Head, or neither would happen, or something else momentous would. Another warden's assistant, this time from Mexico.

After breakfast she went down with her pails to the same spot on the river. At mid-morning a canoe came around the bend in the river, and it was the German.

'Flora,' he called out, before his boat had reached the shore, 'do you have office down here?' and laughed his nervous laugh.

He wore an old shirt and cut-offs. It was his day off, he announced. This time he helped her with the picking, treating each ripe cluster like a string of pearls, and in two hours they had filled both pails. At last, when the heat and the mosquitoes began to get to them, they went over to the river, she in her bathing suit, he in his cut-offs, and waded into the cool boggy water.

'Do you think we could do this in half the rivers of Europe, ya? Only now do we begin to clean them up.'

She admitted she'd never been there.

'This country. Fantastic. In my see-zus I try to discover why Canadians seem to hate it so much.'

3.

He returned on the third afternoon, once more on a day off, and brought some food in a cooler for both of them. 'Some nice patriotic Canadian cheese and sausage,' he said. They sat and munched by the riverside. 'No more wisits from your landlord?'

'No more wisits,' she said.

'Here's to the landlord. *Zum Wohl der Herr.*'

'What did you mean by people here hating their country?'

'Name chust one thing about this place you love. One thing.'

She thought a moment. 'Bears are okay. This valley. I like the wild flowers, Mom's apple trees – no, they dried up and died … deer, I like deer. Grouse, nice fresh air.'

'It's all disappearing. The family farm, good farm land, topsoil, pintails, mallards. Not so many big bucks any more, hm?'

'There's lots of everything around here.'

'No more grouse habitat to the north? No more grouses to the north. Spray with some kinds chemicals, no more hatches. No more marshes up on the flatland, ducks can't nest. Shoot all the big bucks, fewer deer, smaller deer. I tell you, Flora, everything you love you kiss goodbye like your mama's apple trees.'

'That's horseshit.'

Now he was sounding like some kind of government man. 'This is what they said to people like me when there were lots of buffalo, lots of vooping cranes, hm? Ever hear of the pinnated grouse?'

'Should I?'

'No, because it's gone. Forgotten. Anything that nurtures, anything that grows up to be beautiful, it becomes a target. Around here, if it runs on four feet, hop into the snow machine and bang-bang cowboy. The natural flora? Poison it. The topsoil? Grind it down wiz tractors, plough it up and vatch it blow away, ya? Vatch it pile up in the ditches.'

'How do you get off preachin sermons to people who live here? A foreigner, for God's sake. I suppose things are just rosy over there, are they?'

'No, no. The land is in a great death agony all over Europe. This I know. I have seen the figures.' He turned to her, looking dolefully around him. 'I am worse than foreigner. I am an alien from a dying planet. That's how I see myself. I have come down to Earth to send a warning.'

4.

On the fourth day it rained on and off throughout the morning, so she waited until noon to go down to the river. He was waiting for her, this time back in uniform. He was looking grave. He said he could only stay for his lunch break. They shared a mug of tea and some date squares she'd brought along and ruminated beneath the big poplars by the riverbank.

'It's a fantastic country,' he told her, breaking a long silence. 'Utterly fantastic. But when I warble like this to the guys around here, the young guys, they say things like, "I can't wait to go somewhere else." The farmers with moneys, hm? They tear their living out of the soil, chust so they can go to Texas for the winter and spend it all. I tell you, Flora, they hate this place like it was a prison cell.'

'But there's people like that everywhere.'

'People everywhere don't live in Paradise. They chust live in the world. They live in apartment blocks and suburbs and refugee camps and ghettos and places where the seasons have no meaning. Where day and night ... I am being a bummer, ya?'

'Ya.'

5.

Another rain came and went in the night and the morning was sunny. Mernie spotted her daughter from the main barn, in her bathing suit, heading for the lower meadows with her pails.

'Flora, we got more saskatoons in the kitchen than we ever had. You want to lend a hand, I got lots of work for you in here.'

'Can't get a tan in the barn,' she sang out. 'I'm on holidays, remember?'

Beside the path through the woods down to the lower meadows a small creek gurgled with fresh rainwater. Everywhere the dripping trees seemed to exhale humidity. The wind down on the meadows was laden with timothy, sweet-grass, clover and all the re-opened life of the valley.

She was sure the warden's assistant would show up.

He brought two bottles of wine in his cooler. They drank wine, ate berries, and went wading again in the shallows.

'I'll never leave here,' she said. 'I got no ambitions to fly south.'

'You're special,' he said. 'You talk to the bears. When I go beck to Germany, I will write my see-zus and then maybe write clever speeches for the Green Party. But you will talk to the bears.... What are you looking at?'

'You.'

'You look in a funny way.'

'I was just thinkin,' she said, 'if I took away your ideas, what would be left?'

'More ideas.'

'But after all the ideas, after the last idea, then what? This wine must be gettin to me. Who are you when you're not makin speeches?'

'The rest of me is a travesty. I am,' he smiled, 'without a personal life. I am a head full of facts and eloquence and a few good jokes.' His nervous chuckle sputtered like an apology.

'You never been married, never wanted to have a family?'

'Once in a while I have a ... pash, you call it? My biggest pash was for my astronomy teacher *im Gymnasium.* What about you?'

She told him about her marriage, at first haltingly, a veteran who rarely speaks of battle. She felt bolder as the story went on. She even told a fuller version than the one she had given to Head Kreutzer.

'Well, your boo-sing creep of a husband is a fool, ya?'

'Yup.'

'You should wait for a tall blond alien with flashing white teeth and forget about these *Höhlenbewohner,* hm? Why are you laughing?'

'Purple teeth.'

'Und zo are yours.'

The whitey-blond hair, the way his skin went from fair to brown from day to day, the nervous explosions of apologetic laughter, the bulging purple teeth, the eyes as blue as a lake, those last words, *Und zo are yours,* the berry taste of his mouth: these things blurred into her dreams and lived there as though at last they had found a place on the earth to reassemble and call home.

She nicknamed him Whitey.

At the end of the fifth afternoon, a little wobbly and serene, Whitey went back down the river intoning benedictions. *Gott bless Flora. Gott bless Canadian wine. Gott bless the creatures ... the creatures. Gott bless the creatures!'*

Their lovemaking was done on blankets in the shade of some huge gnarled poplars in the last of the hot afternoons. It was a place close to the river so they could cool off. They soon became reckless and went everywhere naked through the woods together. To escape the mosquitoes they would rub river clay on their bodies, or else climb the rounded dry knoll well above the river bottom but well below the ranchlands, not far from Flora's youthful hiding place among the lower meadows. They christened this knoll Gopher Mountain. On a dare she would stand on the knoll and stretch out her body for all to see, but no one saw. She showed her secret hiding place to the young man and he looked on it with such reverence that he seemed to be contemplating an ancient graveyard. She tried to persuade him to enter the copse but he wouldn't. He said the brambles were too thick.

They had a week of afternoons in all without so much as a suspicious look from Flora's mother. And years later, whenever Flora smelled the peculiar blend of poplar leaves, timothy and clover, or smelled ripe saskatoons, she would remember the summer of 1978: how the breeze would greet her body like the breath of God, divide against her face, and tremble behind her like the joining riffles of a creek.

6.

On the sixth afternoon they were lying naked on Gopher Mountain looking down on the forest and the river below. Suddenly Whitey jumped to his feet and yelled out into the valley, 'Eros! Eros! Eros!' He blocked out the sun as he stood above her. He looked like a tree or a cairn.

'Lost your dog?' she said.

'Something I always want to do.'

'What were you yelling?'

'I must explain,' he said. 'Once upon a time, in the high mountains of Soana, there was a young student seeking after truth. If you're a German you have to find truth up in the mountains. And this young guy, he climbs away up to a willage. The people in the willage tell him stay away from der Ketzer, this old man up in the alpine meadow. He's crazy. But he's a young man in search of truth so he finds the old guy up there.'

'What's a ketzer?'

'I can't think of the word in English.... Heretic? Ya. Anyway, it's a beautiful day, chust like this. Out on the meadow the ... how do you say *die Ziegen* ... the goats are chumping around and making little goats, and there is already der Ketzer, looking himself wary much like a goat. You

116

almost expect he makes his love with the animals and the grass and the flowers, hm? And I forget what happens. I think maybe he tells the young student what truth is, but what I remember is even better. The old goat of a man, he stands on this rock and he sees the birds and the bees and he yells out, *Eros!* He sees the goats going at it, ya? And he yells out, *Eros!* And he looks around him – if I were the young student I think I would have fled – and he yells out, *Eros!*

Whitey squinted at Flora, somewhere adrift between his pious and his gleeful state, and said, 'Always I want to be der Ketzer chust once.'

'Well, you answered my question,' she said.

'I did?'

'If we strip away all your ideas, what we got left is a horny old goat.'

'That's good,' he said, and went silent. 'You know, the whole problem with man is the head.'

'This is more ideas, right?'

'Only one more learned discourse and I promise you my lips are closed. Eros is the life force, ya? It is the enemy of – what? – thought, consciousness, science, of logos. Eros is opposed to all those things we can think up to make us secure from the caprice of Nature. Houses, lights, the … uh … *das Gesatz* … the laws, uh … the morality, storm cellars, scientific discoveries and applications, insurance policies. So we subject our land and our seas to the … laws of balance sheets, the laws of mathematics, and forget the laws of Nature, the delicate exchange of ecosystems, the nurture of the soil, ya? Because it's all so primitive, hm?'

'You have nice eyes,' she said.

'But Logos, informed by the wisdom of Eros,' he said, 'that is another thing. Make me king of the world, Flora, and I would bring back Eros, saucy and big-bellied with life. There would be sign-board adwertisements and television chingles.'

Flora closed her eyes.

'Eros and Logos, the heart and the head in a cosmic marriage. I like that,' said the young man.

He said a great deal more but her attention drifted and returned, drifted and returned. All these new words. She'd never keep track of them. Ketzers and gene pools, and ecosystems and building a new planet with Eros and Logos coupling in the garden and a Green Party coalition in the next election, and who gives a fat rat's ass.… *I could never be married to this man,* she thought, and fell asleep. When she awoke, the sun was low and red in the south and he was tugging at her to come swimming.

7.

Their last day by the river was hot. Lovemaking turned their bodies into water slides; they frolicked, slept, and lolled about all day long. In the late afternoon as the shadows of the trees lengthened and began to fall on the river, Whitey slept next to Flora on their blanket. He would be confined to the office after this, their seventh day together. They would have to tryst in Melville whenever he could drive over. Flora would be a teller again. She began to resume some of her former severity. *I never did manage to figure out these deposit slips, dear. That's all right, Mrs Finnerty, I'll fill it out again for you.*

Beside her, the young man murmured, 'I am der Ketzer.'

Shortly after Whitey had left, Head Kreutzer showed up. A new hatch of mosquitoes engulfed them, so Flora walked her friend up the path to Gopher Mountain, wondering if he suspected anything. He seemed oblivious, even when he sat on the knoll where the tall grass had been flattened.

'Nice view,' he said.

They wandered down from the knoll among the long shadows toward the poplars on the riverbank. She was thinking it would be her last trip down here for a long time. At that moment she spotted the bear. It was sniffing Head's case of beer, the same scruffy old male she'd seen a week ago. She almost wanted to yell her salutations. The wind shifted and the bear became aware of them. It padded slowly into the saskatoon bushes and merged with the gloom of the thickets.

'I told you y'shoulda had a rifle,' Head exclaimed.

'What for?'

'You never know,' he said.

'He's just showin you it's all right.'

'Those are his berries,' he said.

'They're everyone's.'

'I doubt he's wild about sharin em.'

'He's letting us see that he lives here,' she said. 'He thinks you left him a gift.'

'Yeah, great.'

'He's got no reason to attack us. We're not chasin him. We're just walkin around.'

Head went for his canoe, keeping a considerable amount of space between himself and where the bear had disappeared. Flora held her ground and lingered by the poplars. Head returned clutching a paddle.

'You ask me,' he said, 'he was showin us the door.'

'What are you doin with that?' she said.

'Come on,' he said, nodding to the east. 'I'll walk you up as far as the road.'

FOUR

1.

Hunting with Steve and the guys felt wrong; she knew that now, but she could not turn back. It felt wrong as soon as she approached the lower meadow with Steve and saw the top of Gopher Mountain rising from the river like the head of a bald man. She could imagine what Whitey would say, or how the animals would clench inside as they approached, and she felt like a trespasser.

From the middle of the narrow meadow Neville beckoned wildly. 'You want your chance, Harry?' he cried. He and the boys had spotted some fresh tracks in the new snow, a lot of them. Neville spoke with the excitement of a younger man. 'You an Steve go halfway up on the left side of the bush. Spread out some. We got em corralled. Head an Clyde are up the other side an Goober's got the east end.'

'Who's doggin?' Flora asked.

'I'm doggin,' said Neville. 'There's been a big mother in that bush. Ain't nothin gettin by this time.'

This time? Flora looked back at the bush in question, a long thin copse of willows and dogwood running down the centre of the meadow, only a few hundred yards from her old hiding place. 'This time' meant that Neville would spot the tracks in the fresh snow better than Clyde could ever have done. That other time. Goober's favourite story.

Steve took up a position about a hundred yards ahead of Flora. There was a draw between them where the water drained in the spring. Steve scanned the bush with the same sort of fervour she saw in all the men.

Neville never barked when he was the dog. Perhaps he assumed that no one would ever mistake him for the thing he was hunting. But occasionally he swore, and Flora could hear this from time to time as he stumbled on a deadfall or took a willow branch in the face. He was moving fast.

There was a minute's silence and then he started to scream; it was like a plea: 'Shooooot the buggers!'

All she could see was Steve, who looked back at her across the dip in the meadow. Then Steve yelled something and his gun went up. A doe leapt out of the bush and bounded into the draw between them, so close she could see an old scar on its shoulder.

'It's a doe!' she cried, and Steve put up his gun.

The doe bounded down toward Gopher Mountain and the river. Out came Neville, spitting twigs, glaring at Flora.

'Do you want some venison or dontcha?'

'That was a doe,' she yelled back.

'Is history about to goddam repeat itself? Do you for chrissakes realize how long it'll be before we get another shot like that? *By the Jesus!*' Neville lurched back into the woods.

Steve and Flora shrugged at each other. Apparently the rules had changed. All around them the snow fell in heavier flakes, slanting into the hills in the late afternoon light. Steve turned his back to Flora, trying to see where the doe had gone. Once more her father swore and crashed into some deadwood. She wondered why this time he would swear first and crash second, and another doe and a fawn bounded out. Once more they chose the draw between Steve and Flora as if it were some sort of safe passage. Steve was still gazing down toward the river. She cupped her hands to call to him. At that moment the buck emerged from the trees, silent, unmistakable. Appletree. The antlers were almost too massive for those of a white-tail. He seemed to be eyeing Steve, then he jerked around to look at Flora. As Steve turned, the big buck began stiffly to trot their way.

Again came Neville's voice: 'Shoot! Shoot! Shoot the bugger!'

The buck passed equidistant between Steve and Flora. The gun was at her shoulder, Appletree centred in her sights, and something red – Steve. He in her sights, she in his. Even at a hundred yards she caught his expression of absolute concentration.

'No!' she cried.

Neville crashed out of the bush.

Steve put up his gun, stumbled backward and fell.

Neville fired and missed. The buck was too close for a scope. He tried to eject the shell. Again and again. 'Harry, by all that's sacred!' he groaned.

The great buck halted to look at her. It seemed to sense something even before Flora threw the gun back up to her shoulder, and bounded down the draw toward Gopher Mountain.

Steve picked himself up from the snow, shook his hands.

Neville tore at his bolt.

The buck wheeled to the right suddenly and made for Flora's bush.

Flora swung her gun and fired.

2.

On their way back to the trucks they saw the moon come up, nearly full, with a copper blush. It lit their way through the meadows. No one spoke.

Whenever he saw a slender shadow that somehow seemed separate from the surrounding trees, Neville wondered if it was a deer. Each time, he would clutch his rifle even harder (though not so the others could notice) and tense up his shoulders. He was tired. The hunt was over and he knew it, but he kept thinking, *if I get half the chance, even if it's a night kill*

...

The last illegal deer he dropped was a doe he and Clyde doubled on by the top road. They had field-dressed it on their own land in full view of a construction crew, and one of the men must have gotten right on the phone, because there was no love lost between Neville and those crews. They never seemed happy unless they were chewing up half the trees on the prairie. The wardens got there before Neville or the boys could throw the doe into the truck. It had to be one of those bastards on construction. The guts were steaming and the snow was red, and the older of the two wardens dove in hands first. Neville, I'd swear this buck has no penis, he said. How do you figure that? Oh, I wouldn't know about them things, Neville told him. I don't have no university degrees like you guys. Does this look like a penis to you, the older one says to the other, that whiteyhaired one. The younger one says, I got university degree, and where I come from those things are called waginas. You oughta know, says Clyde. Guys like you pee sittin down, dontcha? The older one says, do you enjoy picking off does any time of the year, pregnant does like this one? And Neville says, do you enjoy takin orders from a frog in Ottawa?

'You look all in,' Neville said at last to Flora.

She was picking her way along the trail ahead of Neville, stumbling, righting her stride, and carrying on. She shrugged at his observation. Likely she was brooding on how close she had come to nailing old Applétree. Change the subject, he thought. Change the goddam subject.

He wanted to tell Flora how he and Clyde had mouthed off to those wardens, how it was almost worth the fine and having their guns confiscated to see the look on their faces. He wanted to tell her, but he thought better of it. He'd probably told her often enough. Besides, any time he went on about the wardens, Flora would up and defend them just to show him how independent she was. It was that perverse streak that ran so deep in Mernie. Those bastards, he thought. They probably dined on venison that very night. It made him mad to think of it.

Neville's last legal deer was a spike buck, only eighteen months old. And did he taste fine. Neville wanted to shout, *It wasn't always this way, by the Jesus.*

Before Flora came along, Neville and Head's father Harry Kreutzer could go out every fall with a team of horses and have two or three bucks or maybe an elk before dinner time. Neville and his friend Harry couldn't walk out to a haystack without seeing a dozen deer in broad daylight. When Neville was a boy he never knew a winter without deer sausage and mooseburger. They almost ran out of places to hang up the antlers.

Flora had heard it all before.

They climbed out of the last meadow in single file and found the trail through the spruce groves that led to the trucks. The moon had turned silver and cast diminishing blue shadows across the snow. Neville's rifle was on safety, but his arms, his entire torso, were cocked as though he expected the old days to come back again … before the goddam city hunters and their jeeps and their all-terrain vehicles, and those assholes from town runnin down fawns in their goddam snowmobiles and before the goddam wardens in their boy scout uniforms and their candy-ass government jobs takin orders from that frog playboy who wouldn't know a backhoe from a butter knife and all those goddam railway crews shootin deer from a sidecar and those seismic bastards with their overland vehicles leavin gates open like they owned the place –

Flora stopped suddenly ahead of Neville. Everyone had stopped. In a clearing to Neville's right stood something the size of a sawhorse. A coyote? So be it. Neville snapped off his safety.

When he fired, the whole woods seemed to crack back. The animal went down on its back legs. They rushed to the clearing as the creature tried to crawl into the spruce. It was a fawn of six months. The lower spine had been shattered, but still it struggled to reach the nearest clump of spruce trees.

All their scopes, apparently, were fogged.

'Anyone got a knife?'

'Left mine in the truck.'

'Every time I bring my skinnin knife, I end up never shootin nothin.'

The fawn turned to look at them. It seemed to know that its mother was somewhere else and that this was the end, but it tried one last time to haul its body across the last bit of clearing. Game little chryster, Neville thought.

He called Flora over. 'Our scopes don't work so good close in, eh? How about you kill it?'

Flora moved forward into the half circle of men. 'This is a fawn,' she said.

'Yeah, well,' Head mumbled.

'You couldn't make ten hotdogs outa this one,' she said.

'Flora, just do it,' said Goober.

She looked at them all.

The fawn began to bawl, and Flora seemed to be frozen to the spot. It was a curious childlike bleating, high and piercing. Neville wondered if these men had ever heard a fawn bawl before. He thought of his grandson and had a brief flash of his dream of the previous night.

'Jesus,' muttered Steve.

'Kill it,' said Neville. 'Get it done with.'

Head reached over for Flora's gun, gave her his own, cocked hers, raised it to his shoulder and fired. The fawn pitched forward into the snow.

As he gutted the fawn in the moonlight, Head brooded on Flora, how Mate had run out on her and how it was no wonder. She couldn't be one of the boys and she couldn't be one of the girls type thing, but she kept trying to be both. Isn't that just what Mate had said?

After a while Goober came over and held the flashlight for Head. Goober tried to think of one thing he might say to Flora. The first thing that came to his mind was, Too bad about just nickin Appletree, Harry. But he thought better of it. Maybe something like, C'mon, Harry, the boys are waitin. Let's go get pissed. Something like that.

Clyde broke out the beer and offered it around. 'Victory drink, eh? First one ta-night.'

Neville pissed in the snow and drank his beer at the same time, a sad fatigue carved by the moon on the lines of his face. I don't give a good goddam, he thought fervently. Harry gets the sausage from this one.

'I've been wondering what it must feel like to haul a rifle around when you heart's not in it,' Steve said to Flora. She shrugged. He sat beside her in Goober's half-ton waiting to see her lean forward so the moon would illuminate the side of her face. A few hours earlier he had decided to tell her his philosophy of hunting, that the real hunter loves the thing he kills. Somehow that seemed a bit beside the point. He thought and thought about what he might say to her to redeem the moment. He felt a soft 'plop' in his lap.

'Here's your gloves back,' she said.

Later, when Head had washed up in the snow, he sat next to Flora in the truck where Steve had sat. They were all about ready to move out. He said, 'You done okay out there, Harry.'

Without turning in the seat, she said, 'Well, if I done okay out there, I guess you and the boys must of done fabulous.'

3.

When Steve awoke, the fires were faded, the sun up, and there were voices outside. One of them was Head's. Steve rolled out of his bag and peered through the kitchen window. Head was talking to a man in a yellow jeep. He was handsome, stocky, wore his hair long, and wore shades. He wondered if he'd seen him at the Ski Shack. He looked familiar.

Head was clutching a large wad of bills. He seemed torn between the need to pocket the money and the need to count it. 'Yeah, well,' he said to the fellow in the shades. Their conversation, apparently, was over.

Steve yawned. He felt only half rested. He'd been dogged by bad dreams all night long. At first it was obscure creatures chasing him through the woods. Then it was a weird spectacle down at Neville's corral. A bunch of guys gathered to watch the rooster with no head. Taking bets.

'You're up!' he shouted. 'Jee-zus.'

'What was that all about?' said Steve.

'That's for me to know an you to find out. Hey, are we goin huntin or what?'

Steve dressed for his last morning in the woods. He would take it easy today. He hoped that Neville and the boys would be too busy on the ranch to hunt. He also hoped he could see Flora one more time. But briefly. Because then it would be just him and Head, two guys with one thought: get a buck and get out.

Head threw Steve's .308 up to his shoulder and swung it at the bear hide on the wall.

'Can you tell me one thing?' said Steve.

'Pow.'

'Seriously.'

'It'll cost ya.'

'That rooster over at Potts. Once he got his head chopped off, could he still make out with the hens?'

Head laughed. 'How the hell would I know?'

'Seriously.'

'Mernie didn't seem to think so.'

Steve told him part of his dream, that the men were betting on whether the rooster could cover a hen within a specified time limit.

Head only stopped laughing when the bacon started to smoke. 'I'm sharin the cabin with a certified loony,' he said.

'Hey,' Steve said, 'what was goin down out there?'

Head wore a mischievous look. 'Sell me your .308, scope an all, I'll tell ya anything. I'll even not bullshit ya.'

'Who was that guy in the jeep? I keep thinking I've seen him somewhere.'

Head regarded Steve out of the corner of his eye, crammed a piece of toast into his mouth, washed it down with instant coffee, and said, 'You seen him once last August or so in the weight room with me.'

'Of course.'

'That was Mate.'

They packed up the truck so that Head could lock the cabin. While Head was outside, Steve took a quick look into the utility room. The tarp was thrown into the corner and all the antlers were gone.

'Well, Neville,' Head declared, stretching his long arms, 'if you folks are workin today, me an Steve'll hit the lower meadow again. That okay by you?'

'Give er hell,' said Neville.

Flora came into the kitchen carrying her baby. She moved past the men and spoke in hushed tones to her mother. Steve vowed that before the day was over he would make her laugh.

She turned to look at Steve. There seemed to be a purpose in her staring, but no visible emotion. Her gaze reminded Steve of a way some animals have of looking at people. She brought Carey over and said, 'Would you hold him?'

Steve grunted in reply, reddening.

'Last night you was wonderin what's it like to hold a rifle when your heart's not in it,' she said. 'Well, here's my answer.' She handed him the baby. 'Don't worry, his cold's almost gone. And he's shot his wad this morning, so he ain't even loaded.'

Mernie laughed, Neville smiled, but Flora remained impassive and joined her mother where the pantry joined the kitchen. They were doing pies together.

Steve held the baby as though it were an expensive urn. Head settled back down into his chair, brooding at Flora's backside. Neville left at Goober's bidding. The kettle rocked and snored on the stove.

Steve discovered Flora's baby regarding him with what seemed to be a look of appraisal. There was something extra-terrestrial about the face, the elflike ears, the precocious mop of whitey-blond hair, the unusually well-defined nose, the adult look in those pale blue eyes, the dispassionate inspection the baby seemed to be giving him. *We have landed and we are being held by a hoser from the city. We may have to bail on this one. Over.*

'Are we huntin or what?' Head finally asked.

Steve looked at Flora for release. She was spooning saskatoon berries into one of Mernie's pie shells. She licked the spoon and a listlessness like a cloud seemed to drift over her face. Sometimes Cora got that look.

But Cora was different. She wasn't so ... Various terms for female malaise presented themselves to Steve: screwed up, unreadable, bitchy, hot and cold. None of them seemed to work. Ornery? Contrary?

Head put his mug down and rose to his feet. 'Time to hit the road, Schuyler.'

'Maybe yiz can get a grown-up one this time,' said Flora.

'Maybe you should join up with them wardens,' Head replied.

'It takes more guts to hunt down a buncha game hogs than it does t'shoot a fawn.' She glared first at Head, then at Steve.

'Don't look at me,' Steve said.

Carey began to bawl. For a moment Steve had forgotten that the baby was on his lap. Carey's pale face was now red and contorted. 'Jeez,' he said to Flora, 'I think I scared the kid.'

4.

Steve and Head made it all the way down to the lower meadow before they found the tracks of Appletree. They led from Flora's bush back out to the lower meadow and meandered from browse to browse. This had Head buffaloed.

'He's not runnin, he's *feedin* for God's sake. Look where he lifts his foot. He's goin slow as hell.'

'So?'

'Well, Schuyler, it's obvious. He's not runnin from anythin, he's feedin. Look, if you had six hunters on your trail last night an just got nicked by a bullet, would you stop for some horse duvers?'

Steve gazed at the hills where the buck's trail wandered.

Head continued, 'Harry said that Appletree must of got past us in the dark. After she nicked him and we had him surrounded. Remember? When she was in there doggin,' he said, pointing to Flora's Bush, 'an we was all on point. Are you with me?'

Steve nodded.

Head went on. 'We had him surrounded an Harry says, "He's gone." Remember?'

'Yeah.'

'What did she say to you, Steve?'

He thought a moment. 'She said Appletree must have been going like sixty. It was too dark to see him escape.'

'Right. He was goin like sixty an there's no runnin tracks.'

Head retraced the path of the big buck on the meadow. 'Steve, he was goddam *walkin* outa the bush. *Browsin.* There's no other fresh tracks.'

Steve pointed to Flora's bush, from which the tracks had emerged. 'Let me check the thicket,' he said. Steve liked solving mysteries.

He waded into the thicket where Flora had walked the previous night immediately after she had fired at Appletree. He followed in her footsteps. The sun was high and bright, and Steve could even see the bluish trails of mice and chickadees in the snow. Here and there among Flora's tracks were the splayfooted tracks of Appletree. At various points along the trail their tracks came together and made a single path in the snow. He followed her trail into the middle of the thicket until their footsteps and hoof marks circled a little marsh, and still there was only one path, as though Flora and Appletree had been taking a walk together.

Steve waded silently through the snow. He did not want to give away his position. Just in case.

An odd feeling came over him, as though Flora were here in the bush, watching him, eyeing the way he held his gun.

In his dream the previous night he'd held a revolver, his old cap gun from when he'd lived on Albert Street, and the headless rooster was just beginning to feather one of the hens when Flora showed up, naked, for all the men to see. But instead of putting on a show for the guys at the corral as they clapped and whistled, she seemed to be in a state of wild distress. She looked right at Steve and said something to him, she looked him right in the eye, it was an urgent look.

He stumbled on something and had to catch his balance. It was a huge antler.

'Kreutzer!' Steve yelled. 'You're not gonna believe this!'

'Is he dead?'

'No. Hang on,' Steve called, glad to hear his friend's voice close by.

He circled the little frozen marsh to the left. He followed the same trail around to where he had begun, to the place where the buck had left Flora's path and wandered out into the meadow to feed. Near this place, where the willows and grass were thickest, the buck had apparently bedded down for the night, right on the path. So he must have remained in this thicket until well after Flora and the hunters had gone home.

Steve did the circuit again. It was a flowershaped path. In one place Flora had broken trail on her own. This side trip had taken her to the centre of the little pond where she had stopped to pee.

And from this vantage point, from the ovule of the flower, so to speak, she could have seen – Steve did a complete circle, his eyes like the lenses of a film camera; he saw aspens, cattails, wild rosebushes, willows – she could have seen everything.

'She must have seen him,' he told Head.

Head was inspecting the big antler.

Steve said, 'I mean after she took that potshot. She went in there and saw him.'

Head squinted at Steve, his mouth open.

'Weird, eh?'

5.

Flora remembered she had fired the gun because Neville had told her afterward. She remembered Neville pleading, *Harry, by all that's sacred!* and Steve slipping, and a jolt somewhere inside of her body (like one of those old-fashioned flashpowder photographs in black and white) that made her different after, frozen in time and somehow broken (she would never manage to explain how or why), and a whiff of gunpowder: the great buck seemed to stumble, lurch, and toss his head, then gather for another leap. Up he went, bounding like a jackrabbit, and never stopping until he was swallowed up by the thicket. And there he must have waited.

Something else had happened, something broken off and lost between the flashpowder jolt and the buck's wild dance, and this too she tried to reassemble, staring at the falling snow and the edge of the woods.

She found herself walking toward the trees. Neville strode past her, red and puffing, eyes to the ground, his big nose snuffling. 'You nicked him, Harry. I seen it.'

They hurried to the edge of the woods and peered through the trees. Neville found the trail but no blood. 'Goober an Head went around,' he yelled to Steve. 'They're waitin on the other side. We got im trapped!' Neville barked out orders to Steve like an officer. 'If he goes left an runs for the ridge, you take him. If he goes this way, he's mine.'

The two men walked in opposite directions along the fringe of the bush, waiting for the big buck to plunge out, but he stayed and they could not spot him. Flora walked behind her father, lost, like a girl in a dream, the falling snow like dream snow, her father a dark shape like the father long ago who would come in from the hallway to tuck her in at night and she pretending to be asleep. Wave after wave of dissonant sounds. She kept thinking about the buck, remembering the words of the warden's assistant, *The whole problem with man is with the head,* seeing once more the head of the buck on the bead of her gun barrel.

She stumbled on something and picked it up, an antler at the edge of the bush, a huge one, cracked and shattered near the base. *Oh, please, God, please.*

Neville's voice seemed to come from very far away, and in the fading light he was even more like a figure in a dream.

'You go for him, Harry. We'll pick him off if he makes a break for it.'

She picked up his trail and moved slowly through the bush, her bush, unfamiliar now because it was almost dark and almost winter. She was shaking. She went slow as a porcupine. She found the tracks easily but no blood.

Forgetting to bark, she lurched over the thornbushes and deadwood, deeper into the heart of the thicket. In the centre was her little frozen pond, perhaps thirty feet across. The buck had gone toward it. Instead of heading out the other side of the bush toward Goober or Head or Clyde, the tracks veered left and circled the pond. She followed and they doubled back toward the meadow. *Oh please, dear God.* She could hear the voices of her father and Steve not a hundred feet away, so she wondered what would possess the big animal that he would head toward the men instead of away from them. But a few yards from the edge of the bush, the tracks went left again, back into the thicket. She stumbled along in his trail, peering through the fading light, tired now, having to urinate, hearing the men call her name. They expected something from her. She would not answer, though, or the buck would hear her. Back around the little marsh she went and realized the buck had chosen the same trail.

She stopped. If she was following him, then he was following her. They could go on walking the same circle till after dark. She looked behind her and to her left across the little pond. There was still only one broken trail, his and hers. (It went right by that clump of willows where she had touched the moose calf, while across the pond, the cow had munched on lilies. She had touched the calf on the flank and it scarcely acknowledged her presence, the surest guarantee of her invisibility that she could hope for. Then the calf joined the cow and they both looked her way.)

She felt a steady pain along her arm and realized that all this time she had been carrying the antler. She dropped it on the trail. It felt as though she were leaving a note for Appletree. She carried on. Again she heard her name called but she had made up her mind not to bark. She went around the little pond once more to be sure he hadn't left the circle they both had made. But he stayed on the track and again circled back toward her father, and around again just before the edge of the bush. She came upon the antler and her heart sank. She'd been expecting to see him this time. It was almost as if he hadn't received her message, or didn't trust it. She peered through the woods. The dark was falling. There was time, perhaps, for one more trip around the circuit. She stayed on the path and began once again to circle the little marsh, and a semicircle away from the antler, she stopped, looked around, and waited until she could feel the cold settling into her bones, saw nothing, heard only the occasional call from one of the men. Then she stepped inside the circle, onto the ice, and headed across toward the antler. In the centre of the pond she stopped and looked about, took down her jeans and peed in the snow. When she stood up again she sensed something behind her, something like the bear in summer. Slowly she turned around. The big buck stood on the trail by the marsh, head low, watching her. In the dim light she could still make out his one remaining antler like the branches on her mother's apple tree.

'I'm sorry,' she said.

FIVE

1.

Flora deposited Carey on the sofa, drew up the blind, and opened a window in the tiny living room. The snow had almost melted.

'Bok!' cried the baby. His cold seemed to have vanished.

Outside on the street Steve was leaning against the Toyota truck while Head checked their gear in the back. Already Head was sulking, back in harness, beginning to see toilets and sewer pipes, or so it appeared to Flora. *Know what I do t'get ridda the stink?*

'Bok!' cried the baby again.

She picked him up, exposing his face to the sun, and peered at him. 'Are you my fella?' she said.

The baby smiled. *Bok*, was his answer, and she laughed.

'Come see,' she said, and carried him over to an arched recess in the living room wall where she kept the phone. Out of sight behind the phone was a polaroid shot of a man's face. He wore a foolishly happy smile. Flora showed her baby this photo.

'See Daddy?'

'Bok,' said the baby.

Flora laughed again and returned to the window. Still laughing, she looked out the window and caught Steve and Head looking in at her from the truck, as though she were ... It took a moment to figure it out. Never seen someone laugh before, she wanted to shout, but squinted back and tried to imagine both of them with rifles raised, aiming. Yes, that was the expression they wore.

2.

In Toronto it was a bit before midnight. Cora would be in her nighty but not yet asleep. Unshowered, tired, and half-undressed, Steve dialled her number. He sat on his mattress on the floor, fingering some unopened mail on his pillow. He was depressed.

'You asleep?' he began.

His voice was hushed, as though someone were listening, and he smiled nervously into the mouthpiece. 'I would've but where I was this weekend there weren't any phones.... Out hunting.... The Assiniboine Valley, away east of here, way out in the boonies. We had this neat cabin. Guy named Kreutzer, you know, the plumber? Real nice guy.... Yeah ... yeah ... I wondered how those got there. You put them there last June?... Of course I still have them.... Yes, they kept my hands nice and warm....'

They spoke for some time, Steve's voice modulating from taciturnity ('It's no big deal, y'know') to a gentle chiding tone that, for Steve ('You always worry about that, you shouldn't worry about that'), was unfamiliar territory.

Then later, 'Of course we should be seeing each other at Christmas, of course I'm coming down there! What are you saying?' he cried, his face suddenly stricken like a child's. 'Where's all this coming from?'

He looked out over the mess he had made of his apartment, his gym socks and sweats tossed in a heap on the sofa, a case of empties and spilled Cheezies on the matching chair, his rifle and hunting clothes sprawled like a dead soldier on the bedroom floor.

'I phoned you because I missed you, because I was feeling ... you know.... I phoned you because I thought you'd be wondering ... What are you saying? This doesn't sound like you.... I don't have my reservation yet, no, but that's just a formality. I'm *coming* to Toronto.... I *phoned* because, because I thought it was time we stopped kidding ourselves, it's time to cut the crap....'

He listened with his head on his hand then held the phone at arm's length, his other hand reaching out as if to feel for rain, his eyes rolled toward Heaven, then resumed his huddled pose and listened as she spoke.

'Just let me ask you one thing.... Never mind that.... Cora!... Well, of *course* it bothers me!'

Later, after the late news on television and the weekend review of sports, and a couple of beers, and much pacing, after he'd made up his mind that *he* would not be the one to call back first, Steve opened his mail. The last piece was a small parcel with no return address. It was wrapped in brown paper (an old grocery bag?) and tied with old string. There was a note and something light in a small plastic bag. He opened the plastic bag before reading the note because the thing in the bag smelled funny.

'Jesus!' he barked. It was the head of a chicken, long dead. The note read as follows:

Dear Mr Schuyler, Inclosed is a trophy head for the wall of your apartment. Our club members felt this head wold be more use to you than to its original owner. When you do the mesurments, you will note that this head realy ranks up thier with the national trophys for chickens over the last decade or more, this head intitles you to a lifetime membership in the Kreutzer Hunting Lodge so when this here chicken starts to talk to you you lissen. But when you start to talk back, you know its time to come hunting again come out here PDQ where the hunting is fine. Bring this here head with you and show it at the door then we will know you are one of us.
Your sincerely, H. Kreutzer, President.

Steve was in no mood for a joke, but as he read and reread the letter, a sardonic half-smile came to his lips. Before showering, he wrapped the chicken head in the note and placed them back in the little plastic bag. He put the little package into the freezer compartment of his fridge because he didn't want to stink things up.

At some time in the early morning he dreamt once more he was being pursued in an apple orchard by men with guns but this time couldn't find his cap pistol. One of his pursuers had a grin like Head Kreutzer. They drove him out of the orchard and he fled through space. His cries were heard across the galaxy. Even Cora heard him, every time she picked up the telephone.

3.

At an altitude of approximately 36,000 kilometres, a number of synchronous satellites orbit our planet. They are called synchronous because they stay in one position over the earth, and their motion is synchronized with its spin. During the time it takes for Earth to rotate once on its axis, the satellites also complete one orbit; like Zeno's Achilles or lovers on an urn, they are embarked upon an endless pursuit.

One particular satellite, looking somewhat like a huge bottlecap and with attached brush (the kind one finds on bottles of white correction fluid or nail polish), floats above the mid-Atlantic in a cold infinity of stars. It has been seen as a speck of grit in the Big Dipper and a fourth stud on Orion's belt. Yet one is mostly struck by its forlorn disconnection from everything else in the universe; everything, that is, except its apparent loyalty to a specific swatch of spinning sea.

A discarded remnant, perhaps, of some passing intelligence? An icon from some religion whose prayer books have been burned, theologians buried, tablets long since ground to dust? A piece broken off a larger machine? In fact, it is potentially all of these things; it is a communications satellite linking two ground stations, both with powerful antennae that rise like antlers in the night. One of these stations is near Boise, Idaho, the other in Goonhilly Downs, England.

Perched upon this satellite with a specially tuned listening device, we could hear the many signals coming in via Boise in November of 1979, one signal wavering through space from Melville, Saskatchewan: 'I thought I'd show Dad I could drop a buck; I mean those guys think I'm useless as balls on the Pope, and damn it, they had to see ...' and another signal, via the downs, coming in from Hamburg: 'You mean you have tried to bring down this great creature, this Appletree, on purpose?' Back and forth the signals go as our satellite follows the globe rolling like a gutter ball through the universe. 'You get caught up sometimes. In someone else's thing?' 'Ya.' 'And you figure, what the hell, go with it.' The voices seem to lose their connection, so verbally they grope for each other in the dark until the signals become stronger, the right words spoken again. 'Bless you, Flora.' 'I seen him again and didn't say Boo, I just walked out an told the guys he'd taken off, and they believed me!' '... der Ketzer.' Interference. Thunder somewhere over the Downs. 'What?' 'Ketzer. The one who defies orders ... holy orders ... the technocratic imperative.... Brüderlichkeit, ya?' 'What? Yeah, anyway, those buggers, they couldn't nail a buck so they went an shot a fawn about the size of our dogs. I'm tellin you, Whitey, I've had it with huntin.' 'My God....' Pause. Static. 'You still there, Whitey?' 'Vitey, I love that name.' 'I got his antler. The guys, they give it to me.' 'Flora, I must go to work. Next time....' Pause, crackle. '... reverse charges, ya?' 'Ya, Whitey.' 'I love that name.'

4.

Another kind of signal, drifting from the hocks of a doe in oestrus, carried by the night wind across the meadow and floating through a grassy thicket, brings up the head of the greatest buck in the valley. His single antler weighs like the memory of a bad fall, but he struggles out of his grassy pallet stiffly to his feet.

The doe stands several hundred yards away in the centre of the meadow. She is the one with the old scar on her shoulder. She has stopped feeding on the alfalfa to listen. Something unfurling inside her is blowing musk to the November wind and her big tail twitches side to side.

☆ Protection

'Schmuck, you tell me to get behind Wiener, I get behind Wiener, so pass awready. I was in the clear!'

'In the clear yet, you call that in the clear? The time you take getting behind Wiener I could change my socks and underwear!'

That's how I remember Pinsky during practice, putting Segal in his place. Segal, already an angry young man ten years before his pilgrimage to Allen Ginsberg, already tortured by dreams of glory, the victim of a body too long and spindly to give any quarterback confidence in him. Pinsky, perpetually venting his rage on boys a head taller than he was. Segal stalks away from Pinsky on his fourteen-year-old giraffe legs, and Pinsky lopes back to the huddle, spits on his hands, claps them twice. A new scrimmage is seething to be born somewhere beneath his brush cut.

And I remember a boy almost fourteen himself, a gentile, though not yet conversant with that word, sulking as he stands on the curb of Westminster Drive. He wants to play too, but he thinks these Jews should ask *him,* and he is angry because they find him so easy to ignore. He rubs a spot beneath his nose where the peach-fuzz itches, like his body, to proclaim his manhood, the spot where my moustache now grows. I remember his goyish anger, less volatile than Pinsky's, less frequent than Segal's, but anger all the same. He is thinking *If my stupid parents had been satisfied to keep our old house I'd be playing end both ways on Carpenter's team and not hanging around this stupid neighbourhood the only unJewish kid my age on this crescent and if my brother's stupid friends hadn't chased Alvin Pinsky into Mrs Bercovitz's backyard I'd be out there now even if I wasn't Jewish and if I was in high school with my brother I'd be playing in a real league not just a stupid pick-up league.* But he knows that beneath all his excuses for not playing that day is the fact that he, Drew Edmond, the only non-female gentile his age on Westminster Drive, has laughed at Alvin Pinsky.

Less than a month before, it was Pinsky, not Drew, who'd wanted to play. I can run, I can pass, I can kick, said Pinsky to Drew's brother Hank. Hank was quick-witted, tall, built for speed, and sixteen. I can catch, Pinsky continued, I can call signals, I can block. You just don't say that to

Hank and his friends. They're all sixteen and they play high-school football. You don't go shooting off your mouth at those guys, because they don't take anything from anybody. You learn to ask questions if you're younger and smaller, and wait to be invited. Drew Edmond knew that. Anybody with any brains knew that. And you *especially* don't go shooting off your mouth if you're wearing a brand new pair of *red* running shoes. Pinsky was dead before he opened his mouth. It was Hank who coined his new name, Little Red Running Shoes. They all roared as though they'd learned how to laugh from watching cowboy movies. They knew Pinsky was what they called a hotshot and they weren't going to let him off easy.

I remember Pinsky better than I remember anyone in that neighbourhood, and yet I always more or less despised him. He looked to me like a shrunken version of Jerry Lewis, except his voice was perpetually hoarse from yelling, and his functional range was usually somewhere between fervid self-absorption and hot-headed rage. He was a small boy at a time when boys wanted to be able to hold their own in rough company. I'm sure he had all the attendant small-boy complexes. He over-compensated for his size in many ways: he practised his foul shots under the hoop on his garage for hours, he trained for running with a stopwatch, like an Olympian. His mouth seemed twice as sharp and loud as anyone else's in junior high. And though my brother's gang had chased him into Mrs Bercovitz's backyard, ridiculed him with impunity, no one in our lower school ever picked on Alvin Pinsky. He was street-wise and had bodyguards. And they were almost always gentiles. He had lots of Jewish friends who could have done the job, I suppose, but with Alvin's runt instinct for survival, he must have seen an advantage in keeping on good terms with the non-Jewish warriors in the West End.

One such warrior was Artie Hrynchuk, a big freckled boy from one of the poorer neighbourhoods away upriver from our new home. He was a good-natured fellow, but very tough when he got in a corner. Only now do I begin to understand how Alvin Pinsky curried favour with Artie Hrynchuk or other boys like him. I've heard how in prisons vulnerable young men dispense sexual favours for protection, and in mobs how money buys the same commodity. Perhaps no boy near Westminster Drive knew better than Alvin Pinsky that nature's cruellest laws of survival held sway even there. It was a swaddled neighbourhood for a boy to grow up in, but it was not immune to the inevitable. And knowing this before any boy should have to learn it, Alvin Pinsky sought the currency that would protect him from bigger boys. Not only street gangs or punks from outlying areas, but smart alecs like some of my brother's friends, or practical jokers like my brother; boys who might rob Pinsky of his fiercely guarded runt's dignity.

For Artie Hrynchuk, the currency was Jane McKernan. Even without those precociously huge breasts she would have been considered good-looking by our standards at Buckingham Junior High. But her dad owned the Edmonton gravel pit and she was taboo for Artie, who lived with his mother in a shack down by the river flats. Alvin Pinsky, who listened carefully and collected confessions like a prurient priest, soon found out about Artie's burning passion for Jane McKernan. She had lived next door to Pinsky for many years, grown up with him. And because he could make her laugh with his imitations of Jerry Lewis and Bill Haley and Elvis, she had a great affection for him. Alvin was her little guy.

So before he had the slightest idea what go-between meant, Alvin Pinsky became one for Artie Hrynchuk. He must have been pretty good at it, too, because before long the three of them were seen smoking cigarettes on the river bank and heading out for sodas at the Pat. Then it was just Artie and Jane. And finally, when Artie's case had been argued at home to the dour Mr McKernan, Artie's half-ton could be seen parked on Jane's driveway nearly every night of the week. Artie never forgot it and no one laid a hand on Pinsky when he was around.

There were plenty of bullies at Buckingham Junior High, fights during the noon hours, and little pockets of anti-Semitism of which I was only vaguely aware when I was thirteen. Almost no one I knew would call somebody a dirty Jew. Somehow, such an insult never produced the potent sense of release that you got from swear words that have their origins in scatological or genital lore. And among the parent generation of relatively wealthy wasps, what anti-Semitism did exist was disguised as something else. At thirteen, it never occurred to me to interpret the use of the verb 'to jew' as an index of anti-Jewish sentiment.

It was punks and troublemakers (we called them *zoots*) who used racial slurs. When Bunny Fillion called Segal's sister a dirty Jew, he got five on each. When I told my grandmother about the incident, she told me that she felt sorry for boys like Bunny Fillion, who were too ignorant to realize that Jews were no worse than Chinamen, Indians or Bohunks. I'm sure now that Granny didn't feel the least bit sorry for Bunny Fillion, or for persecuted minorities for that matter, but I suspect she didn't know it.

I didn't play that day I watched Pinsky put down Segal, or that week, or any week in July. But when the Asiatic flu hit in the first week of August, and kids my age clear across town were running fevers for as long as three weeks, my luck changed. I, Drew Edmond, was the first kid on the block to get the Asiatic, and when Alvin Pinsky's team started to get decimated by it, I was all better. The word must have got around. It wasn't Pinsky who came to my door, of course. It was Marvin Fuchs and Big Al Rudnunski. They didn't have to explain things. I knew why they were there. I even forgot to get proud and play hard to get. Big Al let Marvin Fuchs do the talking. This was more than a dozen years before Fuchs defended his Ph.D. thesis at Columbia, but even then he was a word wizard. In fact, he was the most pedantic thirteen-year-old I ever met, but so good-natured and considerate that the guys I knew usually managed to forgive him his intellectual superiority.

'Drew,' he said, and looked me right in the eye as I stood halfway out the door of the back porch. 'Due to an oversight ...' (nervous laugh from Rudnunski) '... which is to say, ah, Alan and I and a good *number* of our teammates ... think that you'd make quite a strategic addition to the, ah, team.' (If you don't think a thirteen-year-old kid would talk like this, you didn't know Marvin Fuchs.) He stopped. A joke and a grave concern for propriety seemed to be warring on his face. The joke won out: 'Especially now,' he said, and we all laughed.

The first game they played, I dropped a Pinsky pass in the first quarter that was right in my arms. Wiener told me I needed someone to kick my ass for me. But in the third quarter I grabbbed an interception and ran it down to the Oliver team's thirty-yard line. Segal hugged me so hard I was afraid he was going to kiss me. Even Pinsky clapped me on the back.

So, after victims of the Asiatic started to trickle back from their sick beds, Pinsky kept me on the team. I wasn't that fast or that big or that tough, but I could catch passes and I didn't try to tell Pinsky how to run the offence. I, Drew Edmond, was the only gentile on the team, so I felt flattered to be kept.

Our games were arranged *ad hoc*. Whenever he heard of a team in the West end, Pinsky would phone someone and the game would be set for Sunday because Pinsky's old man didn't want him playing Saturdays.

According to Jane McKernan, the Pinskys were kosher. I didn't know what that meant but I was too self-conscious to ask her. My conversations with her were always brief because I was so much in awe of her breasts and troubled by my fascination.

We weren't a bad team. We won our first game and lost the next two by close margins. But when, in late September, we beat the team from J.P., we were astonished at what appeared to be our prowess. The J.P. team was big and strong. Some of their guys were older than us, and you could tell by the way they dressed and smoked that they knew what life was like on the tough side of the tracks. Perhaps we allowed ourselves to forget that while we had eighteen players, enough to sit six on the bench and relieve the tired ones, they came with only eleven players, one short of a full team. And Ernie Kobluk, their tough fullback, had to watch from the sidelines with his arm in a cast; he'd been fighting again. And Bunny Fillion was down in Bowden serving out a short stretch for car theft. And the Asiatic had sidelined Shag Muler, reputedly the toughest kid in Buckingham Junior High. Looking back, I'm sure that's why we won. We beat them by two touchdowns.

Though I took scant notice of it, there was some bad feeling at the end of the game between Al Rudnunski and Vernon Kiss. I'd known Kiss since I was seven or eight. He was the only rich kid on the J.P. team, big for his age, loud and pushy. He had a feline smile that never spread beyond the limits of his mouth. Like Alvin Pinsky, he travelled with tough kids from the meaner streets of West Edmonton, but unlike Pinsky he really was mean. I saw him pick on Marvin Fuchs before Marvin grew up and filled out solid. I knew that Vernon could take me in those days or I would have lambasted him when he beat up on Marvin.

I noticed, too, at the end of the game with J.P. when the shoving started with Rudnunski, that Vernon had not exactly undergone a moral rehabilitation in the intervening years. I'm not sure why he picked on Rudnunski. Maybe because Big Al was such a gentleman. Everyone liked him. He was smart as a whip but he disguised this with his self-effacing manner and the jokes he made about his fatness. He could have handled Vernon but he chose only to push him away.

'C'mon, ya candy-ass little kike!' said Vernon to Al, and we were suddenly quiet. A funny thing to say, too, because Rudnunski was neither little nor in retreat. 'C'mere!' Vernon snapped. Al was right there, immovable at that moment as he had been at right tackle during the

game. Immovable as he was to be eight years later when he quit his last
year of law and joined the Israeli army.

We all moved in close. First, one of the smaller guys from J.P. tried to
calm Vernon down, but he was adamant and he hurled his teammate
back. Then Kobluk came between them, solid as an oak tree and his arm
out of the sling now. Vernon backed off. He respected Ernie like a fox
terrier respects a pit bull. Ernie was smart enough to know that eighteen
to eleven was not comfortable odds. Their team gradually moved away
and not a blow was struck.

Perhaps it was more pride than masochism on Pinsky's part that made
him accept a return match from the J.P. team. Their captain phoned up
Pinsky and seemed friendly enough. Pinsky, not one to let the safety of his
troops get in the way of his pride, accepted.

'You crazy little putz, why?' asked Segal. A bunch of us were lounging
in the shade of Pinsky's garage.

'So why not? We got a hole in the schedule. And this time it's at
Glenora School. Neutral ground like.'

'I don't know,' I said, but I wouldn't say any more. I don't remember
if I was afraid or just trying to be sensible, but even to appear the latter
would have been interpreted by Pinsky as cowardice. He riled me many
times, but Pinsky was no coward. Perhaps Stanley Segal feared Pinsky's
reproach as I did; he didn't argue much with Pinsky after his initial
outburst.

'We can get Hrynchuk this time,' said Pinsky.

'You crazy already?' said Wiener. 'Hrynchuk told me he's starting to
work weekends. Sundays yet. Besides, he's from J.P. If he plays for anybody
it'll be for Kobluk.'

'Ix-nay,' said Pinsky, and spun the ball straight up in a spiral, caught it,
spun it up again.

None of us asked what this talk about Artie Hrynchuk was all about.
It was like asking your sergeant before a raid if you thought the platoon
had a snowball's chance in hell.

'Hrynchuk's in the bag,' said Pinsky, and suddenly, with another game
against J.P. looming four days off like a thunderhead, I got the feeling that
Artie Hrynchuk had become our protection as well as Pinsky's. I imagined
Hrynchuk in ways that I would have imagined the Lone Ranger a few
years earlier. We had no doubt at all that he could handle Vernon Kiss and

Fillion. Once he'd even taken on Kobluk and come out on top. But could he handle Shag Muler? Maybe. Muler was a tall bony hatchet-faced boy. His feats as a brawler were passing into legend. We didn't hate him, but there were times we feared him.

When we arrived on our bikes for the game Sunday afternoon, Hrynchuk's truck wasn't there. What made things worse was that their team had all its big guns back. Bunny Fillion was fresh out of Bowden, smiling around a broken set of teeth, exhorting his friends. Shag Muler was hanging loose and smoking like men I'd seen in gunslinger movies. And Butch Bullmer, a tough kid from the country, who just stood around taut and low to the ground, solid as a fire hydrant. One of the St. Denis brothers, smoking in a white shirt with the collar up and wearing a pair of zooty pants, and the other St. Denis brother combing back his ducktail. They must've had almost two dozen guys there and they looked more like a hit squad than a football team.

Most of us had football sweaters and a couple of our guys even wore shoulder pads. But most of the J.P. guys wore black leather shoes or boots and not one of them had a football sweater. I assumed that in J.P. they considered running shoes or football sweaters to be sissy. It never occurred to me back then that their families couldn't afford such luxuries.

There were several guys from J.P. I'd never seen before, and when we'd tossed the coin and begun heading to our end of the field to kick off, one of them came with us. I asked Marvin Fuchs who he was but Marvin had no idea. The newcomer seemed to move with a certain authority for a small fellow. He was thin, pale and otherwise nondescript: a scruff of hair the colour of dust, no eyebrows, prominent cheekbones that made him seem hungry, small pale blue eyes that took in everything.

'You know him?' I asked Segal in a discreet whisper. Segal only shrugged. 'Well?' I persisted. Segal pinned the ball for Irwin Wiener, our kicker.

'Get onside, Drew,' said Segal grimly, and then, 'No. And that's the whole point, see?'

No, I didn't see. I looked over at the new fellow once more. Instead of running shoes he wore light-blue socks that seemed a couple of sizes too big for his feet. He had no football sweater either, just a white T-shirt and a pair of baggy jeans with a red strap on the left thigh, where carpenters hang their hammers. At our school it was a tradition that no one wore a red strap unless he wanted it torn off at noon hour. This fellow didn't seem bothered about that. His jeans were faded, so that red strap had obviously remained unviolated for some time. I couldn't get a fix on him. There was something old and aloof about him, though he was probably not much older than we were. I remember thinking, as Irwin Wiener raised his hand above his head like real kickers do, this new guy has never been in a classroom. Even more than the invincible Muler, this fellow struck me as belonging to that world beyond my neighbourhood where boys didn't have mothers and men slept on the river bank and smelled of lemon extract. It was the hungry mouth and the watchful eyes. I thought, *what's Pinsky up to now? Is this guy a stray his mother feeds?*

No one scored in the first quarter. Kobluk made some first downs on us through the left side of our line, but every time he tried the right side Rudnunski stopped him cold. Their quarterback could throw, but we had guys like Wiener, Segal, and the new guy who were tall enough or fast enough to knock the ball down. We didn't get any interceptions, but they couldn't connect with their long passes.

Offensively we were almost nonexistent. Pinsky tried passes, but they rushed in and either knocked them down or sacked him. They were hitting hard, very hard. Pinsky got nervous, and we started fumbling on the hand-offs. It took us a whole quarter to get our bearings.

Then their quarterback started connecting and Kobluk started knocking a few heads around and they scored twice and missed both of their converts and we scored once when Pinsky ran back a kick almost the length of the field. It was twelve-seven at halftime.

I was sharing the water jug with Rudnunski. He just sat in the grass and looked battle weary. Vernon Kiss and another guy had been double-teaming Rudnunski. They'd been slugging and kneeing him and he hadn't been saying anything about it. He just sat there big and sullen.

Finally he said, 'They're out to get us, Drew.'

'I know,' I said, 'but we can dish it right back.'

Rudnunski shook his head. At first I thought he meant no, we'd be crazy to try any of the rough stuff on them. I looked over at the guys from J.P. One of them had a case of beer out of his car. He was looking very mean. I'd never seen a case of beer at a football game before. I wasn't yet fourteen and I was from Westminster Drive and nobody I knew drank beer on the school grounds.

Marvin Fuchs and Stanley Segal came over. Again Rudnunski said,

'They're out to get us,' and I knew then what he meant. 'Us' meant Jews. They didn't want just to win a game, they wanted more than that. They were going to humiliate us and send us home bleeding.

Marv Fuchs spoke soothingly to Rudnunski. I couldn't hear what he was saying but it looked like an old rabbi talking to a reluctant Sampson. I remember it now as a conversation entirely in Yiddish, but this is probably my own addition to the story. Pinsky came over. He had a bad scrape on his knee, he was aching from being sacked, he was tired from his touchdown run, but he was too furious to be afraid.

'Get your knee into him,' said Pinsky. 'And if he comes at you from behind, give him the elbow. Like this!' And for Pinsky it was merely a matter of technique.

But we all knew, we Jews, that once Rudnunski clobbered Vernon Kiss, Shag Muler and his storm-troopers – Kobluk, Fillion, Bullmer and all the J.P. zoots – would be on us like an SS regiment. If Pinsky knew, he wasn't showing it. Nor was Wiener, our most accomplished fighter. Pinsky and Wiener were talking quietly to the new guy, who I swear had not opened his mouth since he arrived. He looked over at the other sideline at Kiss, Fillion, Bullmer, Kobluk and Muler, no emotion on his face. Only a trace of stoatlike hunger.

Kobluk kicked off. He tried one of those short bouncers that was supposed to travel only the minimum ten yards so the kicking team could recover it. But Kobluk toed it a bit too hard, and it drifted magnetically into my arms. I hadn't handled the ball once in the entire first half. A buck fever of dread and elation pounding through my system, I charged straight at the horde of oncoming Philistines. The fastest half of our team was well behind me and two slow guys, Marvin and Big Al, were beside me. A ball carrier is supposed to wait long enough to pick up his blocking, but I was too anxious to be a hero and too afraid of being clobbered to think. I got ahead of Big Al and Marvin and cut over to the sidelines and the whole J.P. pack was right on my heels, so I tried to run through a couple of them and someone caught me from behind. But I'd taken the ball into J.P.'s territory, and outside of Pinsky's touchdown run, it was the furthest we'd penetrated all game. When I went back to the huddle several guys, Pinsky included, slapped me on the back. That was the last good moment I had in the game.

Pinsky called a short pass to the new guy. Wiener lined up next to me on the left side of the line. We were to draw off some pass defenders by running like hell up the left sideline and Pinsky would just dump it over the line to the new guy.

The ball was snapped and Wiener and I took off and Shag Muler took off with me, but suddenly he stopped. I thought Pinsky must have unloaded to the new guy but I was wrong. Someone was down. I trotted back. Everyone milled around the injured player. It was Rudnunski. He was rolling around on the grass, groaning and swearing.

Vernon Kiss was there commiserating. 'Jeez,' he said, 'Al, I'm sorry.' This in a high nasal voice that sounded pretty phony to me. 'Are y'all right?'

Al said, 'Fuck you, Kiss.' It was his thigh, it must have hurt like hell. His groaning came louder.

'What's the matter?' snapped Pinsky.

'Fuckin *kicked* me when I was *down*.'

'I never did!'

Vernon Kiss was very tense. Wiener came over, looked him in the eye. 'You been kneein Rudnunski since the goddam first quarter, Kiss.' Kiss looked stricken because Wiener was very tough. Kiss and I grew up with Wiener. When he was mad he was nothing short of sadistic and right now he was very mad. He was snarling. 'You wait till he's *down,* an he can't protect himself, then ya give im the knee!' Wiener was getting his anger up, his fists were clenched, he was almost ready. 'Too *chicken* to face him. Ya gotta wait till he's *down!*'

Up stepped Shag Muler, raven-haired, dark-eyed, an axe-blade face jutting forward at Wiener's.

'Fuck off, Wiener!'

'Yeah?' said Wiener, but his snarl had suddenly gone off key. He knew he could break Vernon Kiss in two, but he also knew no one could take Shag Muler in a fair fight. Like Kiss, Wiener always avoided fair fights.

'Come on, you guys,' said Kobluk. Rudnunski groaned once more. I looked up and Fillion was there too, a bottle of beer in his hand. The bottle was empty, and he held it by the neck and tapped his hand nervously with it. His eyes were disturbingly blank. 'Come on,' said Kobluk, 'break it up.' He stepped between Muler and Wiener, straddling Rudnunski, who was still holding his leg, swearing and groaning. Never big on brains, Wiener thought he was safe, so he reached past Kobluk and gave Vernon Kiss a shove. Muler leapt over Rudnunski to face Wiener again. He shoved him hard and Wiener told him: 'Go to hell, Muler! Can't Kiss fight his own battles?'

'What'd you say?'

'I said, can't Kiss – '

'The other thing, suckface!'

'I said go to hell,' said Wiener quietly. Muler shoved him again.

'Come on, you guys,' said Kobluk.

'This is ridiculous,' said Fuchs.

But now Muler padded very slowly after Wiener, who suddenly looked much less than the guy who gave Segal a bloody nose the month before, a head shorter than the Wiener who half-drowned one of my old friends in the science room sink. Wiener's voice was practically bawling and Muler hadn't even hit him yet.

'Wiener,' he whispered, soft as a zephyr. 'Wiener?' Wiener backed off and Muler kept coming, real slow. 'Wiener?'

'What!' bawled Wiener, and Muler spat right in his face, but Wiener wouldn't fight. Muler slapped Wiener's face, but still he wouldn't fight. He grabbed Wiener's arm and twisted and Wiener howled. And then Wiener wrenched himself free, swung around and belted Muler. He belted him very hard, right in the gut. Muler just stood there. It was a good solid punch and we all knew it, and Muler just smiled. Then belted Wiener full in the face and Wiener started howling again. He was an enraged six-year-old boy. With sickening dread, we must have all realized that Muler had not finished with him.

I remember that moment like a photograph. Muler was loose, his voice purred, and he was smiling; Kobluk just looked on; Marvin Fuchs looked as though he was witnessing the birth of his blackest prophecies; Big Al, up on one knee now, his own pain momentarily abandoned; Fillion vacant-eyed, no longer tapping his beer bottle on the palm of his hand; Bullmer with that obsessed smile some men wear at ringside; Segal no longer raging but perfectly stoical, as if awaiting the signal from the leader of a firing squad; Wiener howling no more.

I conjure it in detail because that's when the new fellow stepped up in front of Wiener, faced Muler, pointed to his own cock, and to Muler said, simply, 'Bite this.' Nobody laughed or moved. The only sounds were Wiener sniffling and the autumn wind. As many J.P. mouths caught in mid-breath as Jewish mouths, and as if we hadn't all heard him the first time, the new fellow said it again, softly: 'Bite this.'

He was forgettably drab in his red-straps and white T-shirt, his oversized socks. He was several inches shorter than Shag Muler, smaller in every way. And yet quite unforgettable. Those prominent cheekbones, slits for eyes, that thin scruff of hair the colour of dust, that face of a hungry mink. His hands were down by his sides, and every boy on the field, finally, knew why he was here. Muler looked down on the newcomer, and though his face was as impassive as his adversary's, we knew that Muler would strike first. Shag Muler. Not cruel like Fillion was reputed to be when drunk, not mean like Wiener when he bullied smaller boys, but dangerous when convinced of the rightness of his cause.

Perhaps he would have relished that first blow more, aimed it better too, if it had been launched at Wiener. I remember it as an overhand right and it caught the pale boy hard on the left ear, but his follow-up left missed, and though the fellow's ear flushed pink, he moved away, eyes on Muler, without a flinch of pain, instead summoning Muler to try again. So Muler slapped him, his admonishment for little boys who use foul language, and the pale boy came in on him. It was too fast to record, but I remember Muler clubbing at the dusty head as a gorilla might pound his own chest and the pale kid, no boxer either but a toe-to-toe slugger, slashed up at Muler with uppercuts and brawling overhand rights, both men landing until something had to give. Two sounds snapped out of this squawl of arms: one, the crunch of bone on bone; the other, the wrench of gristle, as Muler went down, sank slowly to his knees, both hands over his left eye, little rubies of blood seeping between his fingers.

'Hang on! You, hang on!' said Kobluk needlessly, because the new fellow was just standing there over Muler, as poker-faced as he'd been all afternoon; Fillion, drunk, wasn't moving; or Vernon Kiss, whose mouth was still open; or Wiener, who'd forgotten his own hurt; or Segal, at a loss for words for the first time I'd ever known; or Pinsky, who reminded me oddly of Frankenstein beholding his monster. Then Kobluk went down on his knees and held Muler's head for a better look and Marvin Fuchs handed Kobluk his handkerchief, saw Vernon Kiss's baleful stare, withdrew.

'Goddam butted me,' mumbled Muler.

I approached Rudnunski, Fuchs and I helped him to his feet, and now it's me Vernon Kiss glares at: I am the Jew he has hated for years.

'C'mon, you guys,' Pinsky said eventually. We headed for our bikes. As I climbed on mine, still surrounded by my allies mounting theirs, I noticed that our nameless champion was gone.

* * *

I might not have remembered it all in such detail except for what happened today. I was sitting in a bus on Jasper Avenue, cursing my Honda for losing its muffler at precisely the most inconvenient time. Already I could hear my wife Rachel kvetching. When *your* parents used to come for supper we were *always* on schedule, but when *mine* come all the way from California, you couldn't make supper on time if you had a day's head start.

My goy parents used to profess so stridently to have accepted Rachel that we both knew they hadn't. I would get nervous before those occasions, come home early, fuss with the food and our toddlers, and generally get in Rachel's way. My parents are gone now. But when Shim and Ebie come up from L.A. it's all sweetness and light. I mean I really *do* love them.

Anyway, while I stew about this, I'm reading an article in today's paper (the one I write for) about a group of hate-mongers who plan to set up a colony somewhere in Central Alberta. And suddenly, Alvin Pinsky sits right down beside me. He doesn't recognize me. It's been twenty years at least since I've even seen the guy. He is taller, almost average height, still quite thin, though he's filled out some. His jacket and trousers are beige, summer weight. Everything about him is cool. Yet there is that same coiled fierceness, that same impatience as he waits for the bus to leave the curb. It's easy to imagine him on his way back to the huddle, a new scrimmage mapping itself like hope or war in his head. I half expect him to spit on his hands for traction.

Before he recognizes me I say, 'Pinsky, *pass*, for God's sake. I was in the clear.'

He turns and gives me a look that is many things: flight, circumspection, shrewd appraisal, annoyance. I am the pursuer, the hotshot's next client, the wise guy perhaps.

'Drew? Edmond?'

He still has a brush cut, or perhaps he has returned to one, so I know he won't go for the thumbs like the old radicals do. We shake hands warmly. I suspect, from his perusal, that he notices the paunch I've acquired, the lines of worry. Perhaps in my eyes he sees just a semitone of envy: he is a man now, five foot seven or eight, still athletic, a jogger perhaps. At any rate, no longer the runt. I make a little joke about what success has done to my mid-section and he counters with something about how lack of success has kept him lean. His voice is still raspy, hoarse.

He sells real estate, claims to have 'Little Jerusalem in the bag', by which he means our old neighbourhood. He's working on his second marriage and has two kids. He had a problem with the bottle but claims he gave it up for chain-smoking.

Then, switching subjects as fast as a quarterback with a broken play, he says, 'Guess what. Muler, remember him?'

'Who wouldn't?'

'He's tits up.'

'Shag Muler is dead?'

'Happened yesterday. He was found dead in his own bedroom. Hrynchuk phoned me about it. I bet you'll read about it in your paper tomorrow.'

'Artie told you?'

'Right. He kept in touch with Shag. Apparently Shag had his own construction company. He had it made, for God's sake.'

'How did –'

'Bang,' says Pinsky, index finger to his temple. 'Hrynchuk told me he had a drinking problem, didn't get on with his wife. Mixed marriage.'

'Ouch,' I said.

'Wha?'

'That hits home. My wife is Jewish.'

'Sheesh,' says Pinsky.

'Did Shag Muler marry a Jewish girl too?'

'Muler *was* Jewish.'

'*What?*'

'Hardly anyone knew. Muler kept it quiet. In his neighbourhood … you know? Very tough neighbourhood.'

'I always saw him as a kind of Doberman for the SS boys.'

'Sure,' says Pinsky.

'At least that's how I saw him when I was Jewish.'

We both laugh. Then I remember another warrior. I have to ask Pinsky, after all those years. 'That other kid,' I say, 'the one who took Muler on, remember?'

'The one who got him with a head butt?'

'Yeah. Who was he?'

I remember asking almost everyone on the team about the strange warrior who beat Muler. Segal, Rudnunski, Fuchs, every one of them gave me the same answer: Pinsky's not saying. I remember asking Rudnunski a year or two later when we were in high school. And he still said, Pinsky's not saying. I heard theories, mind you, but no one could agree on the boy's name or where he came from.

'You never found out?' says Pinsky.

'How could I? It was the best-guarded secret on the street.'

'You probably saw his picture in the papers up to about ten years ago. Name's Redl, Willie Redl.'

'The boxer?'

'Yeah. He was from the East End back then. Friend of mine knew him from boxing at the Y.' Pinsky grins his old shrewd grin. 'He was our protection.'

Willie Redl. My God, I had been asked by my paper to write his obit for the sports page. He had been the Canadian welterweight champion. A local guy, Butch Bullmer from the J.P. team, had managed him for a few bouts. Then Willie went to Cleveland in the early sixties. He fought the best out there. They say he was ranked for a year or two in the top ten. But the years multiplied like the scar tissue on his face, and before he died in the East Jasper Hotel, he had the physiognomy of a Neanderthal with the pox. Our protection. Who art in earth. Cauliflowered be thy ears.

I say to Pinsky, 'That feels like a previous century.'

'Ah,' he says, only half listening, 'it's a brand new era.' He says this like a proud member of the Chamber of Commerce. A brand new era.

Doesn't he see the headline in front of me? SURVIVALISTS SET UP SHOP IN ALBERTA. Pity the non-Aryan who wanders too near their fencelines. Protection becomes infection, hatred dons a bright new mask. *We have come to this ranch to study our scriptures and our weapons,* says the redneck in the caption photo.

The bus rolls to a stop. 'See ya,' says Pinsky. He hops off and strides down Twenty-fourth. That surprisingly long stride. Except it's no longer the walk of a small boy compensating for his size. It's the walk of a man who has places to go, things to do.

This meeting will make for lively talk around the supper table. My Years as a Jewish Athlete. I will hide the newspaper. Shim and Ebie will return to California with their illusions about Canada intact. They will think that hate literature is an American industry. They are so old and small, especially Rachel's dad. Each year he seems to shrink and bend a bit more. Her parents bring out the parent in me and I get protective around them.

And sometimes I cringe at the things we used to say as kids, the racist jokes. If I tell that to Rachel, she'll resurrect her old suspicion that I married her out of some vague sense of guilt. Guilt, for God's sake. I don't think I've ever convinced her that she is the great buffer between myself and despair.

I won't even talk about the schoolyard skirmish. And if Rachel asks me where the paper got to tonight, I will say, *Paper? What paper? Let's go to bed.* Shim and Ebie will be exhausted. Rachel and I will tiptoe up the stairs. All night long we will cover each other like blankets and in the morning it will be a brand new era.

☆ Meeting Cute at the Anger Motel

Marcie and Robert were up at dawn and off along the highway, but in the first hour Marcie said hardly a word. Robert peeked at her. She was fussing with her hair, biting off split ends with her incisors. These teeth protruded a bit, and she thought they were a bit too much on the horsy side. He considered them very attractive.

Marcie remained silent nearly all the way to Rosetown, when at last Robert shot another furtive glance in her direction. She was squinting at something up the road on a dusty siding. At first it looked to Robert like an empty chair turned sideways, then it became a wheelchair with an arm sticking out and the thumb pointing up at the sky. Robert drove on by.

'Stop! Stop the car!' Marcie cried. 'It's a person! It wants a ride!'

'Maybe,' he said, 'we should just kind of drive back and have a look? Not commit ourselves.'

Marcie gave him a look.

It turned out to be a girl, or possibly a woman. Robert swung the car around to her side of the road. Before Marcie could get out and help, their hitchhiker had clamped onto the back door, opened it, vaulted inside with the use of her hands, grabbed her wheelchair, collapsed it, and hauled it in after her. The entire manoeuvre took about twenty seconds.

And there she sat in the back seat, less than four feet tall, no legs to speak of, stubby arms, some well-defined fingers, a large head with a big wide mouth. Her hair was cut short. She listed to her left and looked gravely up at Robert and Marcie.

'Hi,' she said. 'I'm Grace.'

A hot wind was blowing up dust from the southeast.

'Lordy, it's a sizzler out there,' Grace said. 'I must of sat in that spot for a good hour.' She sounded nasal and sped-up like a voice in an animated cartoon.

'You do this often?' Marcie asked her.

'Only once the snow is gone.'

After a silence of some miles Marcie asked Grace if she was going to the Calgary Stampede.

'I'm mainly off to see my boyfriend. He's in a band. They have a gig in Calgary. Where you folks off to?'

'Hope, B.C. To visit his parents,' Marcie replied.

She wondered what kind of a band. And would Grace's fellow be similarly disabled? If so, would he play an instrument? And how do you ask questions like that without sounding like a complete idiot? After a while she said, 'This guy, is he a rock musician or what?'

'Folk rock I guess you'd call it. He's on the road a lot these days. But that's okay. Me an him, lately we've been needing our space.'

Marcie could not stop peering back at Grace as she spoke. She had a lateral lisp and slushed out her Ss through her big wide mouth, always listing a bit to her left. She looked like a doll made by a deranged man.

Whoever she was, she had managed to foreshorten another bout of this *thing* between Robert and herself.

Marcie drove the last lap with Grace sitting next to her. She thought mostly about marriages she had known, good and bad. Finally she said to Grace, 'Are you and this guy in the band engaged or something?'

'Oh, God no. I can't see that happening. Winston is so young, you know? And I'm too independent.' Grace jerked around on the front seat and gave Robert a smile. 'You guys are hitched, right?'

'Yes,' said Robert.

'Men these days,' Grace said, peering back again between the bucket seats. 'This latest crop, I mean. They don't seem very big on making commitments. I'd like to have a dollar for every woman I've counselled because her man was having an affair. I feel I can say this to you. You don't strike me as the playboy type.'

Marcie glanced at Robert's face in the rearview mirror. He gave Grace a bleak nod and stroked his absent beard.

'Say, haven't I seen you somewhere before?' Grace said, but Robert was apparently off on a new round of brooding. 'I have the funniest feeling I've seen your husband somewhere before.'

Robert was thinking of all the people who ever insulted him or rebuked him or ostracized him; or when he was a kid, all the kids who had been mean to him and all the teachers who had punished or ignored him and all the girls who had teased him without trying to understand what he was really like and all the times he got blamed when it wasn't his fault; and all the women who had turned away from him, even when he was just trying to help them. He came up with quite a list.

The fight had started the previous night at supper in an Italian restaurant. Robert was going on about how he missed his old guitar, the one his father had sat on. Marcie reminded him that when he had the guitar he'd scarcely ever played it. It was Marcie's private opinion that what he really missed was his freedom – those days after he had dropped out of theology but before they had met. His days as a grad student in psychology. From what Marcie could piece together, Robert would have been lean, bearded, a bit on the unworldly side of things, but on the verge of some big discoveries. And of course good-looking. If he could not preach to people, he would counsel them in that same gentle and reassuring voice. That relationship with confused young wives and students on campus, it must have been a bit of a turn-on. That was Marcie's opinion. Back then there were reasons for Robert to wear a beard and play a guitar.

The dinner with Robert was supposed to be a romantic evening. Candlelight, a litre of the house red, the whole bit. And Robert, for some reason, chose to reminisce about the good old days.

'Gloria said she never really noticed me until I picked up that guitar.' Gloria was the religious one with the knockers.

Marcie countered with allusions to some of her lovers.

'Lovers?'

In the first year of their marriage she would have called them boyfriends, but apparently the gloves were off. Robert asked how many there had been.

'Counting Whatzisname?'

Robert very definitely did not like hearing about Whatzisname, but after all, hadn't he started it? You bet, and so Marcie jumped in with both feet. She gazed at the chandelier, counting on the fingers of her left hand. Then she began to count on the fingers of her right hand and Robert became upset. She realized that she had gone too far. She made an honest effort to minimize her confessions. 'Well, if you rule out, you know, the quickies, I only had four.'

'The quickies.'

'The one-nighters.'

In that clinical Jesus-type voice of his he asked her to continue. He wore a weak, suffering smile, as though she were talking about torture or rape and not fun or love or whatever.

She should have gotten the signals – no, she had gotten the signals, but it was too late to turn back. Robert extracted more and more details about the one-nighters. There had been four of these as well, including Whatzisname, a prominent director of television drama on a speaking tour who proclaimed that, in comedy, lovers should 'meet cute'. As Marcie went merrily on, Robert's round and comfortable face went from a weak smile to an obsessed gawk. When she reached a point in her revelations about Mikey, a big old bear of a guy with a motorcycle, Robert groaned like a man in torment. She stopped talking. She didn't know what to say. She asked how he felt about all this.

He said it made him feel unlucky.

Robert spotted a motel on the east side of Calgary that had a vacancy, a small miracle at Stampede time. The sign said *Wrangler Motel.* Their room smelled like an abandoned cigarette factory. The air conditioner roared with a whiny insistence and dripped all over the floor. The shower stall was rusty, the toilet seat cracked, and on the wall of the front room was a velvet painting of two lovers in a sleazy embrace.

Marcie urged Grace to come in with them at least long enough to phone her fellow. When Robert returned with the last of the luggage, Grace was digging around in her bag.

'I got some dope here. You guys indulge?'

This question made Robert nervous. He allowed that he had nothing against people who took the odd puff now and then, but he said no thank you. He glanced uncertainly at the bathroom door behind which Marcie was taking her shower.

'I knew you were both all right,' said Grace, pointing to her head. 'Intuition.'

A series of thoughts occurred to Robert: that Grace's musician would not be found, that he was a fiction; that he, Grace and Marcie would be locked into a threesome all the way to Hope, B.C.; that he and Marcie would be cajoled into puffing a bit of Grace's dope; the proprietor would smell it outside their door and call the police; the press in Saskatoon would pick up the story (how, he had not quite imagined); and he would be fired, Marcie would be fired, and their trial would be held before a court on national television. His father would see it and have a heart attack.

'Home grown,' said Grace, wistfully.

Robert excused himself to get some beer.

When he returned from the off-sales there was a man sitting next to Marcie on the bed with a guitar case between them. The man was aboriginal. He looked lean and strong, had a sparse moustache, and wore his hair down past his shoulders. It was as long as Marcie's.

Grace said, 'Bob, this is Winston.'

'Robert, actually,' he said to Grace, but she was looking at Winston.

Marcie suggested they all have a beer.

'Honey, I'm sure these people must have things to do, places to go.'

'I tell you, Bob,' said Grace, 'I was never one to outstay a welcome. We'll have a beer with you and then be on our way.' Grace sipped her beer and rolled a joint. The joint did the rounds and Marcie did not hesitate. After a while she seemed to relax, took the towel off her head, and her blonde hair fell damp around her shoulders.

She turned to Winston. 'How did you two meet up?'

Grace pointed the joint at her friend. 'You tell them, Winston, and I'll have your head.'

Winston said to Grace, 'It'll cost ya.'

'You tell them how we met, Winston, and I'll tell them all about your former profession.'

Winston addressed Robert and Marcie.

'When I first run into her I was in a halfway house. And before that I was a guest of the govmint.'

'Yes,' said Grace, 'he was a bad boy. He took an airplane for a joy ride once.'

'What?' said Marcie. 'Are you a pilot?'

'No, I just seen how they done it. Up north, ah? I was a guide up north.'

Marcie's face was aglow with a dreamy look. If one of the guys at the studio where she worked had offered her a joint, she would likely have given him a lecture on respiratory problems. But each time one of Grace's joints did the rounds, she took her turn. Marcie looked suddenly younger to Robert, like Marcie Nordstrum, the girl he had courted. If only he could be alone in this room with *that* girl, or even with the Marcie before the quarrel. But no, that could never be. He half wished he had married a plain woman – and not just plain, but given over entirely to wifely pursuits. Sometimes her job as a field producer for the station seemed more important to her than his own job seemed to him. He looked up and saw Winston eyeing him.

'Jesus, I been here all this time, thinkin I know you from somewheres.

It just come to me. You're that Loblaw guy on the afternoon show.' Winston unlimbered from the bed and thrust out his thumb in an old-fashioned hippy handshake. He said to Grace, 'I seen him lots of times. This guy's a star, ah? *LEAN ON ME,* right?'

'Right you are,' said Robert.

'Right on, Saigon.'

This old expression got them all laughing and Robert launched into a detailed description of the show. At least he tried to. Grace's dope was beginning to act up a bit, and he would reach the midpoint of a long description of how to counsel people live on television, forget what he had been saying, and be at a loss to finish his sentence, but he'd finish it anyway. Everyone would crack up and Marcie shook so violently with laughter that Robert thought she would fall on the floor.

Winston said, 'Hey, Bobby, all that stuff behind the camera, you must like that stuff, ah? You're such a relax kinda guy up there.'

'Frankly, Winston, it stinks!'

They all laughed like a family of coyotes.

'By the way,' he added for Winston's benefit, 'it's Robert.'

In the general uproar Grace managed to get another case of Pilsner. Now, how did she manage that?

'How ever do you do it?' Robert asked her. 'You get around on that thing like an old golf pro.'

'Oh, it's not so hard once you know how. There's still one thing I can't stand, though, and that's doing laundry.' At this, Winston began to laugh so hard he couldn't light his cigarette. 'Oh, you be quiet, you old buck. He should try it some time.'

'Tell em!' shouted Winston. 'Tell em!'

'Not unless you get out that guitar,' Grace said. 'Let's have a song.'

'Tell em!' he cried, and fell over laughing on the bed.

Grace turned to Marcie.

'You asked Winston how we met? Well, I'll tell you. I always do my laundry in this little shopper's plaza on Thirty-third? Maybe you know the one. Next to the old bakery? The washing machines are all right because I can sort of rise up on my chair and lean on them when I'm taking out my laundry. But those dryers. I wish to Jesus they weren't so low. Here I go stuffing in my sheets and clothes, and Lordy, I pushed so hard I fell off my wheelchair and right inside! Well, those doors? They're magnetized. And this one went and shut on me. As soon as it shut, round and round I go.'

'How could that be?' cried Marcie. 'Did someone press the button?'

Grace was looking Robert's way.

'Laugh if you like, but this bugger had quite a while to go on the cycle, and I had no idea when it'd stop. I hollered and I prayed but no one heard me. You know, I think I was about passed out from the heat, the next thing I saw was this Indian guy staring at me, his eyes wide open? Winston, I think it was your turn to pass out. Anyway, when I saw his face I said to myself, this is the loveliest face I ever saw in my entire life.'

'Hey,' cried Winston, 'is that why you screamed at me?'

'Well, Lordy, it was *hot* in there. And you sure took your sweet time pullin me out.'

'I didn't know what I had. I had to make my sessments.'

When Marcie stopped laughing she said she had to admit, that was the best meeting story she'd ever heard. 'You two really met cute.'

Robert wished she wouldn't use that term, and on this he brooded in silence. Not that he and Marcie hadn't also met cute. Back then she had been just a studio technician and he was the guy with the popular new program. Everybody in the studio called him Shrink. He noticed Marcie Nordstrum right away. Who wouldn't have, with all that pale blond hair, that tall gawky bearing, and her amazing flash of teeth when she smiled? But he hadn't the nerve to approach her until one day she came into the cafeteria with a black eye. She tried to cover the damage with sunglasses, but the second he spotted that shiner, Robert brought over his tray, sat down, and in a few minutes they were laughing like old friends. A few days later they went to a movie. She agreed to go with him if he promised not to ask her about the shiner.

Saskatoon, late October, Marcie's flat, basement of a large house. Marcie and Robert drinking herbal tea and chatting. The possibilities of romance, at this point, were remote. She handed him a guitar, similar to the one his father had sat on. He played something and sang, and Marcie was delighted. What song was it? Surely he hadn't forgotten. Whose guitar? Probably it belonged to the guy who'd given her the shiner.

Anyway, the lights had gone out. Just like that, a district power failure. Robert recalls a fit of giggles. 'I can't find the teapot,' Marcie said.

He said he would find it and moved slowly toward the sink. Marcie must have been moving out from the sink, because they drifted blind into each other's arms. And Robert said just the right thing: 'I would love to kiss your shiner.' He kissed her on the black eye and the other one, and then all over her face, and a great wave of something radiant seemed to flow between them. And stayed there. The moment was like a gift from God, totally unmerited. The opposite of getting struck by lightning or run down by a truck. There was a special word for it. It was on the tip of his tongue.

'For these thy gifts, O Lord, which we have already eaten, um ...'

'Go ahead, Marcie,' Grace whispered.

'... ah, may we all be truly thankful, amen.' Marcie smiled. 'I guess I've never said grace after a meal.'

'This is how I start all my readings,' said Grace.

'Okay,' said Robert, 'give me the low-down.' He let out a big belch. Marcie gave him a look. This belching thing had always irritated Marcie. She had a conviction that handsome men – and Robert was a handsome man – should not belch. This was a hard point of view to argue, so she almost never mentioned it.

The four of them were gathered around Robert's pizza. Grace drew an imaginary line across his platter with a white plastic knife. The top half was his day life, the bottom half his night life.

'You are often disappointed by people's behaviour, Bob,' she said. 'People disappoint you.'

'Yeah,' said Robert with a kindly smile.

'But you get along okay.'

'Right.'

'But there's this chaos,' Grace went on. 'Your luck's on the spin cycle type thing. You've stopped moving forward, stopped fighting. Your dream is right before you but you can't grasp it.'

Robert and Marcie darted glances at each other. He began to stroke his absent beard.

'How do I get this luck back?'

'That's Winston's department,' said Grace.

After a silence Winston said, 'Bobby, you need liddlebit medicine, ah?'

'What kind of medicine?'

Grace said, 'He means you've lost your totem, Bob.'

'My totem.'

Robert looked blankly at Marcie.

She smiled. 'A few years ago your father *sat* on it!'

Grace turned to Marcie's pizza.

'You're the opposite. See this area?' With the plastic knife she pointed to the top of Marcie's pizza. 'You haven't eaten these two pieces here, but you've eaten everything else, even the crusts. It's all tidy. You like to tidy things up. You like to be in control. You resist changes. Lifestyle, old age, things like that.'

'Holy shit,' said Marcie.

'Women envy you, right? Marcie Loblaw, what a neat person, right? You get your identity from what you do, not from who you know. And right now you're lucky. Very lucky.'

'How can you tell all that?'

'It's all here. And look, you've eaten up everything in the lower half, the part Bobby here wouldn't touch.'

'So,' Grace continued, 'you know where you're coming from, you remember things … the past … your dreams are all about the past.'

Grace tried to explain, but Marcie kept thinking how at twenty-seven she still wore her hair long, exactly as she had when she was eighteen at the Tech. Marcie kept staring down at the pizza platter.

'Why am I lucky?'

'Well, you're lucky and you don't know it, so you try to keep things under control. Never give too much away, never wear your heart on your sleeve type thing. And you hardly ever make mistakes.'

Marcie resumed the hunt for split ends, snipping them off with her teeth.

Robert stared at his face in the bathroom mirror. Without the beard it was not so attractive a face. On the advice of his producer, he'd shaved it off for *LEAN ON ME*. The show had become popular as an afternoon feature in Saskatoon, then other stations had picked it up. He liked the popularity but he missed the beard. He could hear Marcie's brush trailing through her hair. It went slowly, as it did when she was lost in thought. He grimaced at himself in the mirror. He was still stoned. He didn't look stoned, he looked ordinary. He had a handsome face, but it looked ordinary.

Returning to their bed Robert nearly stumbled on the guitar. Winston had left it there, but he was sound asleep with Grace on the hideabed in the next room. Marcie had on her mother's old silk nightie. He watched her arms as she brushed her hair. She had lovely arms and shoulders. The fluorescent bulb above pulsed down on her mane of blonde hair.

'She told me I was lucky,' Marcie said.

'And all your dreams are of the past.'

'Don't start that.'

'I wasn't.'

'Why did she say I was lucky?'

'She said you were lucky and you didn't know it.' Robert crawled in next to her, and with an extraordinary attempt at lightness, said, 'A day from now we could be running naked through an alpine meadow and making love in the flowers.'

'It's not all it's cracked up to be, you know.'

'What's that supposed to mean?'

'Alpine meadows,' she said. 'Sex in the sun.'

Marcie was remembering how she got the shiner. The words that triggered the blow were, 'I will go out with whomever I please whenever I please.' The one she addressed these words to was a fellow named Jay, a spoiled boy with dark eyes, dark hair and a voluptuous mouth. Sex in the sun. A field of mountain flowers by the bend of a stream. It was like trying to live inside a romantic movie for the type of people who called movies films. She was bitten by horseflies and mosquitoes and gouged by roots. She and this man had lived together in Saskatoon for less than a year and broken up so many times she had lost count. She liked to correct his grammar because he was vain. She figured it was the 'whomever' that brought on the blow. The other man, in this case, was Whatzisname, the director, who'd had a night to kill in Saskatoon. Into this soap opera Robert had stumbled with his tender and caring voice. She had gone around with him, lived with him, married him, but she had never been able to tell him that she loved him. (She had never told that to *any* man, except maybe in jest, as in *I love you to distraction, I even love washing your socks and underwear.*)

His name used to be Bob but he always insisted that people call him Robert. Maybe he had a point there. Too many jokers would jump at the chance to change Bob Loblaw to bah blahblah. She glanced at him next to her on the bed. He looked as though Jay's fist had passed through her and struck him.

'I'm sorry, Robert,' she said. 'It was only a remark.'

He lay with his hands clasped reverently over his chest. When he died that's just how he would look.

'Come on, Robert, where were you when they passed out the cool?'

'I'd like just once,' he began falteringly, 'to think there was maybe one or two things we could do ... together ... of an intimate nature ... that you hadn't already done with some –'

'I was young. Weren't you ever young? I didn't know what I wanted.'

'Some of them got to you. Did I ever get to you?'

'Of course you got to me,' she said, spitting out the word 'got'. 'I married you. I didn't marry them.'

'You would've. If they'd asked.'

'Some of them did ask.'

'I know. Just the wimps.'

She scoffed at him with her eyes.

Stroking his chin fiercely, he said, 'I'd like just once for you to name one terrific thing about me. One reason for living with me. One thing I can do that none of those … *gigolos* can.'

You make terrific hollandaise sauce, she wanted to say.

Robert swung his legs out of bed and his foot struck Winston's guitar setting the strings ahum in a hollow discord. Head drooping, he remained on the edge of the bed.

'It's like you're all loved out. It's like you gave so much to those guys there's nothing left for me.'

He stared at the window, waiting for her to respond, but she couldn't. 'You're never really *with* me. All you've got left is this dried-up lukewarm –'

'That isn't true!' she cried, and a great spasm of grief began to roll through her. He turned his head around and watched her for a moment, and then he just got up and left the room.

The street was filled with noisy drunks celebrating the Stampede. He turned away from the noise and kept walking for a good mile, when suddenly he remembered the song he had played for Marcie on the guitar on their first date. It was a Debbie Boone song called 'You Light Up My Life'. She had never liked the song, she said, because she had never heard a man sing it. The song had made him feel wild. *She* had made him feel wild.

That's it. That's what would win Marcie back. He would sing and play that particular song on the guitar for her. He turned back towards the Wrangler Motel. The first R was shot on the neon sign, so it said the *W angler Motel*.

The fan grew louder and receded, louder softer, around and around went the fan, around and around went Marcie, flying through the hot night as the guitar played on … she was inside someone's guitar, hot and spinning, she could see the round hole, going round and around, she was surrounded in golden sound, forever in this infernal machine and no one would ever find her. Someone was thumbing the bass strings, and the whole guitar was humming... humming over her eyelids... she was humming too, her head was humming, her body was humming... if only the boy with the guitar would rescue her... he sang:

> *If I could fly, if these wings was mine,*
> *I'd fly up north to the old trapline.*
> *I'd fly up north and return to you,*
> *I'd fly up north like the eagles do.*

Marcie opened her eyes. The room was dark. She tiptoed out of the bedroom. A neon sign from the street threw little pink and blue strobes on Winston's shoulders. He sat on the hideabed and sang softly so that his voice was barely audible above the moaning of the air conditioner. His right hand rose and fell on the strings. He was all alone. Grace was gone, her wheelchair was gone.

She crept over the cool linoleum back to bed. Her dream had faded but Winston's song sent back a vibration of it, and she shuddered. She left the door of the bedroom open so that she could hear the rest of the song. She closed her eyes again and lay on her belly listening. The bass strings seemed to hum the beat ba bum ba bum up through the mattress plucking little strings in her body. Before she could call it back, a low moan winged its way out of her as a high string bent into a cry...

The music stopped. She heard Winston shuffling across the room. He was coming towards her. He was standing above her. She couldn't see him but she could sense that he was there. The cigarettes, the man smell of him.

'Winston?' she whispered. 'Don't stop playing. That was nice.'

Robert backed out the door of the motel with a vision, it numbed his mind, the elegance of lean and sculpted limbs and tangled long hair, black and blonde, as though the lovers in the velvet painting had come to life.

'Oh God,' he muttered. 'Oh no. Not this. Anything but this.'

He staggered down the street for several blocks before he saw Grace gliding ahead of him on her wheelchair, slowly, as though she were visiting an art gallery. He ran up to her, kneeled on the sidewalk, held her wheelchair so that she would see the depth of his pain, and then he wept.

'Do you believe in magic, Bob?'

He just looked at her.

'Bob, if you're going to get back on your feet again, you have to believe in magic.'

'I've just come from a motel room where my wife is in the arms of –'

'You can spare me the details, Bob. I knew what they were about even before they did it. That's why I'm out here and they're in there. But if you'll pardon my frankness, Bob, you're acting like a cripple.'

'That's a funny thing for a cripple to say. No offence intended.'

'None taken, Bob.'

'You must feel as bad as I do,' he said. 'Is this the first time he went and did something like this to you?'

Grace waited until he had recovered sufficiently from his weeping to blow his nose.

'You have to realize, Bob, that Winston doesn't mean to hurt me or anyone else. He's like a man on a journey and so am I. We were just each other's resting place for a while. My guess is that, with Marcie, Winston will think he's maybe got himself home at last. He'll be strutting down the street tomorrow as proud as a peacock. But next week or so he'll be on the move again and your wife might have to make some sudden adjustments. She might just find herself on her own for a while. Oh, that Winston, he is such a willful little boy sometimes. You know, I think he's gone a bit far this time. That's it, Bob, you just let it come. No use in holding it all in. A man could drown in all the tears he keeps inside.'

After a while, Robert got up on his feet and began to wheel Grace away from the busy avenue and down a quiet dark street away from the noise of cars and parties. The more he walked the less stoned he felt. After a while he asked Grace what she had meant about magic.

'Well, Bob, I was thinking about a small bit of mischief we could do. I don't mean out-and-out revenge, of course. But golldarn it, you and me, we've got an account or two to settle, wouldn't you say?'

'Go on.'

'Well, it seems to me that without any money or credit cards, your wife is going to look considerably less attractive to our Winston, and without his guitar, he is going to look a damn sight less attractive to your wife. Do you see where this thing is going, Bob?'

'Maybe.'

'How would you like to be the owner of a fine old Gibson Flat-top?'

'But Winston. Wouldn't he –'

'Don't even think of it,' said Grace. 'He borrowed it from someone's back trunk about a year ago.'

Robert came to a stop. He turned the wheelchair around. He headed back up the street towards the motel.

'I might just owe you a favour,' he said.

'Come to think of it, I could use a change from my routine.'

'What do you mean?'

'Well,' said Grace, 'I've always been a great admirer of your program. Some of my clients refer to it from time to time.'

'The ratings are a bit down these days. It's nice of you to say so.'

'Maybe you need a new angle, Bob. Maybe you could use a partner in crime?'

As they talked, they neared the motel. Now two letters were gone from the blinking sign. It read *W ang er Motel.*

Marcie drew her knickers off, discreetly, working them down beneath her dress just in case someone should see her out there in the back yard. She began to throw them for a nice little spaniel that had come waggling up to her. Then woops, she threw them too far and they went over a big fence, but the little spaniel was so eager to get them that he sprang up over the big fence and sprang back with the knickers in his mouth and she cried out *Good dog! Good dog!* and the spaniel (he had long drooping ears and fine glossy feathers between his toes) leapt right up into her arms. *I love you,* she cried. *I love you.* Saying these words, just saying them, felt like the most wonderful release in the world.

But now the little dog was fading, and she could hear a man breathing next to her, the beautiful Indian man from last night. His name would not come. She decided that she would just keep her eyes closed until she could remember it. Then everything would start to fall into place. What to say if Robert walked in. What to do about Robert. But first, the name. The name of the man who would soon be waking up beside her. It was so embarrassing.

☆ Luce

For us, Witiko can only scream with laughter
watching us pinned down and wiggling
scorched by the burden of our nightmares.

From *Children Shining on the Moon*
  – Ahasiw Muskegon-Iskwew

ONE

In the winter of 1936 my father's plane went down on a vast lake
somewhere north of Whitehorse. There were three in the plane. The pilot
was a man named Walmsley. He was badly hurt on impact when the plane
skidded across the lake and crashed into a snow-covered rock on the shore
of a small island. Apparently this man died a day or two later. This left
Father and a Cree Indian named Amos Whitehawk, who had surveyed
with my father for several months. Both escaped from the plane with a
few cuts and bruises.

My father knew very little about survival in the bush, so at this point
Amos took charge of things. They made a provisional sort of igloo by
shovelling snow all night long into a large hump, letting it harden, then
digging inward and upward to clear out a chamber about seven feet across
and four feet high. The chamber was above the level of the entrance, so
the heat generated by their bodies built up and drove the cold air down to
the entrance. On extremely cold nights they would sometimes let a
candle burn, and the temperature of their little igloo remained slightly
above freezing. They had a .22 rifle, some tins of sardines and some cocoa.

The bush plane remained in full view by their igloo on the leeward
side of the little island. After each snowfall, they made a point of sweeping
off the top of the plane so that the searchers would be able to spot it.

The thing my father remembered best about his conversations with
Amos during their fifty-three-day ordeal was what he said about Regina,
his sweetheart. The longer they remained stranded up there, the more

Amos extolled her in his quiet way, until this woman, whom Father had never met, gradually became synonymous with warm houses, homecooked meals, affection, cups of tea, feather beds, everything civilized, everything that was not bush. By a process I can only describe as religious, she became the home to which their minds returned each night when there was nothing left to eat and nothing visible to hope for.

Eventually their plane was spotted from the air, their position relayed by radio, and they were rescued. They arrived in Whitehorse in reasonable health and became celebrities overnight. Their story was reported and broadcast from coast to coast.

My father and Amos had little in common, but owing to their miraculous return from oblivion, they remained friends long after Father had met and married Mother. Amos returned to the Lake Windigo Reserve northwest of Edmonton, married Regina, and raised four children. Sometimes we took summer holidays in a rented cottage less than two miles down the lake from Amos and Regina's house. Hank and I got acquainted with Regina and the Whitehawk kids, but since the kids were quite a bit older than us, we usually stayed at the cottage when Father and Mother paid their respects.

Every August Dad and Amos would sit in the Whitehawks' cabin in silent comradeship, or take an equally silent walk down to Owl Cove or up the tracks to the trestle. I might be wrong, of course, but I got the impression that Father was paying tribute to Amos in lieu of talking to him. Mother and Regina had lots to say to each other, and sometimes talked for hours through the long afternoons. Regina was a short, stout, friendly woman who liked to laugh a lot. To Hank and me she was no more an icon of hope than her husband was. She and Amos were merely a bit more pleasant to be around than most of our parents' friends, which meant, I think, a bit more accepting of us as children.

Within a year of my sister Regina's birth, her namesake, Amos's wife, died. The Whitehawk kids grew up and left the reserve, but Amos remained. He was a large man, reputed to be very strong, clumsy on his feet, philosophical about the solitude to which fate had consigned him; stoical, we called it. He trapped and netted fish through the ice in winter, guided fishing and hunting parties in the summer and fall. Our parents never exposed their friends from the city to Amos because they assumed that his long silences would not be understood.

Amos and Regina were the only people my father ever actually worshipped. Such was the irony of my father's friendship with Amos: the more he worshipped this quiet sensible man, the more he isolated Amos from himself and other people; and the more Amos kept his thoughts to himself, the more he became, to our eyes, a statue in the park, a memorial of someone who was more perfect than human.

Whenever my kid sister Regina asked about where she got her name from, the above account was more or less what she got. It's all true. Some of my facts came from the files of the *Edmonton Journal*, for which I write features. I wrote the story down a few years ago, before our parents had passed away. Just a piece of family history. They all liked it. I've always been the family historian.

Last June my sister Regina gave us her own interpretation of family history. 'I was a passion that couldn't be prevented,' she announced to brother Hank and me. The occasion was her twenty-seventh birthday. 'But you two,' she said, licking a glob of icing from a candle, 'you two were planned. I mean, how boring can you get?'

'That's right,' I said. 'One night Mother and Father's TV set broke down. They had nothing else to do. It took less than two minutes. Hank and I took turns peeking through the keyhole. They yawned when it was over and went to sleep. Right, Hank?'

Hank gave me his older-brother look.

'Mom said I was conceived during troubled times,' Regina said, undaunted. 'Is that right?'

Kind of a dumb question to ask your brother, when you come to think about it. She was looking at me because on matters of family history, Hank is hopeless. He has no use for the past.

'Not really,' I replied. 'Elvis Presley was at his peak, Joseph McCarthy was in decline, John Diefenbaker was going full tilt into chiefdom –'

'Jackie Parker was winning Grey Cups,' Hank offered. 'I passed grade ten with honours.'

'That's not what I meant,' she said, smelling a conspiracy. 'That is not what Mom meant. She meant troubled times for Dad.'

Hank and I traded looks.

'Something was going on back then, wasn't it. Drew?'

I glanced Hank's way. Either he wasn't letting on, or by this time he'd managed to put most of it out of his mind.

'Something was always going on back then,' I said. 'How should I know?'

Regina was holding a knife in one hand, a birthday candle in the other. A wave of laughter and squeals burst from the kitchen where our partners and kids were gathered. A happy family reunion. I was determined it was going to stay that way. I could now see the direction this thing with Regina was headed.

'We've had this conversation before, Drew,' she declared.

The candle in her hand reminded me of Father and Amos's igloo, but the knife ... this was one of Mother's old kitchen knives, the blade thin from many sharpenings. It reminded me of fishing in our old rowboat at dawn; we called our boat the *Titanic* ...

'Reggie, every family has its ups and downs. Try getting married, you'll see. How should I know what was going on back then?'

Reggie shook her head. 'No. Mom always said that when I was on the way, "Dad was going through some difficulties," and she never elaborated.'

Once again, I looked over at Hank. He was not just silent, but silent with a purpose, as though to remind us that there were certain things you didn't discuss at the supper table.

'Did he have a mistress?' Reggie pressed on. 'That's it, isn't it.'

Noisily Hank expelled a chestful of smoke, which is his way of scoffing. 'I am going to help my wife with the dishes,' he said, giving me a vigilant look. He has a way of defusing perilous conversations.

'Stop fidgeting,' said Reggie, when Hank had gone. 'And stop looking down at your shoes. You know you're going to tell me.'

Regina does this to me all the time. So does my wife, Rachel, so did Mother, so do my two little daughters. I fight back but eventually they win. I'm surrounded by women. They don't realize it's their job to adore me. The only family member who ever adored me was our dog. Alas, now dead.

So. Right there on her twenty-seventh birthday, I told her. Hank be damned, she had to find out some time. It took about half an hour. The story kept growing on me. When I finally finished, Regina just stared, wedging her thumbnail into her teeth. At that point Rachel burst in.

'What is this, a funeral? Reggie, you pregnant or something? Uh-oh. Is this, like, a *family* matter?'

I shrugged at my wife. Regina didn't even look up. All she said was, 'You should write all this down.'

* * *

One night last July I had a dream. It was a few weeks after I'd told Regina her birthday story but before Rachel had taken her little holiday from wifedom. I was a boy, lying in bed once more at Lake Windigo. I had tied some fishing line around my big toe, the kind of strong green cord we used as a handline. The other end hung out the window. It was there for a reason but I couldn't remember what it was. There were voices outside my window. An old man cursing in a weird language I didn't recognize. A girl whispering my name, soft and sexy, like Bubby Bothwell. Someone else (Mrs Bothwell?) singing 'Teddy Bears' Picnic'. And Freddy Bullmer with his teeth knocked out, or his dad, or a composite of both, weeping uncontrollably over a lost love. His voice howled, it was pathetic, and I felt sorry for him. Then a thunderstorm rolled in. (This part may have been an intrusion from the real world, because a storm did break over Edmonton that night.) Suddenly I remembered why my toe had a fishing line attached to it. At the other end was a huge fish hook. On the hook a human corpse was impaled. I think I know whose corpse, but never mind about that.

There came a tremendous tug on my line and I was yanked out of bed. Something was dragging me toward the open window. *No!* I screamed, and *Help!* The thing on the other end was a leviathan fish with horrible jaws that snapped on the surface of the lake just outside my window (I was now in a houseboat). It leapt and thrashed over the waves. I yelled out again, *Daddy, help!* At this point I knew that my dream voice was yelling but my real voice was not. There was a knife – Regina's old cake-cutting knife, originally our mother's – on the windowsill. I was braced against the wall just below my window, holding the line so tightly my fingers were bleeding. If I could just let go with one hand, grab the knife, and cut the cord, I would be safe. I held the line with my right and grabbed with my left. There was a horrible surge, as though I were being hauled by a jet plane into eternity. The knife was in my hand and I was in the water. Just as the tail of the monster convulsed into the bright sky, I cut the cord.

I found myself sitting on an old wooden veranda. It was part of a cottage overlooking the lake. Above, the gulls were wheeling and screaming; red-winged blackbirds, ducks and swallows were nesting; a breeze perfumed with water lilies caressed my forehead. I held a fishing line once more, this time quite a thin line, and someone, also on the veranda, was holding the rod and reel to which my line was attached. A boy.

I know you.

Big deal. I know you.

What was that fish?

I guess that was Lucy.

How do you know?

The old fruit told me.

Who?

The old fruit. You know.

'Who's a fruit?'

Someone chuckles. Rachel beside me. It's a rainy morning. I can hear Sally and Jessica galloping around the living-room. Rachel wears an enormous grin. 'Don't ask me who the fruit is. It's your dream.' Now she is laughing outright.

'I said that?'

She nods.

'What else?'

'Something about Lucy,' she said, offering me a taste of her orange juice. 'One of your women?'

'I never knew any Lucy … wait.'

The dream had receded into the lake. It turned, glided back for one last look at its dreamer. It was eyeing me. I could almost see the line in its mouth, the whole dream free in its own watery medium, saying catch me if you can. I grabbed a pen and an old envelope, little flashes going off in my head.

'What is it?'

I sat there, not quite looking at Rachel, but not absolutely shutting her out, and I remembered the woody rotten smell of the aspens in late summer, how insanely the loons would call at sundown, the ebb and flow choruses of the frogs, the fish smell of the old boards on the public pier, the musty smell of my own bedroom, and how the ratchet would buzz when a good fish struck. I began to write. Three words.

'What are you writing? Yoo-hoo.'

'"Butch Bullmer",' I said with a big smile. '"Nineteen fifty-three."'

TWO

The summer I was twelve Butch Bullmer told me that old Mr Hook was a fruit. If my memory serves me, we were untangling my fishing line on the front veranda of our cottage. Aubrey, the dentist with the cottage on the point, was also supposed to be one.

'What's a fruit?' I said.

No doubt Butch would have squinted up from the tangle of camouflaged line and given me his pained look, the disdain of the worldly for the innocent. 'You don't know what a –'

'Sh!' I hissed and glanced at the Bothwells' backhouse. The bony white shins of Mr Hook protruded from the doorway. As he often did on sunny mornings, Mr Hook was reading on 'the old D.V.' (his name for it). He always kept the door open to admit the sunlight.

'He can't hear us,' said Butch, returning to his lapful of snagged line. He pecked away, swearing softly through a huge wad of bubblegum. 'A fruit's some guy always lookin for a feel.'

'You mean like a prostitute?'

'Na-a-oo!' he bawled, laughing in that raucous way he must have learned from his older brother Freddy. Back then Butch would have been about eleven years old, the youngest of five kids, and the only Bullmer my mother would tolerate. The others, according to her and Mrs Bothwell (her mentor as to the right sort of people), were a bit ratty. Butch's oldest brother Freddy ran with a pack of rough boys from the town just across the tracks (literally and figuratively) from our beach. We were the cottagers; they were the townies.

'Well, how'm I supposed to know?' I protested, when Butch had stopped laughing. To this day, I see Butch holding his head in his hands. He opens his fingers and peers out at me through the slits.

'Piss off,' I said.

He swore softly, shook his head and began pulling out long loops of fishing line. 'You're too goddam civilized,' he said. 'You don't have to be so goddam civilized.' This from a boy a year younger than me. If we hadn't been going fishing that day, and if that fact hadn't illuminated me with the sort of light that transforms all things unpleasant, I might have hit him.

My friendship with Butch was based on mutual curiosity. He was very impressed with my father, who for some reason enjoyed talking to Butch. As well, Butch was quite impressed with what he considered to be our progressive ways. I had a camera called a Brownie Box, which worked. I had an autograph book which, by 1953, had been signed by nine members of the Edmonton Eskimo football team, including Rollie Myles. I had a pair of two-tone leather shoes that I scarcely ever wore, handed down from brother Hank, brown on heel and toe, beige on top and sides. My parents owned a short-wave radio that picked up American stations on summer nights. Butch had areas of expertise, however, that gave him some advantages. He had two older brothers who were unquestionably streetwise and two sisters who knew things none of the girls in my neighbourhood knew about, or admitted knowing. Butch possessed a rudimentary code for these things. He had begun to master the street language on numerous matters guaranteed to shock, and at that particular age I thrived on shock.

Zipped up and tucked in, old Mr Hook emerged into the sunlight. He hobbled stiffly across the Bothwells' patch of lawn and into the little guesthouse at the back of the yard. He was carrying his book, a leatherbound copy of the poems of John Milton.

'How dya know?' I whispered.

'Here, hold this,' said Butch, handing me the rod and reel. 'Crank er,' he said, and as he held on to the snap swivel at the end of the line, I reeled him in. He pulled hard on the line in order to test the reel. Butch Bullmer, my talking flounder. My father called him the Mad Russian.

'Howdya know Mr Hook's a fruit?'

'He pinched my sister's ass.'

'Oh.'

He had also invited my brother Hank across the fence to view some pictures. Hank had a glimpse and quickly fled. He refused to tell me what was in the pictures. Other kids on the beach had not been as quick, and their bottoms, regardless of size or sex, had felt the horny pincers of Mr Hook.

'Sits in there all day an reads dirty books,' said Butch, indicating with his scabby sunburned nose the Bothwells' backhouse. 'See that book he had?'

'Yeah.'

'That's for beatin his meat.'

'For what?'

'Never mind,' Butch sighed.

I could have told Butch that the book in question was just a bunch of old poems. On one of my night reconnaissance missions with Hank I had found it in the Bothwells' backhouse on a little shelf next to a container of lye. Hank claimed later, on good authority (our grandmother), that one of the poems was about devils. But nothing of any shock value. Its only pictures were delicate little line drawings on the borders of the pages: gardens in bloom, forests, viny trellises. The pictures he showed to children were probably hidden in his summerhouse.

Mr Hook was Mrs Bothwell's father, she his only living child. Her mother, as far as I can remember, was never mentioned. Mrs Bothwell was apparently raised and married in England where Mr Hook had been, of all things, a schoolmaster. Since his retirement, Mr Hook had turned a bit dotty, my parents explained to me. He was considered harmless but Hank and I were under strict orders to have nothing to do with him.

The Bothwells had a peculiar hold over us. It wasn't simply that they were wealthy; it was the English way in which their wealth manifested itself: Mr Bothwell's public-school accent; Mrs Bothwell's obvious supremacy in matters pertaining to music, art and literature; the Bothwells' house in Edmonton, a gloomy stone colossus walled in by an enormous caragana hedge; and always their black Bentley parked on the Crescent.

The Crescent had a name but to us it was just the Crescent. It commanded a fine view of the North Saskatchewan river valley. Between us and the Crescent was what we called the Avenue, a busy wide street that felt like an international border. On the south side of the Avenue was the genteel Crescent. On the north side, our side, were more modest houses. The farther they got from the river, the more modest they became. To live on the modest side of the Avenue, yet close enough to walk to the Crescent, was in a sense to live in a state of permanent aspiration for a house on the Crescent. We weren't wealthy, but we only had to cross from our side of the Avenue to Bothwells' to sense what wealth was like. Rich in that grand way. It had a lot to do with what Mrs Bothwell referred to as the right sort of people; more to do with Bentleys than Cadillacs, more to do with private schools and riding lessons than swimming pools.

Queenie Bothwell's origins were humble, but it never occurred to us to claim her as an equal. She'd found a husband with family money and she had education. She was a queenly looking woman with honey-blond hair. She had a way of talking about things cultural that seemed to silence all the mothers on the block. She either directed or got the leading roles in the plays put on by the local amateur theatre. She was president of the

Community League, the symphony society, and one of the founders of the art gallery. With Queenie Bothwell, there was no *r* in art.

To my father and especially my mother, it was fate that brought the Bothwells next door to our rented cottage at Lake Windigo. The Bothwells' cottage, the one they bought in the summer of 1953, was a much grander affair, a sprawling two-storey frame house with a little summerhouse at the rear which could be used in the warm weather.

Suddenly my mother was the envy of her friends. There were the Bothwells right across the fence, the Avenue no longer between us. My mother and Mrs Bothwell could dash back and forth for a chat or a cup of sugar (at the lake Mrs B did some of her own cooking). My father, I've always suspected, had a boyish crush on Mrs Bothwell. I think he was bewitched by her beauty and by the way she regaled him with stories about that version of England he wanted to believe in: stories about royalty and men of history, stories in which Mrs Bothwell's imperial convictions figured strongly. Although of course she didn't know them, she spoke about people like the Duke of Windsor or Princess Margaret Rose or Winston Churchill as though they had lived on the next crescent over. My mother discovered that Queenie Bothwell tippled. Mother relished this fact and told almost no one.

Hank was not impressed by this new move by the Bothwells. As far as he was concerned, we were being invaded by the neighbourhood tyrant. He meant the woman who had ruined the skating rink. For this, Hank would never forgive her. Up until the previous winter, the skating rink had been a place for free skating and hockey, and Hank, a fine athlete, loved hockey more than any other sport.

When Mrs Bothwell became president of the Community League, she brought with her some changes to the PA system, which included a record player, outdoor speakers, and some 78s of her own choice. She had not been pleased with the hockey games. She said they were raucous and bred unruly behaviour. (She may have had a point there.) Around the time she ascended to the Community League presidency, we heard a music we had never heard before. It was like the first stage of a *coup*. Vienna waltzes, popular ballads, and a lot of what some people might call nursery music. Two of Mrs Bothwell's favourites were 'Dickybird Hop' and 'Teddy Bears' Picnic'. To add to the mortal tyranny of these songs, these monuments to sissydom, the singer had a cherubic warble to her voice, a tremolo that hovered over us at the skating rink, benignly, like a huge tea cozy.

If you go down to the woods today
You're sure of a big surprise.

The surprise, of course, was the bears. But why, if you went down to
the woods today, did you need to *go in disguise?* What disguise did the
singer recommend? These were teddy bears, not real ones. At six o'clock,
so the song said, their mummies and daddies would take them home to
bed because they're tired little teddy bears. The bears had the aura of Mrs
Bothwell, which was the aura of the nursery: the idea that children must
grow up feeling safe. Mummies and daddies indeed. After I had reached
the age of six or seven, my parents ceased being mummies and daddies.
These, Hank instructed me, were sissy names. They were Mother and
Father in polite company and Mum and Dad in all normal circumstances.
It was babies who needed their mummies and daddies. We occasionally
needed a mum or a dad.

So when we discovered the Bothwell family next door to our rented
cottage, we were plunged into a rebellious mood. Hank first, and I under
his tutelage. We feared coming into the stifling shadow of Mrs Bothwell's
wing, we feared the ridicule of the Bullmer brothers, we feared Mrs
Bothwell would not approve of yelling and violence and all the things that
made a young boy's life bearable. We knew we had the moral high
ground.

Mr Bothwell was a nervous dapper little man with delicate skin. He
frequently cut himself shaving. He had a Home Counties accent and a
melodious voice, but by some quirk of nature or upbringing, perhaps an
arrested boyhood, he had difficulty pronouncing his Ls and Rs. He would
say things to my mother like, *Thank you, Gwadys, but we'd wather walk to the
wink.* Bothwell was an ineffectual kindly man. He brought family money
to Canada and a knowledge of accounting and administrative practices, so
he retained some sort of standing among the bluebloods and mandarins
on the Crescent. He was given a chair on the board of governors of the
university, a position he considered to be largely ceremonial.

One day at the lake, a wonderful thing happened. Old Mr Hook
moved into the summerhouse behind their cottage. Having parents who
were as ordinary as lawns and driveways, as conventional as the Kiwanis
Club, as robust and cheerful as potluck suppers, we yearned for the
aberrant. Given an authoritative book about the Orient, Hank and I would
search immediately for the Chinese tortures. Given a book about cats, we

would race past all the kitties to get to the man-eaters. The only thing we cared to know about certain aboriginal peoples was their habit of eating other people. Mr Hook, with his pinching ways, his gory anecdotes, his mysterious pleasures, his habit of reading verse in the old D.V. with his pants down and the door open, became our favourite grotesque. We didn't *like* Mr Hook, but Hank and I did allow him to inhabit our imaginations.

At home there were certain subjects that were forbidden. Whenever my parents wanted to discuss something to do with pregnancies, money, death, someone's operation, or someone they disliked, they would do so in their bedroom in subdued voices. This same voice Hank and I adopted when discussing such subjects as cannibalism, fights, girls, pranks and secrets. As far as the subject of Life was concerned, it was *shush, the boys may be listening,* or *shush, Mum and Dad may be listening.* The ultimate breach of etiquette would be to discuss Life in an intelligible language with a member of the opposing age group.

That's the rule Mr Hook always broke. It was as though, in retirement, he became a composite of some of the impudent whelps in his school. They say he died in a mental hospital in the late fifties. If he were alive today, I suppose people might call him a pedophile. Not violent, not a child rapist or a dealer in child porn, but a low-level pervert of minor interest to the authorities. In addition to his enthusiasm for fondling and pinching, he seemed to have a compulsion to break all the rules of classroom decorum that he had enforced as a schoolmaster. I am reaching back to him, of course, just as I am reaching back to myself, unconcerned about the extent to which these memories have become shaped by my imagination, but my memory of Mr Hook's impact on me is very sharp. I can see him before me now as though his ghost were leering at the undies my wife sheds on our bedroom floor. *Give us a look,* he would say.

'Give us a look, lads.'

Butch and I peered up from our unsnagging operation. Mr Hook was standing at his fence. Butch and I probably exchanged cautious glances.

'I say, lads, give us a look.'

Butch brought him my rig. The line was unsnagged, the snap swivel attached to one of the eyes of the rod. The reel that had caused the trouble still wouldn't work. My promised fishing trip with Butch was

slowly slipping from my grasp. Mr Hook held the rod in both hands as
though he were warming up to cane someone.

'Fancy catching some fish?'

'Yep.'

'Luce, is it?'

'Sir?'

'Never angled for the luce? Never killed one?'

'What's a loose?' asked Butch, addressing Mr Hook in that scornful
tone he reserved for me on matters pertaining to sex.

'It's a bit like a shark,' he said, and our ears must have perked up.

'It lurks in the weeds,' he added, waggling his hand in the direction
of the lake. 'It's very long and tapered, it's like a cutlass, and it has a pair of
clamps for jaws.' He held his hands together, palm to palm, fingers
straight, and clamped them together several times so that his long yellow
fingernails clicked. 'They've rows and rows of backward slanting teeth,
d'you see, so their prey cannot escape.' His old knuckles cracked as his
fingers bent into fangs.

'How come we never heard of em?' asked Butch, the question
reasonable, the voice derisive.

'Because,' said Hook, without the trace of a smile, 'they feed on
children. Not often, mind, only at night, and then only in August … when
the frenzy is on them.'

'What a load a horseshit,' said Butch to me, so that Mr Hook could
hear him.

Appalled at Butch's bad manners, I broke in, 'Have you seen sharks?'

'Aye.'

'Have you seen them attack people?'

'Not too recently, no.'

'I bet they're awful,' I said. 'I bet they just come up outa nowheres an
chomp –'

'My son was in the Navy,' said Mr Hook, staring at nothing. 'Jerry
subs blew him out of the water in the North Atlantic. He and his mates.
They had a choice between burning petrol and sharks. I think –'

'Yech,' said Butch.

'I think they chose the sharks. Which, if you take my meaning, the
sharks … chose them. Ripped them to bits,' he whispered, one fist
clenched, eyes red and fervent and unfocused.

We said nothing, just stood looking at Mr Hook; likely we were wishing that he was back on his side of the fence. Not that we feared the things he talked about. I think we believed that his world was no more ours than the tea-cozy world his daughter seemed to be fashioning for us at the skating rink.

Mr Hook brightened. 'Would you young gentlemen like to see some pictures of sharks? I've a few back in the old D.V.'

No thanks, I hear us saying to him in one voice, and we retreat.

The next memory of that day is my father in the kitchen, tinkering with my fishing reel, the one I was to use if only he could fix the ratchet. My fishing plans had already been postponed from a morning to an afternoon excursion; now it threatened to become an evening excursion or none at all. I was being very patient with my father, who (for a Dominion land surveyor) was not particularly good with his hands. He was humming the first line from a current song entitled 'Slow Poke'. Just the first line, over and over again. He picked away with his screwdriver, and seemed to be operating in slow motion.

'Nearly finished?'

Father looked up briefly from his tinkering. His pipe was in his teeth and he wore a sort of grin, which was really just the straining of his jaw muscles. 'Can't tell.'

'What's a loose?'

'Mm?' Father looked up again, cocked his head slightly to the side, and drew a bead on me by squinting over the tip of my fishing rod. He was always doing that, a habit he may have picked up in survey school. All you had to do was come into the room and he would line up his sights. In his living-room chair he would squint over the top of the pointed lampshade on the sideboard, as though it were a plumb-line and you were a stadia rod or a surveyor's chain, and aim approximately at your chest. 'How do you spell it?'

'I don't know. It's a fish.'

'Look it up,' he mumbled around his pipe.

I went into the small bedroom that served both as a sewing room for my mother and a study for my father. He had what amounted to a religious faith in books, particularly those volumes that specialized in general information: how-to books, *The Book of Knowledge,* encyclopedias and dictionaries. For such a small cottage and so short a span at the lake, we had a pretty big library, and the owner of the cottage allowed us to keep our books there from year to year. Since I didn't know how to spell the word, I failed to locate it and began to assume that Mr Hook had been fabricating in order to impress Butch and me.

But my father found it. 'Luce,' he said, and spelled it for me. 'It's an English word for *Esox lucius.*'

'What's that?'

'Just a jackfish,' he said, and showed me a picture of a northern pike. Hank had caught several that summer. We ate one for breakfast. It weighed about two pounds and was very bony. The luce was as ordinary as Edmonton. Another victory for reality.

From a book I've kept to this day, Father read the following passage:

Pike are considered to grow much larger in Europe than in North America. European stories of ancient pike and of individuals over 100 pounds are largely fanciful and in the same category as stories of pike that pulled mules and milk maids into ponds. The most legendary is the Mannheim Hoax or Emperor's Pike. This story first related by Gesner in 1558, told of a pike 19 feet long, weighing 550 pounds, which was caught in a lake at Wurtenburg in 1497. This monster was said to have an engraved copper ring around the gill region that told of its release there 267 years earlier by Emperor Frederick II. The skeleton, preserved in the Cathedral at Mannheim, was found to contain vertebrae of several pike. Because of the difficulty of authenticating records of large pike, the world record is contested by the following: a pike that weighed 53 pounds, was 51 inches in length and 36 inches in girth, caught in Lough Conn, Ireland; a reportedly authentic Scandinavian pike of 57.2 pounds caught in 1892; and the 74.8 pound pike reported by Berg (1948). Berg also recorded the maximum weight of this species as 143 pounds. This is doubtless an uncritical quotation of some of the fanciful individuals in the European literature.

I mulled this over for a while. I was all on the side of the fanciful individuals, but in my mind I suspected Mr Hook of telling a stretcher.

'Why does Mr Hook call the backhouse the old D.V.?'

'He has funny names for things. He's English.'

Later on that week, we had supper with the Bothwells, which annoyed me. I still had not gone fishing. First, it had been the broken reel. When the reel was finally fixed, the weather turned stormy for several days. And now it was this interminable visit. As we sat around the great oak table with four Bothwells and old Mr Hook, I could see quite plainly that the sky was clear again, the lake calm. Everything was ideal for fishing. No one would have gone near the jackfish to spook them. I could almost see them gliding past the big public pier as they sometimes did in the evenings. Bronze and olive on their sides, orange fins, beak-like jaws, snake bodies. And how long did I have? One hour? An hour and a half at the most. I was convinced that the next day would be stormy. Unlike my mother, I had no faith whatever in the weather. Fishing was always now or never.

On came the dinner. Hank and I were silent while Miranda, the Bothwells' eldest, complained to her mummy and daddy about the behaviour of Shanghai Lil. This was her horse, an enormous chestnut mare stabled a few miles down the lake, and quite possibly the only creature Miranda ever loved. My mother claimed that Miranda had a *behaviour problem*.

'We trot through the gate,' Miranda explained, 'past the first fence, then around the corral. We go clockwise and we're trotting, we've always done it that way, but now Lil wants to gallop, suddenly she's mad keen for it. Daddy, she's never done that.'

Down the long line of Bothwell hands came my plate. The meat, I could tell, was roast beef. It had been roasted grey and juiceless. On the side of the plate was a boiled potato with no gravy and what looked like a puddle of seaweed. This, I determined, after some furtive prodding, was a spoonful of mixed vegetables, one of which was broccoli. They had been boiled into a greenish-grey mush.

'Drew?' said my mother, and I put down my fork. 'Mrs Bothwell has asked your father to say grace.'

Father mumbled something down at Mrs Bothwell's end of the table. I don't know what he said; I'd never heard him say grace at anyone's table.

'I think someone's been riding her,' said Miranda to her father, after a suitable pause.

'I bet it's Freddy Bullmer,' said Bubby Bothwell, whose real name was Robin. Freddy, who was sixteen, worked at the riding school caring for the horses sometimes, and was rumoured to have the hots for Miranda. Whenever Miranda taught swimming lessons, Freddy hung around the pier, gawking and smoking.

Miranda turned to Bubby, who was my age, threw down her knife and fork, and glared. This was the rage of the pampered princess, I remember thinking. Miranda, at fourteen or fifteen, was slim and regal, and had contempt for Bubby who was plump of body and rather moist of disposition. 'It isn't Freddy,' said Miranda in a soft menacing voice, her perfect starlet's nose aimed a foot or so over Bubby's head.

'Oh, no,' Bubby simpered. 'It couldn't be Freddy. He's too *nice*.'

'If you think I'd give that little slime the time of –'

'Miranda!' cried Mrs Bothwell, who looked very beautiful, her eyes blazing with an emotion I'd never seen in my own home. 'Bubby?' She turned to her younger daughter. I watched these three females: Miranda, a paler blonde than her mother, hard, elegant, and dangerous, to my way of thinking; Bubby, plump, dark, and soft, her skin flushed like a clear sky at dawn; and Mrs Bothwell, Hawaiian tan, honey-blond hair, glazed delft eyes, and otherworldly demeanour. She smiled, clasped her manicured and shapely hands as though in prayer, and turned to her husband. 'Georgie, I do wish you'd speak to the stable about this. What if Randy should fall?'

Mr Hook said, 'The mare's in heat.'

Mr Bothwell said, 'I'd wike to know more about it before I –'

Mr Hook said, 'The mare, all she wants is a good –'

'Daddy!' said Mrs Bothwell.

'I love your photographs,' said Mother to Mrs Bothwell. Mother had seen them many times before.

From my chair I could see the lake in all its evening glory. The sun would soon be setting. The lake was as smooth and shiny as the Bothwells' oak table. The air would be warm, the mosquitoes down. The perch would be cruising past the reeds. And the jackfish prowling, flashing into the schools of perch, gorging themselves. It was almost too much to bear. I began to fidget.

'Eat your supper,' my mother hissed, then pointing to one of the many framed photographs on the dining-room wall, 'Such handsome boys.'

'Which? The ones in uniform?'

'Yes, are you one of those sailors, George?'

'Oh, my goodness, no,' said Mrs Bothwell, lowering beautifully the angle of her vision to the floor. 'Brother Alex and a friend.' Her voice had become a whisper and she smiled. 'They both died in action.'

'Oh, dear,' said my mother, her hand to her lips.

'And, I am proud to say, died rather … gloriously.'

There was a pause, then Mr Hook began to squawk, 'They died feeding the bloody –'

'Daddy!' cried Mrs Bothwell. Her face was stricken with what seemed to be unbearable pain.

'I just love that little girl!' said Mother, a bit desperately, pointing to a picture of a child swaddled in a satin nightdress in the arms of a large matron.

'That is Georgie,' said Mrs Bothwell.

Hank and I guffawed at Mother, but no one else did.

Later, several lifetimes later, dessert was served, an eggy liquid custard. While we ate, Mrs Bothwell chided her father. It seemed a curious inversion: mother to son. 'Now you wouldn't act so cheeky if we didn't have company, would you.'

Mr Hook was sulking. This seemed odd to me. When Butch Bullmer was plainly scornful of him, insulting him to his face, he seemed not to mind. He didn't even seem to hear. But when his daughter scolded him he pouted in the most obvious way.

'I've a good mind not to bring you out here ever again. You wouldn't like that, would you.'

'Pelican,' said Hook.

'Now, you said you'd behave, Daddy, you promised.'

'Aren't we the snotty one,' he replied, his voice and his old wattled head shaking. 'Suddenly it's all la-di-da.'

'Daddy, I shall have to ask you to leave this room. You're ruining everything for the Edmonds.'

Fiercely, Mr Hook turned to us. 'She's a bleeding Aussie, she's two-thirds kangaroo.'

'Daddy, that's not fair,' said Mrs B, in what I considered to be the accent of an English lady of high degree. She was very pale now, suddenly haggard.

'Daddy,' said Mr Bothwell, 'we know all about Mummy's histowy. Now don't let's go on about it.' He said this in a very sad and suffering voice, which in no sense seemed put on. I would have thought that to be born in Australia, with all its crocodiles, boomerangs and poisonous snakes, would be a wonderful thing. Apparently Mr and Mrs B did not think so.

'Well, that's that,' said Mrs B as her father tottered muttering from the room. 'There's an end to it. Let's stop being so *gloomy* everybody. Bubby, show Hank and Drew your collection of dragonflies. Bubby is our bug collector,' she said to Mother, hugging Bubby rather violently. Bubby seemed in no mood to show off her dragonflies.

'*Go rift in your bubblebath!*' came a cracked voice from the pantry.

'Daddy!'

My mother always seemed to know what I was thinking. She had no interest in fishing or cleaning the wretched things when they were brought to her. But she must have known how much it meant to me to catch a northern pike. Up till now the boat and the equipment (which came with the rented cottage) had been Hank's. Hank was a better swimmer and given older-brother privileges. Mother singled me out for an early retreat from the Bothwells' supper table.

'Drew has a very important mission,' she said, and I sprang to my feet.

'Oh!' cried Bubby. 'Tell us!'

'He will,' interrupted my mother, her face aglow with conspiracy, 'if he succeeds. Now off you go, Drew. And remember, not a second after dark.'

I said my thank-yous in the manner rehearsed with Hank and Dad before we had arrived at the Bothwells', and left my mother to fabricate my mission as best she could. My mother was one of the most adept employers of the social lie I have ever known.

Our rowboat, the *Titanic,* was a leaky old tub painted orange and staunched with many cans of black oakum, which had dripped down the sides of the boat like the stripes on a very old tiger. We were told that for decades it had been used by a commercial fisherman on the lake and had simply outlived him. As long as the water was calm, the *Titanic* was a safe boat. Every time there was a storm, however, the waves would find it where we had left it beached on the shore by the boathouse, ease it back into the lake, and sink it. These recurrent captures of our boat made me wonder if the lake wasn't a living thing with insidious intentions. After each storm we would have to lead the thing back into the shallow water and drag it up on the beach. For a small boat the *Titanic* was extremely heavy. Often half the beach would come down to help. It was an excuse to get together, a ritual event after storms, none of which the *Titanic* could ever seem to resist.

When I raced down to our cottage from the Bothwells', I was not thinking about the *Titanic.* I had forgotten about the three-day storm. I threw on my life jacket, grabbed the rod and tackle box with one hand and the oars with the other. Thus laden, I tore down the path to the pier. There remained less than an hour of daylight. The sun was sinking beneath the rim of hills to the west of the lake. I raced through still air scented with lush dripping flora; I could feel the air flow past me in a cool silver wind. I was without a plan of action, like a released animal. I didn't even check the *Titanic* as I raced past its usual mooring place and out onto the public pier.

A guy was there, swinging something around his head like a bolas. I thought of Mrs Bothwell, two-thirds kangaroo, leaping in terror, pursued by this Aborigine glowing in the sunset. In those days I thought the bolas was an Australian weapon; I'd never heard of gauchos.

The pier was shaped like a T-square; it had a wide docking area perpendicular to the walkway. The fellow stood on the docking area beside the emergency siren. It was Freddy Bullmer fishing with a handline. Still flopping at his feet was a small jackfish.

'They bitin?'

'Shoulda seen it last night,' he mumbled. He yanked his hook out of the water, pulled off some weeds and began to swing it. With each orbit around his head, the line got longer and longer. I hunkered down on the pier so the hook wouldn't strike me. He got his whole body into it, like a discus thrower. At last he released the handline, and the coils at his feet leapt up and out like a striking cobra. The lure splashed a good fifty feet toward the raft in the deeper water. He brought the spoon in, hand over hand.

'Howdya learn that?'

'Injuns,' said Freddy, which no doubt meant Amos Whitehawk. He and Butch knew Amos better than I did.

'Seen any big ones?'

'They're all out there,' he said, pointing to the raft. 'Gotta have a boat.'

I leapt to my feet. 'I've got one. You could come with me.'

'Gotta be outa your friggin mind,' he grunted, pointing back toward our boathouse at something beside the pier. I ran back to where the *Titanic* was supposed to be beached. It lay in three feet of water about one hundred feet offshore, completely sunk. I snatched up one of the oars and heaved it at the boat, muttering curses. Oblivious, Freddy Bullmer hauled in his line, an enormous silhouette against the sunset, a warrior standing in a blaze of orange. I swore louder so that he would hear, selecting my vocabulary from Butch's repertoire, curse words that would guarantee me a manly status in Freddy's eyes. It seemed the only appropriate response at the time.

'S'matter?'

'First it's my reel, then it's the weather, then we have to sit through a stupid friggin supper at Bothwells', and now this stupid shitty-ass boat.'

Freddy continued to cast.

'Can I cast over here?'

'No one stoppin ya.'

I looked down the shoreline to where the cattails gathered and out into deeper water where the raft lay. I'd swum out there in the daytime but never with a fishing rod and tackle. It was out of the question.

'Wish I had a boat.'

I snapped on a red devil and cast. It splashed almost at my feet. My line was once more snarled in a savage backlash. I had reached my limit and began to vomit cuss words into the setting sun.

'Edmond, don't getcher girdle in a knot.'

Freddy had never called me by my name before, last or first. He was four years older than me. He was wild, a hero among boys, a heartthrob among girls, and a villain among parents. We feared and admired him.

He lit a cigarette. 'Reel's fucked, eh?'

I nodded.

'An you're in like Flynn with the Bothwells.'

I looked up at him.

'You wanna catch a big one?'

I shrugged. I was probably close to tears.

'C'mon, Edmond, you wanna catch a big one or dontcha?'

'Yeah.'

He bent over and fumbled with a handkerchief. He stuffed the handkerchief inside an old canvas bag that contained some fishing lures, and he summoned me.

'C'mere.'

I followed him to the other side of the pier. Leaning against the siren was a large black inner tube.

'Look,' he said, like a commando chief before a raid. 'Strip off yer clothes an paddle out to the raft on the tube.'

'But my reel won't –'

'Take this.' He stuffed his handline into the canvas bag.

'But what'll you use?'

'Never mind that. You do me a favour?'

He pulled out the bunched handkerchief, held it up in the air and chucked it back into the bag. 'There's somethin wrapped in this. You take this – never mind what's in it – you take this to Miran ...' He paused and gave me a very intense look. The planes of his face were angular and bony, it was a hungry face on a lean head, and his hair was combed into a ducktail. 'You keep a secret? Eh?'

I nodded. This was Life he was talking about; I knew the tone.

'Take this to Miranda Bothwell. Tell her it's tonight. She'll know who sent it.'

'Okay, but what about your fishin stuff?'

'Keep it, fer chrissakes, it's no big deal.'

'Boy.'

He took the small jackfish and heaved it away out by the raft. I stared at the inner tube, then at the glassy water all aflame in the sunset. I wondered what Freddy would think of me if I didn't have the nerve to leap in. It would be cold, it was always cold after a rain. Freddy had turned to wash his hands in the lake. I looked out at the raft and began to strip.

'Attaboy, go get them buggers. And you lose my little present, I'll be playin pool with your balls by sun-up.'

Now down to my undershorts, I tossed the tube into the water and cannonballed into the lake. Freddy gave me a flashy grin that reminds me now of Sinatra or Gene Vincent, if anyone remembers them. He handed me the old canvas bag. Shivering in the water, I took a quick look at the casting rig. The line was dark and very thick. It was wound like carded wool between the notches of the small board to which it was tied. On the end was a large red devil, its paint scratched by the teeth of many jackfish. I slipped the inner tube over my head, clamped onto the fishy-smelling bag with my mouth, and paddled vigorously out toward the raft, snorting and wheezing like an old Labrador. The water was cold. It made me kick and paddle all the faster. When I'd hauled myself and the inner tube aboard the raft, I turned to thank Freddy. He was striding off the pier. I called out but he didn't answer. He just loped into the shadows.

Up the hill where the cottages stood, everything would have been lacquered in golden light. Down below the hill where Freddy had vanished, and out on the water before me, it would all have been in shadow. To the west, auras of gold and crimson. Above me, a pale moon. I might have seen a school of perch swimming by, striped, like miniature tiger sharks. As I was unwinding the cord from the spindle I might have heard an owl hoot, the rise and fall of choruses of frogs, a loon shrieking lunacies at the coming night.

I remember swinging the big lure around my head, just like Freddy had. It was easy. I was the gaucho now, shivering and tense in my clinging shorts. The line grew longer and longer, my body twisting to widen the orbit of the lure. I was totally, simple-mindedly absorbed. When the spoon shattered the sunset, I was part of its magnificent violence. As my spoon sank, it seemed the outward tentacle of my reach; I was a hunter, full of menace and passion.

Something jerked my line. I struck back and I had one. It came slowly spiralling in, a larger jackfish than the snaky creature Freddy had taken, its sides flashing bronze as it twisted and lunged lazily by the raft. I hauled it in, clutched it with both hands in the middle of its slimy body, and brained it on the diving board. It slithered out of my hands and I had to pick it up and hurl it down on the raft many times before it stopped twitching. Slime, fish blood, scales all over my body, fingers bleeding, exultant, I ripped the hook out of its jaws. This was easy, I thought, casting again. Wait till Hank sees this. Wait till Dad –

Another tug on my line, this time stronger. I yanked back and it was gone. I worked feverishly now, scarcely aware of the cold, hauling in the line hand over hand, laying it in loops at my feet, anchoring the spindle with my foot. The light was fading fast and there was time for one or two more throws. I watched my hook come up from the depths, yanked it out of the water, began to swing it around and around. If only Butch could see me, or Freddy himself. I sent the hook high and looping into the sun's waning reflection, let it sink, counted to ten, then did a slow retrieve.

Pulling in the line, I had the feeling of being watched. So real was this feeling, I kept looking over my shoulder. I seem to remember hearing someone whistle from somewhere up among the cottages, but otherwise nothing. Squinting out over the water, I could make out the pale curve of Freddy's discarded jackfish floating about twenty feet in front of me. When my line was about halfway in, something nudged it. Not a strike, more like a slap, and my arms flinched as though whatever was watching me had made a grab at my goosepimpled flesh. I spotted my lure as it wobbled up from the depths. A blackness appeared in the dark. A hole beneath my lure. A black hole about the size of a man's head, coming up as my lure came up. And surrounding the hole, an open set of jaws, a huge open maw.

I gasped. A thing as big as I was, a green long thing with eyes wide and cold, a hungry thing, drifted after my spoon.

I yanked it out of the water. The fish glided past, its tail swept right out of the lake and the water erupted with a smack. It was hovering just beneath the surface. It turned, very slowly, tilted its head and faced me, grinning. I was fixed at the far end of its gaze; I stared back, frozen bird to ancient serpent. Without moving a fin, as though it were too immense, too ancient for movement, boar grizzly floating backwards into his den, it sank back down into the lake.

Terror surged through me, swam slowly over my soul, and right then I stepped on something hard. I bent over and picked it up. It was a ring. Standing on the raft, it seemed to me that this ring must have been flung up out of the dark water by the fish itself like a forbidden gift from the underworld. It felt strange in my hand, a heavy silver piece, like a ring in a dream. I tossed it into the canvas bag.

And then it hit me: I had to get back, and all I had was an inner tube. My legs would have to dangle down into the water. Mr Hook's words cruised back through the darkness: *They feed on children. Not often, mind, only at night, and then only when the frenzy is on them.*

At this moment I may have been searching the water for a sign of the thing I had seen. Freddy's dead jackfish had floated closer to the raft. It bobbed belly-up in the gently lapping waves, just under the surface, a white arc like a sliver of moon. There was a sudden rush from beneath the raft, a huge rolling motion like a cloud engulfing the moon, and the small jackfish was gone.

That decided it. The only way back was by boat. I had to call for help. I thought of Hank, but lately Hank had been acting very jocky, with a sort of practised taciturnity. He would go out of his way to look unimpressed with me, he was quick to ridicule, he'd say things like, 'Who do you think you are, you've never even walked across the trestle.' I couldn't call for Hank. And Freddy, by now, would be across the tracks and into town. Butch would be at home. Mom and Dad would still be at the Bothwells'. The idea was to call someone but to avoid letting them know that I was afraid.

Shivering, I went over to the inner tube and slashed it with my red devil. In a minute or two it was deflated. I had to make things just right so that my calls for help would seem justified. Besides, who would believe that a muddy old slough like Lake Windigo harboured a monster?

I would call for my dad. He was a stalwart man who didn't go around blabbing things. I would tell him that my inner tube had burst when I was casting. I would admit that the adventure had had a certain foolishness to it, but as evidence of my initiative I could show him my dead jackfish on the raft.

'Dad?'

A little louder. 'Dad?'

An echo returned, a timorous little plea to the night: *Dad?*

'Da-a-ad!'

Da-a-ad!

I yelled it again and again. The more I cried out and heard it flung back at me, the more I was reduced to cowardice and rage.

'Da-a-a-a-adday!'

My voice and its heartless echo soared out so high and strident my throat grew hoarse. It went from entreaty to anger to fury. What right did he have sitting in the Bothwells' place when his son was out here perishing in the cold? I couldn't even sit down; I was freezing. I huddled and hunched and danced around the raft, aware that as I shook my platform, sending out little waves, the grinning monster below would know my situation and might come back from the nightmare that had released him. He would know and he'd be waiting.

At last, perhaps around ten o'clock, a voice, unmistakably human, floated out to me. A soft voice, one word. It sounded like *bro* or *dro,* and it came from somewhere beyond the reeds.

'Who's that?' I called, and began to make out a rowboat coming towards me. It was Amos and Regina, and Amos was calling my name. I waited till their boat came near so I could speak in a whisper and people on shore wouldn't hear of my predicament and think me cowardly. Regina reeled in her line and Amos slipped the oars as their boat drifted up to the raft. 'I need help,' I said finally. They stared at me shivering in my jockey shorts, as though I could do nothing that would ever surprise them.

'Gonna catch yer death,' said Regina.

'My inner tube's bust,' I said, which did not quite explain why I'd been yelling like a cut calf.

'Your mum's gonna think you gone an drownded, huh?' Regina clicked her tongue and then she started to giggle and Amos joined in.

I had to tell them something. They would think I was a pretty poor example of an Edmond male. After all, they had both, in a sense, rescued my father from real horrors, from death itself. On the bottom of their boat was a potato sack containing some fish they had just caught. I assumed, therefore, that since they were Indians and knew this lake intimately, I could tell them the truth.

'Amos,' I said, 'I saw something down there and I swear to God I'm not exaggerating. I mean I never even dreamed I could ...' Amos was rowing us over to the public pier with an impassive face. I wanted him to pick up on my excitement, so I did exaggerate. 'I saw a fish so big,' I said, extending my arms in that classically suspect way of anglers, 'he was bigger than a person!'

'Yuh,' said Amos, neither denying nor corroborating my story.

'I swear to God,' I said. 'Cross my heart.' Did you cross your heart to Indians? Butch would know.

'Jackfiss?' said Regina.

'I guess so.'

'We know dat one,' she said.

'Yiz seen da bad one,' said Amos.

The way he said it – no, the way I received it – I thought he meant some figure out of Cree legend, like Weesakijack or Windigo. But no, this apparently was a real fish. 'He tears up da nets in winnertime,' said Regina.

I climbed up onto the pier and they handed me my lone jackfish and Freddy's equipment in the old canvas bag. My teeth were chattering.

'Yuh,' said Amos again. 'Yiz seen da bad one.' He looked up the lake and back at me as I shivered on the pier. 'Some day we'll get im, ah?'

* * *

I'm writing this thing in the same cottage we rented all through the fifties. Rachel has just gone off to the city. Something has gotten into her. We had a nice session of mutual accusations. Sometimes it seems to get worse between us.

It's become creepy around here. Whenever Rachel and I are apart for more than a day or two, whatever the reason, I get spooked by things. The distance between us now, that's my version of the Abyss.

Sally and Jessica are at Camp Windy-a-Gogo eleven miles up the lake. In a week Rachel will pick them up and we'll all have a pow-wow here. Sort a few things out.

She keeps insisting that something has changed me. I'm only half there. I haven't been pulling my weight with the kids. She wakes up and sees me sitting on the edge of the bed, just staring. I'm moody. I claim she's just picking away at little things, looking for excuses so she can have her midlife crisis as soon as possible. She's bored with being all things to all three of us. She's just bored. And she won't admit it.

Who knows? Things change between people.

This cottage has changed, but not in every way. It's been renovated, has a new owner, but it smells basically the same: the must of mouldy linen, upholstery, and rotting vegetation laced with woodsmoke and a million stove-cooked meals. The old D.V. is still next door, huddled like a derelict in the willows behind the Bothwells' big cottage. So much is flooding back.

On the morning of the second day here, before the girls left for camp, I made a big discovery. Bubby Bothwell now owns the cottage next door. Her parents are dead. She has three children and an Australian husband who builds sailboats. My girls love him. 'He has a motorboat too,' says Jessica, who rates people according to what they own. Miranda, I've discovered, has had three husbands. She is childless and, at forty-five, still a jetsetter. Bubby says she's fond of saying things like, *Strasbourg in April? No one skis there any more. Do you know who skis there in April? Fiona and Basil. Definitely NQUTD.*

* * *

Miranda. I had a message to deliver. Down the path came Bubby and Hank to see if I'd caught anything. Apparently they had not heard my screams for help. One look at me, blue with cold and in my underwear, and Bubby ran back for a towel. Hank dashed out to the end of the pier and got my clothes. I decided I would tell them what happened. Shivering in Bubby's huge towel, I blurted out my story. Even Hank was impressed. We were all three of us rather gleefully terrified, and AWOL as far as our parents were concerned – though they weren't yet concerned, since they were still at the Bothwells' having a good time.

Bubby, at my request, summoned Miranda. Even then, at fifteen or so, Miranda looked and played a combination of two roles: the *prima donna* and the *femme fatale*. No other scripts seemed available to her. She smoked, drank, and carried on, mostly with rich boys who had wild reputations. She approached the three of us with an air of extreme condescension. We babbled my story to her, which was a mistake. She simply stared down at us, her weight on one leg, clasping her arms, eyelids half closed, blowing smoke over our heads, and said, 'Dewey-Duck, you probably saw your own reflection.' She never called me anything but Dewey-Duck. It was always a source of resentment.

No, we all cried, it was there, it was enormous.

'It's also your bedtime,' she said. She knew this was a real threat to us. Like her mother, she wielded power with supreme indifference.

I remembered, suddenly, that I was on a mission, had been, in fact, since I'd spoken with Freddy on the pier. I implored Miranda to wait, reached into Freddy's canvas bag, and pulled out the handkerchief.

'Here,' I said. 'This is for you.'

She held the handkerchief out from her body as though it were a dead fish. Of course, it was empty. *The ring!* Freddy Bullmer must have wrapped it inside his hanky, and when my monster thrashed at the surface of the lake and I flinched, the ring must have fallen out of the bag. That was when I stepped on it.

It was still at the bottom of the bag. I found it and handed it to Miranda, and when she glared at me, I shrugged.

Something about my adventure on the raft was beginning to sag. Miranda, with all her princess *ennui,* had begun to de-mystify it. The ring, until now something satanic in my mind, was turning into a mere bauble, the sort of thing that a girl at school would wear on a chain around her neck.

Perhaps Miranda did not quite see it that way. Her eyelids opened well past the halfway point.

'He says "tonight",' I told her.

'Who says?' whispered Hank.

'I'm telling!' cried Bubby.

'You're going to bed!' whispered Miranda.

'Okay, I won't tell,' said Bubby.

'Tell what?' cried Hank as Miranda, no longer bored, dashed off into the trees.

When I came to our cottage with Hank and Bubby, our parents were still not home. We all raced outside and played a game of Hank's devising. There was a treasure and one of us had to guard it. The other two had to get it. All the guard had to do was tag the one trying to get at the treasure and he or she was dead. But if one of us could lead the guard off a ways, the other one could dash in and grab the treasure. If that person could keep the treasure for fifteen minutes by Hank's watch, that made him or her the guard. Bubby said it should be jewels but Hank, who was thirteen and read a lot of thrillers, said it should be secret plans. Instead of being pirates we could be spies. So Hank became the guard and he kept the treasure under a big washbasin in the back yard. For secret plans we used Mr Hook's leatherbound copy of poems. That was my idea. I stole it from the old D.V.

It was well past ten o'clock. The cobwebs across the paths, the sounds of birds and frogs, everything nocturnal, was secret and holy and terrifying. What I mean is, enchanted.

At first Hank was immovable. He just sat on the washbasin and when we came within a hundred feet or so he would make short, threatening rushes at us and we'd tear away screaming into the night. After a while, however, he still had the secret plans but we were still alive and taunting him. Eventually Bubby came a little closer than I had, and Hank raced after her. There was a lot of screaming. I darted into the clearing, grabbed the book, and leapt over the Bothwells' fence.

Having apparently killed Bubby, Hank came racing back to the clearing. He looked hideous. He always played his roles with too much conviction and he loved to scare me. I ducked into the old D.V. but kept the door wide open. If Hank saw the door closed, I deduced, he would know I was inside and he would kill me. It must have worked. Hank raced past the old D.V. and around to the front of the Bothwells' cottage.

For what seemed a long time I sat on the toilet seat thumbing through the pages of the book by the light of the moon. I tried to imagine, as I read some of Mr Hook's underlinings, what a serious spy would be doing with these plans. A passage caught my eye.

> *A dungeon horrible, on all sides round,*
> *As one great furnace flamed; yet from those flames*
> *No light, but rather darkness visible*
> *Served only to discover sights of woe,*
> *Regions of sorrow, doleful shades, where peace*
> *And rest can never dwell, hope never comes*
> *That comes to all, but torture without end*
> *Still urges, and a fiery deluge, fed*
> *With ever-burning sulphur unconsumed.*

I read and reread these lines. They had the aura of forbidden knowledge, and I began to wish our treasure weren't plans for a spy to steal, but something sinister, like the ring of the monster, flung up, as it seemed once more to me, from the bottom of the lake.

On a willow bush outside the door of the old D.V., luminous and blue like the concussion patterns on a broken windshield, was a large spider web. At first I could see no spider. A large moth struck the centre of the web and began to flutter. A huge garden spider rushed out. As the moth struggled, the garden spider danced around it. They both seemed to be dancing, the one feckless, the other fierce. When the moth stopped fluttering for an instant, the spider rushed in. It seemed to embrace the moth with his striped hairy legs and mushroom body. Moth and spider hung there, swaying, silverblue in the moonlight.

Something made me start. It came from a car parked in the Bothwells' driveway, a moaning sound. I thought of old Mr Hook and then of Hank, who might be bluffing. I had to last a little while longer with the plans or of course he would kill me. I crept past the spider web by the door of the backhouse, and remaining in a low crouch, made it up to the side of the car. It was a battered 1950 Hudson. I had seen it somewhere before. From within, there came a prolonged exhalation, as though someone in pain were struggling. Then someone else gasping. Perhaps Bubby and Hank had left the game and had decided to neck? No, that was preposterous. Or perhaps Mr Hook was having a heart attack. It sounded more like he was being murdered or murdering someone. Whoever was there began to rock the car from within, gently at first, then more and more furiously.

The moon shone directly into the car's front window. I raised myself slowly to the level of the side window and beheld a heaving knot of arms and legs, bouncing silver buttocks, and heard the voice of Freddy Bullmer rasping out of the tangle *o yeah o yeah o yeah o yeah o yeah* louder and louder and Miranda groaning something that sounded like a black mass and the huge foam rubber dice bouncing on Freddy's rear view mirror like an evil talisman. Creeping away I thought about the spider and the moth swaying in a lovers' embrace, and how the luce had devoured the smaller fish with a single rush ... *the frenzy is on them*, Mr Hook had said, and the ring, I thought, the heavy silver ring I had given to Miranda: it must have had strange powers after all.

Rachel awake in the hammock. How long has she been looking at me?

'What did you just write down?'

'I wrote, "Rachel awake in the hammock. How long has she been looking at me?"'

'Have you ever played around on me?'

It's a mellow Lake Windigo afternoon. Mid-August, when the stronger winds and slight chill of the mornings bear with them little harbingers of fall, those earth odours of things past their ripeness. It's mostly in what those smells remind you of. You cling to the good things at this time of year as though they're all about to die.

'No.'

'Never?'

'Never. Does that make me sound boring?'

She won't answer me, gives me a sleepy smile. I can't tell if I've ever known her thoughts. Without anyone around, I have these musings more and more. Likely she's having them too. Last night she just drove out for what she calls an update on me. I may have passed my update; she stayed all night.

'Will you ever write something about us?'

'On a day like dis you should esk such a kvestion?' My attempt to imitate Rachel's grandmother.

She says, 'I don't know what you mean by that. It's a pretty ordinary question. You're writing about *her*.' She jerks her thumb at Bubby Bothwell's cottage.

'You have a sexy nose.'

She gives me her you-are-straining-my-patience smile. 'Will you ever write about us?'

I don't think I will. Ever.

'What did you just write down?'

'I wrote, "Some day I am bound to write about Rachel and me."'

'You're such a liar,' she says, closing her eyes.

'Did you know what the Bothwells' backhouse is called?'

'The old D.V. You told me.'

'Do you know what the D.V. stands for?'

'Lemme guess … Defecating Vultures?'

'Yer a riot, Rachel. It stands for darkness visible.'

'I don't get it.'

'Have you ever really looked at a backhouse at night?'

'Only you could ask that question.'

'I'm serious. When you open the door to the can, at first you can't see anything. Then your eyes adjust and you see you're in a dark enclosure. Then you look down at the toilet seat and you see an even darker darkness. The ultimate black hole in the universe. It even smells of sulphur and brimstone.'

'We have the nicest conversations sometimes.'

'Darkness visible. It was Mr Hook's little joke.' I read her the quotation from Milton, this time from a nice shiny paperback. It didn't feel like the same poem. I wanted Mr Hook's old leatherbound volume. I wanted the smell of sulphur, brimstone, and puberty, the arachnoid enchantment of an old backhouse in the moonlight.

'Another riddle of the universe, solved,' she declares, sliding out of the hammock and putting on a pair of sunglasses.

'Where are you off to?'

She looks at her watch. 'A rendezvous with my gigolo. Where do you *think* I'm going?' She does this a lot lately.

'You just got here last night.'

'Okay, what if I told you I was on my way back to Edmonton because I've got a life to lead?'

'I was just asking.'

'What would you do if I started going out? You know, having fun.'

'Fine. Terrific. That I'd write about. Let me know if you run out of money.'

We exchange glares. With her sunglasses on, she has the advantage in this department.

* * *

Others saw my monster. He came to be known as Adolph. Some native people reported torn nets in the winter of 1954. In the spring of 1955, when the ice had melted a few feet out from shore, Butch Bullmer claimed to have spotted him basking in the sun just beyond the reeds. Some kids a few doors down from the Bothwells' cottage spotted Adolph from the pier one morning after a storm, swimming slowly around the *Titanic*. Fishermen came from Stony Plain, Spruce Grove, Drayton Valley, many from Edmonton, some from up north, to catch Adolph, even just to see him cruise the shoreline. He was responsible for what was rumoured to be a fortune in fishing tackle. He swam trailing fishing lines, and fishing lures hung from his bony jaws. He seemed to flaunt them before his would-be captors. He became a reference point for us, a measuring stick for the Olympian, a storybook character as talked about as Wop May or Jackie Parker. We came to know who among the townies and cottagers had actually seen Adolph.

His publicist was Clarence Bullmer, Butch and Freddy's father. Clarence was an old scrapper who cut ice in the winter and hauled it in the summer. He would sit in the Windigo bar for hours telling Adolph stories. What he said depended to a large extent on who was listening. Fishermen would come to the hotel and seek him out. Have you actually seen him? they might ask. And if none of his cronies was around, he'd tell his stories as though he'd been there every time Adolph was hooked or sighted. *We was over by the point – no, by Jesus we was halfways down ta Owl Cove. Well, I swear, I was haulin in this three-pounder an suddenly z-z-z-z-z-! Off she goes like I'd latched onto a German sub. An you know, that bugger had swallowed my fish whole an run out all my line? Snap. Just like that, not a word of a lie…. Well sir, I was mindin my own business drinkin a bubbly behind the icehouse an the missus she's out on the dock, and she hollers, Clarence! Clarence! she says, you gotta warn them kids. There's a sea monster down there…. While back a man from the city standin right over there where yer boat's tied up, he says to me, Clarence, that's a sturgeon or I'll eat my socks. I says to him, Charlie, I says, pass the salt an pepper. That there's no sturgeon, that's Adolph. That's exactly what I says to him…. Right underneath the pier, not a word of a lie, and he wouldn't touch yer hook if you had rye whisky on it, just lyin there. Along comes this Merican lady with a spinnin rod, she says, Anything around here worth wetting a line? I points down ta where we was gawkin, I says to er, How bout that one? Bit on the small side, I says, but he'll be good in the fryin pan. Well, she damn near shit her drores….*

I suppose what happened was inevitable. The community needed more business. In the summer of 1956, some men devised a contest with a cash prize of one thousand dollars for any angler who hauled in Adolph. The first person to break the news to me was Butch Bullmer, and he had a plan. I must give Butch credit, it was a good plan.

He found me one morning down at the public pier watching some men with diving tanks. I was fascinated. They did all their fishing with flashlights and spear-guns in the deepest parts of the lake. I've referred to Lake Windigo as an old slough, but it's actually eleven miles long and about two miles wide in places, so there is plenty of room for a huge fish to hide or to fatten up. It didn't take Butch long to find out what the scuba divers were doing at our lake. He spoke to a tall fellow, who was about twenty years old and very self-assured. 'You can come right up on them,' he said, hefting a large burbot from his rubber dinghy. 'They assume you're one of them.' He held the burbot by a metal arrow that protruded from the top of the creature's head. In a pool of pink slime at the bottom of the dinghy lay several large fish, two of them pike. I was impressed.

'You seen Adolph?'

'No,' said the tall fellow, 'but he's around. We'll get him.'

'You'll never get him,' said Butch. 'Who're you tryin to kid? He's too smart.'

'We'll get him, Squirt,' said the tall fellow with a subdued smile.

'You got as much chance as shootin mermaids.' Butch spat on the pier. 'C'mon,' he said to me.

We went and sat side by side on the hull of the Titanic. 'Fuckers,' he whispered. Butch seemed to be making up his mind about something.

At this time he was fourteen, baby-faced, short and very stocky. I was fifteen and two or three inches taller than Butch. He had become a restless fast-talking schoolyard brawler. He had just been suspended from school. My parents no longer tolerated our friendship. Butch was obsessed with money, always asking people how much their things were worth. With all my we-live-near-the-Crescent complacency, I was not tolerant of Butch's money obsession, and too often in later years I tended to dismiss him.

'I know where he's at.'

'Where?'

'Never mind where. There's a thousand bucks on his head. You gotta promise you'll come with me. I need a Injun Joe.'

According to Butch, an Injun Joe does the rowing while the person he chauffeurs around does the casting and gets to play the fish and be the hero. If it's a big one, the Injun Joe rows the fish clear of the snags and does the netting. I was miffed that Butch didn't even consider the possibility he might be my Injun Joe. He was marching ahead of me on the road that led to the reservation. I remember it as being very hot, and the dust sprayed up around our shoes.

'Wait up,' I yelled. 'Where we goin now?'

He stopped, spat into the dust. 'Are you with me?'

'What if we catch him? Who gets the money?'

'I catch him, I get the money.'

'What do I get, your autograph?'

'You provide the boat an the equipment, be the Injun Joe, you get five bucks an hour,' Butch said. 'That's ten times what you get at that drugstore in the city.'

He was exaggerating slightly, but as a delivery boy I earned less than a dollar an hour.

'Do I get paid even if we don't get him?'

'You'll get yer money.'

There it was, a paid adventure in which the risk was all Butch's. 'Hang on,' I said, and Butch spun around with a scowl. 'You get ten casts, eh? Ten casts. Then you're *my* Injun Joe.'

Butch raised his index finger. 'I need *one* cast, Edmond. One cast, okay?'

We followed the road in through the reservation and down to Owl Cove where a hilly meadow opened out, giving way to a big marsh of several hundred acres.

'Why doesn't Amos Whitehawk do it? He's got a boat.'

'Never mind,' Butch mumbled. 'See that dock?'

I couldn't see a thing in the savannah-like swamp grass. We walked closer. There was a rough path through the tall grass. We had to leap from hump to hump to keep our runners dry, and finally onto an old dock that leaned and swayed as we walked it like the spine of a dinosaur. It led us past the reeds and cattails and out beyond the lily pads. We could see right down into the amber water. Owl Cove is the size of a large pond, a satellite of Lake Windigo with only a weedy channel connecting them. It was always considered Indian land, so very few people from the beach ever went there. From the main lake it was almost impossible to find; you had to know where to strike into the reeds and how far to paddle. That day, this little cove, encircled by a forest of cattails, tall reeds, lined by regattas of lily pads, alive with throngs of red-winged blackbirds, orioles, grackles, screaming gulls and nesting ducks, seemed very much our own private sanctuary. Perhaps I was just a kid who was easily led, but the prospect of acting as Butch's Injun Joe was getting easier to accept.

'Where is he?'

'Comes in here after dark, stays all night. Amos throws him fish every night just after sundown. See?'

He pulled at my elbow and pointed to a dozen fenceposts sticking out of the water in the shape of a corral. Nailed to the posts were at least fifty feet of chain-link fence. Inside the fenced enclosure was a net with a fine mesh in about six feet of water. It contained dozens of whitefish, some of them three pounds or better, lying dormant on the bottom.

'He knows they're in there,' said Butch. 'He swims around and around. Amos uses a dip net, gets a whitefish, an stuns it so's it gets ... convulsions?' He looked at me nervously to see if he had the right word. 'He sees it's injured an comes right in an grabs it. Last night he took five a the buggers, five big whitefish, Edmond. He's a bottomless friggin pit.'

'You splittin the take with Amos?'

Butch didn't answer. He just stared down at the water with a lover's fierce look of longing.

'Eh? Five hundred down the middle?'

'That's between me an Amos,' he muttered, and spat into the water.

We loaded the *Titanic* during the heat of the day, pretending that we were going fishing. Butch had decided on a handline, so I donated his brother's rig, the one Freddy had given me three years earlier the night I saw the luce.

'Three packages of Dad's Cookies?' called Hank. He was lying on the beach next to Bubby Bothwell. They were sharing the same towel.

Butch said nothing.

'Don't tell me the jackfish are taking Dad's Cookies.'

I followed Butch's example. Mum was the word.

'You'll never catch anything. It's too hot out,' Hank continued in that older brother tone.

Bubby turned over on her side. She had somehow lost her chubby schoolgirl look and I could scarcely keep my eyes off her.

'No one goes out before seven-thirty, Drew,' Hank went on. 'You guys're crazy.'

We rowed the *Titanic* right down to Owl Cove. Butch had figured out how to get through the reeds, but he knew we'd never do it in the dark. We hid the boat deep in the rushes where we could reach it from the shore of the cove.

'Why not just tie it to the pier?'

'Don't want Adolph to see it,' said Butch.

I should have known, of course, that Butch was hiding the boat from Amos. His preparations were so clandestine, his mood so tense, I should have been able to read his intentions, but Butch's little adventure had taken hold of me. I had become his Injun Joe without so much as a handshake.

'Show them candy-ass frogmen. Hey, Drew?'

The plan had one major complication. I had to sneak out of our cottage at 2 a.m. There was no way I could tell my parents where I was going or (especially) with whom. An alarm clock was out of the question. And Butch didn't trust me to stay awake till the appointed hour. His solution was to get me to tie some heavy string around my big toe and toss the ball of string out my bedroom window. At two o'clock Butch would creep up and pull on the string, and I would climb out of my window fully dressed. It was too ingenious to resist.

I was afraid to fall asleep that night. I knew that if I did, Butch would come and yank the string, and knowing Butch, yank it much harder than he needed to, and I'd wake up screaming or something. So every time I fell asleep I'd awaken with a jolt and check the clock then doze off again.

According to the notes I had to read to my counsellor back in 1956, I dreamed I was fishing with Butch in the ocean. We were in a ship, going after Adolph, but he kept changing shape. I imagined him first as a whale or a shark and later in the dream as the ancient luce with malevolent grin, as large as the Emperor's Pike. Then I was lying on the raft next to Bubby Bothwell, who was on an air mattress tanning in the nude. I don't remember where Butch was, only that he was there some of the time. I was supposed to be fishing for Adolph but I was having trouble concentrating on both Bubby and Adolph. This was irritating. I dangled my foot in the water. Dark tubular clouds were massing overhead like waves in a storm. *Do you want to touch me?* Bubby asked. *Yes,* I said. *Not now,* she said. *I haven't got anything on.* Someone began to sing, *If you go down in the woods today you'd better go in disguise* ... I knew I shouldn't dangle my foot in the water. Butch said I was asking for trouble, but I would not let Butch boss me around any more. After all, he was a year younger. I felt afraid suddenly, as though something or someone were watching me. It was either under the raft, in which case it was Adolph, or on the other side of the foaming clouds. *Do you want to touch me?* Bubby asked again. *Yes,* I said.

That's rude, she said. *You're rude.* She rolled over on her side to face me, showing me her sex. It was like a rosebud. *What's the matter?* she asked. *Someone's watching us,* I said. *You're silly,* she said. *It's just your imagination.*

Something grabbed my toe, it had powerful jaws. I dug my fingers into the spaces between the logs of the raft but it pulled with a terrible surge. There was a frightful explosion of water, I was being dragged. *Now you're in for it,* said Bubby, who sounded like her mother. *That's exactly what happened to my brother.* Then, *Daddy!* I cried as I went under. I couldn't breathe. *Bloody hell!* said someone, and he was …

Outside my dream. Pulling on my big toe.

'Bloody hell!'

A voice outside my window went crash on the dogwood. It wasn't Butch Bullmer, it was a rasping voice. I freed my toe from its noose and peeked out, kneeling by the corner of my window. Someone in a nightshirt thrashed on the ground like a snared animal. Muttering, rolling over. Someone arthritic. He gathered himself together, and with the aid of the fence, reared up high and ghostly white in the moonlight, reared up pawing the air like some old plantigrade, injured but refusing to die. He glowered at my window with what looked to be equal parts fear and menace. It was old Mr Hook.

I retain the impression that this was not his first visit to my bedroom window. He was rumoured to be in the throes of a long illness and convalescing at that time. No one had seen him basking in the old D.V. that month. In the moonlight he looked very old. His face seemed to have twisted into a permanent grimace. He lurched around in a circle, muttering words like *meddling* and *insolence* as he went, ripping string from his legs, twitching, leering at my window. Could he see me peeking at the corner? Did he think I had set out to trap him? Finally he stopped lurching around in circles and slouched off down our fenceline, trailing string from his leg.

* * *

This lake, this cabin. Sometimes at night they spook the hell out of me. I wish the girls were back from camp. Who comforts them when *they* get spooked at night? I want Rachel here. She belongs here, damnit. We weren't meant for marital crises. That's too fashionable. I want my gals back. They always made me feel brave. Now I'm like Faust writing by candlelight; I might conjure up something I can't handle. Maybe I already have. These are strange thoughts for a nine-to-five features writer.

A dark van keeps cruising up and down the road. I can't sleep. Good night, Rachel, wherever you are. May all the yiddisha-mama guilt in creation give you insomnia.

* * *

It was probably about one o'clock. With great misgivings I re-attached the noose to my toe and climbed back on top of my bed. Dangling outside my window were still about a dozen feet of cord. I didn't want to fall back to sleep. What if Mr Hook returned? I'd have to wake up my parents and Hank, ruining the whole scheme with Butch. I began to regret agreeing to go on the trip to Owl Cove. I was filled with a sense of forboding. What if there was a storm and the *Titanic* sank? What if I had to swim back to shore with Adolph somewhere on the prowl? What if I got tangled in the line or the reeds? Had I remembered to throw in the life jackets? All I could remember throwing into the boat were the mosquito lotion, a big club, the fishing equipment, Mother's kitchen knife, and the three packages of Dad's Cookies. I began to phrase excuses for not going. It would have to be something to do with sickness or injury. Blood poisoning or scarlet fever. Indeed, I could *feel* the fever and the chills ... perhaps I really was sick ... my vision going funny ... I would remain collapsed on this bed ... Bubby Bothwell would get word that I was drifting between death and life, she would visit me ... take my hand, feel my forehead....

The next tug on my line was Butch.

'Getcher ass out here!' he whispered. 'It's quarter past. You wait any longer, Adolph's gonna be a old man.'

The thought, I could have told him, had crossed my mind.

It's chilly, the grass and leaves are wet, my runners are soaked, I try to walk fast and I stumble. The fog hangs ragged in the ditches like unfinished thoughts. I can hear two birds, a robin and a chickadee. The robin's warble is nasal and tentative, a sleepy sound. The chickadee's is two notes: the first is a high minor note, the second lower and extended, floating sadly through the trees, a girl's name with two syllables, she will never come back. I think cold and wet, I think lying in bed, I think Dad's Cookies, I think old Mr Hook ... what would he actually do to someone ...

'It was real weird,' I tell Butch.

'Did he *say* anything to you?'

'I don't think he even saw me lookin.'

'I was you an he tried that again, I'd run outside an kick him in the nuts.'

'It was real weird.'

I make my way down to the lake through spider webs, patches of mist, spongy humps among the cattails. Everything I touch is insubstantial.

Butch locates the *Titanic*. We heave the thing over on its side, dump out the water, toss our gear back in and ease the boat out beyond the lily pads. We tie it to the pier and Butch leaps out to get a dip net hidden in a small thicket. I stand on the pier shivering and try to see things. Butch comes back with the dip net. He begins lowering it into the whitefish corral and scooping whitefish into a big milk pail.

'Get in the boat.'

'What's your hurry?'

'Get in the boat!'

I get in and man the oars. Butch tosses the dip net into the bushes and jumps in. At least a dozen whitefish mill around in the milk pail. I row us slowly out past the pier, ship the oars, and we drift. Butch has a flashlight. I hold our anchor in my lap, a rusty iron plate we found by the railroad tracks.

'Now,' he says, and I drop the anchor.

Butch stands up and shines his flashlight down into the water. It is perfectly calm, not a leaf trembles. We wait there an hour or so. A pale light seeps up from the east. I hear a tiny splash and see a muskrat glide past our boat. Over by the lily pads a family of ducks swims languidly in single file.

'Nothin so far,' Butch whispers.

'Gimme the cookies.'

Butch unravels a few feet of cord from Freddy's handline and ties on a large bare hook. I've never seen one that big. Its shank must be three inches. He ties it to the cord with a multitude of clumsy knots, links the bend of the hook to his index finger, and tests the knot with all his strength. I can hear him grunt.

We munch on cookie after cookie. The stars have begun to fade. I can see the edges of things. Thickets, trees, a crow's nest, a duck, things that loom out of the shifting mist.

'I'm cold.'

'C'mon, show, you old bugger. I know yer down there.'

'What do you think about Bubby Bothwell?'

'Rich bitch.'

'Yeah, but what do you *think* about her?'

'She's the type thinks she's sittin on the Todge-ma Hall.'

'She's got Hank goin round in circles.'

'Gimme one a them whores,' he says, and I hand him a struggling whitefish from the pail. He clubs it once, stunning it, and tosses it into the circle of light the flashlight makes on the water. The fish vanishes then reappears, twitching on the surface.

'Nothin so far,' says Butch for the fourth time or so, then, 'Know what your old man told me? Fifty-three days. Him an Amos. All they had was some hot chocolate an a few tins a sardines. Makes you wonder.'

'They had a .22.'

'Still.'

'It's so bloody cold. Especially on the feet. Wish the sun would come up.'

'Think you could ever eat somebody? I mean if it come to that?'

'Bullmer, you have the weirdest mind.'

'I could. I'd do it. You're up there on a little island with this Indian, a few tins a sardines between you. You know how Indians eat. Twice as much as a white man. An there's this guy, whatzisname.'

'Walmsley.'

'Right, Walmsley. An he's dead. Fresh meat, for God's sake. I mean how long them sardines gonna last with a goddam Indian the size a Amos, eh?'

'They had a .22.'

'But on a little island in the snow in the dark, fifty-three days, Edmond. I mean, do you think –'

'I think you're as weird as old man Hook.'

Butch shook his head. 'You're too civilized. Don't be so civilized.'

Whitefish drum against the milk can. Another muskrat churns past the boat. More ducks venture out from the reeds. Somewhere a rooster is crowing. A loon rears up out of the mist to release an astonished falsetto.

Butch reaches into the milk can, pulls out a small whitefish, clubs it, tosses it in the direction of the loon. The whitefish swims weakly on its side, flutters at the surface. The first whitefish is dead. It drifts towards the pier.

Butch is bent over double, his eyes closed, arms folded, head on his arms. 'If I was a loon,' he mumbles, 'I'd have better sense than to swim around here.'

'If I was a jackfish I'd have better sense than to eat loons.'

'Jackfish'll eat anything that moves.'

'The day Adolph eats a loon I'll give you a million bucks.'

Butch looks up at me and sneers. 'Bubby Bothwell.'

'I think she's nice.'

He doesn't heed me. He is looking toward shore, munching on a cookie. He raises his hand for silence, scans the water, turning around in his seat so that he covers a complete circle, covers it twice. Through a mouthful of crumbs he whispers, 'Hang on.'

The loon surfaces right before our eyes, paddles off into the mist. We see it in silhouette waiting at a safe distance.

'What's up, Butch?'

'Hang on.'

Butch has the big hook in his left hand. He is now standing on his seat, scanning the placid surface of the water. The muskrat swims toward us seemingly without concern. It accepts us.

'One a them whitefish,' whispers Butch as a loon cries from the far end of the cove, 'it's gone.'

The dead one floats by the pier. The live one has vanished. The water is as calm as the wisps of mist drifting both ways across the cove. The loon swims back our way, the muskrat swims across our bow. We are both looking at the muskrat. Then at a glistening back as big as a sunken log; it comes up golden green from the depths and engulfs the muskrat, gently, in its jaws. The muskrat is gone from our vision with a soft *sploosh*, and we gawk at a target pattern of waves from the centre of which the animal has been snatched. When I see Butch's face I know what mine must have looked like that night, long ago, on the raft, and that Butch's *usual* face is a man's mask of invulnerability, but that his *other* face is just a boy's. Like my own.

'Get ready!' he hisses. 'Get ready!'

I haven't the faintest idea what getting ready entails, nor does he. We plunge our arms into the milk pail, I am faster. He snatches the fish from my hands and searches frantically for the club. He swears in a desperate snarling whisper. The club has simply evaporated. Holding the whitefish in both hands up to his mouth, like a cob of corn, he bites down hard on the head, then spits. There is blood on his chin. He tosses the whitefish into the wake of the widening circle of ripples. There is a splash by the pier. The other whitefish, the dead one, is gone.

'Gimme another one!'

As Butch thrusts his hook into the back of the next whitefish I watch the one he has just bitten. It flutters at the surface helpless as a moth in a web. Butch unravels loop after loop of thick green cord. He ties one end to his seat, then stands up and begins to swing the baitfish lightly back and forth through the air.

'When he smells the blood, he's gonna grab this, Drew. You haul up the anchor faster'n shit, okay?'

'Okay.'

'Otherwise he'll get tangled up in the rope.' He swings his bait back and forth, swaying gently. He looks like Freddy on the pier. 'So don't let me down, okay?'

'I said okay.'

He releases the baitfish with an easy fifteen-foot toss so that it lands beside the one with the bleeding head. Butch's baitfish dives and rolls at the surface, dives down again.

Suddenly there are gentle waves everywhere. The whole cove is in motion. Lily pads undulate, cattails sway, our boat rocks. I look up and a rosy light floats through the mist, the tops of the trees are capped wih light, the upper rim of the sun begins to rise like the red eye of a hunting creature. The night is draining from the water in the cove, I can see how the anchor rope stretches down below the surface. I cannot yet see the luce, only imagine him lying at the bottom of the cove, the grinning prognathous jaw, the eyes of purest hunger, watching.

'Drew, *look!*'

The cord slithers from his hand. He feeds loop after loop slowly into the water.

'Get the anchor!'

I haul up the anchor and I whisper to Butch, 'Why don't you strike back?'

'Let him swallow it.'

Holding the anchor, I am suddenly aware that we are *connected* to this thing. There will be no tearing the hook out of the water before it can seize our bait. There are no options. We are going to catch it. The thought immobilizes me, it is too huge.

'He stopped.' The line is limp in his hands.

'Is he still on?'

Butch pulls lightly on his line. He looks like a man testing an electric fence. The line jerks from his grasp then stops pulling.

'When you gonna strike back. Butch?'

'Sh.'

'He'll get away, you're gonna lose him.'

'Shhhh.'

Butch begins to inch his line in, hand over hand. A channel of slowly parting rivulets approaches, as though a breeze as thin as a knifeblade were cutting through the water.

'He's comin this way.'

Butch holds the cord lightly between the thumb and forefinger of his left hand; it is tightly wrapped around the fist of his right. I can see down into the amber water. It looks like a dungeon of weeds, a lair, a place of death and silent screams. A torpedo shape glides slowly into the shadow of our boat.

'Butch, he's right there!'

'Where?'

'Under the boat. He's huge.'

'I think he's ready.'

'Then *do* it, for cryin out loud!'

Butch leans over the side of the boat frowning into the water. 'Where is he?'

'There!' I am pointing to the shadow cast by our boat. I know the luce is there, a darker shadow within a shadow. Butch peers, disbelievingly, at the same spot. He seems to be paralyzed.

'Butch, if you're gonna do it, do it!'

'I can't see him!'

'What does it matter if you can't see him? He's had half a lifetime to swallow –'

And Butch does it: standing on his seat, holding the line in both hands with no slack, like a flyweight throwing a two-fisted uppercut at an invisible heavyweight, he thrusts up at the sky.

Butch's plunge into Owl Cove is like cartoon horror: Woody Woodpecker hurled into a tree, vibrating like an arrow. Or Elmer Fudd, having stepped over the edge of the cliff, tiptoes back on thin air as though trying not to awaken the law of gravity.

Adolph takes off in an explosion of silt, the fishing line still wrapped several times around Butch's right fist. He has judged the moment but not the power of the luce's first run. He leans back into the run like a wagon driver reining in a wild team, then, in a slow inexorable curve, hands first, flies up and out of the boat. When he strikes the water, his body is still in the driver's whoa-back stance. He is engulfed without a sound.

It is several seconds before I notice that the boat is moving into the middle of the cove, several more when I realize that the handline is tied to the *Titanic*'s back seat. Butch would be thrashing halfway between Adolph and the *Titanic*. Scrambling through our equipment I cannot find the kitchen knife anywhere, only the club we thought was lost. I grab the cord and try to snap it with my bare hands – to this day I'm not sure why. I lodge my feet against the seat to which the cord is fastened and pull with the full force of my body. The cord bites into my hands, there is even a little blood, but the line will not break. We have reached the far end of the cove. The reeds are whipping by my head, I am still tugging hard on the line, and in the centre of my mind is a horrific refusal of thought: a thrashing shadow the shape of Butch that I cannot seem to acknowledge. The boat begins to rock, the milk can crashes into my shoulder, we head back into the middle of the cove, the boat drifts to a stop, the cove is stilled, there are writhing bodies of half a dozen whitefish at the bottom of the boat.

When I look into the water, the first thing I see is the green cord making a loop around the boat, the luce swimming slowly past the stern. Magnified perhaps by the water, he seems even larger than I had remembered, though smaller than I had dreamed. Again that grinning maw, the lower jaw extending well beyond the snout. His gills go in and out; his eyes are round, bright yellow, cold, staring.

In my hand, suddenly, is the knife. I wave it at the thing and yell a curse. A shudder seems to flow through the entire length of his body and he shoots under the boat and out the other side. Streaking limp through the water, his right arm extended like Superman in flight, head fallen to the side like Jesus', Butch follows the luce, as though propelled by an unseen force – the thing he is becoming, a thing you only dream of, moaning through the air in the darkest night....

And I'm in the water, the knife in my left hand, plunging toward Butch's body as it drives toward me. I seize his arm in my right hand and slash at the cord, at the arm, at the weeds, then a mighty acceleration brings the amber caverns zooming at my face – something snaps. We are floating up to the light, I can hear whitefish thumping wood, I am bobbing in the lily pads, I am holding on to Butch, starting to thrash, suddenly afraid. I spin around and the boat, like a trained steed, is right there, nudging my shoulder.

I must have pulled myself into the boat and then dragged Butch after me, because somehow I got him to shore. I remember him lying there, gasping for air. His body was twitching, perhaps a result of oxygen deprivation. His eyeballs were rolled up and back into his head so that only the whites showed, as though Butch were in full retreat from some horrible vision. He was making croaking sounds. I tried mouth-to-mouth on him, the stuff Miranda had taught us when she was a summer lifeguard, but it didn't seem to work. I remember tasting fish on his mouth and it revolted me.

I got up and ran to get my parents. The trail leading down to the reservation was blocked by a stalled half-ton. Under the hood, thank God, was Amos Whitehawk. I don't think he ever let an Edmond down.

'Yiz seen a ghost or somethin?'

I babbled something about Butch drowning by the shore. Wrench in hand, Amos took off down the trail with huge clumsy strides, and I strained to keep up with him. When we had waded through the grass to the place among the rushes where I'd left Butch, he was gone. The swampgrass and cattails were beaten down flat, so there was no doubt I had led Amos to the right spot. Amos scanned the place then followed the trail I had made dragging Butch's body from the cove. Suddenly he turned off this trail and trudged along a fainter one towards the old pier.

'Hey, kid!' Amos shouted.

Butch didn't seem to hear. We moved closer to the pier, leaping from hummock to hummock.

'Bullmer!' I shouted, and still he didn't look up. He seemed to be staring at something in the water. He looked very strange.

'What's he doin?' Amos asked suspiciously.

'I think he's looking for Adolph.'

Amos asked me what we had been doing here, and I explained how Butch had been dragged overboard and nearly drowned.

'Hey, kid! Bullmer!'

Butch appeared to be hypnotized by something. By this time we were perhaps a few yards away. His lips were moving as people's do when they are dreaming and no sound escapes.

Amos whispered, 'Dro, you say yiz got a boat here?'

'Over there,' I said, pointing, 'but why don't we just climb onto the –'

'He's gonna jump, that's why.'

As we ran for the boat I had only the slightest inkling of what Amos was up to. The plan seemed to be to come at Butch from the water rather than from the pier. This would discourage Butch from jumping in. But why would he want to jump in?

'You row,' Amos whispered, and once more I was someone's Injun Joe in a gambit I failed to understand.

'Go slow,' Amos said, his big bronze hand on my knee.

We glided out past Butch, did a wide curve, and came back toward him. I expected to see Adolph just beneath the surface of the water at the end of the pier, glaring up at Butch; this is how I used to imagine it. But there was no sign of Adolph. Only Butch, staring at what? His lost prize money? His own reflection? Very slowly, Amos mounted the pier. When he put his hand on Butch's shoulder, Butch whirled around like a trapped animal. I'd never seen him look so fierce.

'Bullmer!' I yelled. 'For chrissakes, it's me!'

Butch scrambled on hands and knees to the very brink of the pier and leapt. Amos caught him by the belt and Butch dangled in mid-air, all tensed, but with nowhere to spring, a somnambulist now captive in a world less real than the one he dreamed.

'Hey, Butch,' said Amos softly to the bundle suspended from his arm. 'Hey, Butch. Ya got no call goin down dere, huh?'

He carried a bewildered Butch by the belt, right off the pier and up through the tall grass to a dry spot by the rail. I tied the *Titanic* to the pier and followed him. Butch lay in the bright sunlight, eyes shut, opening and closing his mouth slowly. He appeared to be eating the air and swallowing it. He kept this up for several minutes. Finally, Amos turned to me and said, 'Go get yer dad. Tell im old Butch gone a little bit outa his mind, huh?'

Mother came too, and Hank, and Bubby Bothwell, who had been out in her back yard writing a postcard to Miranda when she heard the news. No one asked what I'd been doing with Butch Bullmer so early in the morning. Back we came in the car, Bubby in the middle between Hank and me in the back seat. Father stopped our car behind Amos's disabled pickup and we kids ran down to the marsh, Mother and Father close behind us. Hank and I arrived in a dead heat. Amos was talking to Butch in a low soft voice. Butch was on his hands and knees, crawling toward some aspens at the edge of the marsh. He still looked confused. His right arm, the one the cord had been fastened to, was bleeding. I may have slashed it with the kitchen knife.

Amos and my father knelt down beside Butch, prodded him, spoke to him. Mother came over and tried to get a better look at the cuts on his arm. Amos and Father began to confer in hushed voices, a sign to me that something weird was going on. I came closer and heard Dad say, 'I just can't believe it,' and then go silent. Amos put a big arm around Dad's shoulders and Dad wore a look I'd never seen on him, a haunted look, all his perceptions peering in upon something.

My mother also noticed this. 'Doug,' she said, 'what's wrong?'

At last Amos spoke. 'Butch, he's got some sorta bush fever, huh?' Amos's hand was still on Dad's shoulder in a comradely gesture that I can only begin to fathom.

'What's that?' Mum asked Dad, who was worried speechless.

'Somethin happen makes yiz sorta wild for a bit?' said Amos.

Butch, still on his knees, was grasping the trunk of a small tree in order to stand up.

'But his arm,' my mother said, 'it's –'

'No,' my father said, finally, his voice trembling. 'Gladys, we can tend to the arm once he comes around. It's best not to disturb them.'

By 'them,' presumably Father meant victims of Butch's bizarre condition, and he later muttered some things about the effects of shock which none of us understood. Nor, I think, were we meant to. This part of the episode was swept under the carpet.

Like a creature learning to walk, half-ape, half-man, Butch inched slowly up off the ground, leaning on the tree. The more weight he placed on his limbs, the more they trembled. From a certain angle he appeared to be attempting to push over the tree.

'Hank?' Bubby called from the pier.

Hank shushed her. The men went over to Butch, who was now most of the way up, his eyes glazed, face pale. They spoke, one after the other, very softly to Butch.

'Hank!' cried Bubby once more. 'Look!'

Hank left Mother's side and trotted down to the pier.

Butch began to whimper. He embraced the tree as though it were his mother's leg. Our mother went over to him, placing her hand on his back. Her hand went underneath the muddy T-shirt, up and down, and the whimpering grew softer.

'Holy cow!' called Hank. 'Look! Drew, c'mere!'

Mother motioned with her head that I should go, and I ran down to the marsh. Bubby and Hank were leaning over the end of the pier, the very spot from which Butch had attempted to leap into Owl Cove. I must have guessed what it was they were staring at.

What I hadn't expected was that it was dying. It lay on its side, bobbing at the surface, convulsing its tail, gills kneading, pectorals erect, the greatest fish we would ever behold, longer than a boy though not as big as a man. He trailed several fishing lines, one from a fin, and our own thick green handline, the hook buried deeply within his intestines. It had almost leached his old life away. Blood billowed from his gills. I turned to call back to the others. Mother supported Butch; they were walking like lovers or drunks, slowly, side by side.

The men came down to the pier. Amos hauled Adolph out of the water onto the pier and dragged him up on shore. Butch limped down, steadied by my mother.

Bubby clutched my arm and pointed to Adolph's enormous head. 'Look, Drew, it's like you used to say. He's grinning.'

At last Butch spoke. He looked away up at Amos, who still held the handline attached by our hook to Adolph's insides, and half snarled, half whispered, 'I don't care what you done with them whitefish, Amos. That there thousand bucks is mine.'

That's when I was struck with the full force of what we had done; Butch, and I as his Injun Joe, had stolen Amos's fish.

About ten years later, after a brief success as a fight promoter, Butch was murdered. His body was found in the ashes of a hotel fire, but they proved he had died before his body was burned. I spotted Amos at the funeral, wearing an awkward doleful expression.

Seeing that expression reminded me of how he and Father had looked on the way back from Owl Cove in Amos's truck: Butch and the luce in the box, Father and Amos in the cab, looking for all the world like Butch's parents wondering where they might have gone wrong. Mother had taken the rest of us back in our car and nobody said anything.

All seven of us had breakfast in our cottage, each preserving a separate silence, the event having been so bizarre, like a war or a death or a birth, that it absorbed our words. Hank ate hungrily. His silence was the sort one maintains after seeing a brilliantly played hockey game. Bubby's silence was reflective. She ate slowly and stared at the air in the kitchen, wearing a bemused and dreamlike hint of a smile. Mother's silence at the stove, from where she and I passed out pancakes and bacon, was distraught. I can see now that things were dawning on her about what happened to men in the bush, and to one man in particular. Amos was silent, as usual, but his face that day was tinged with resignation or sadness. My father chewed slowly, methodically. Each mouthful seemed a separate incident in the morning's events, which he was putting into proper sequence. Butch Bullmer was the only one who said anything, and that very softly, to the Bothwells' bulldog, Guinevere, which he fed beneath the kitchen table. When he looked at me, which was only once, it was a scowl aimed at shrugging off what must have been the accusations in my own face. When Mrs Bothwell arrived for coffee, I was meditating on the strangeness of all that had happened at the cove, wondering why it was that Mother hadn't really acted like my mother, and Father hadn't really acted like my father, and Butch hadn't acted like my friend, nor Amos like the impassive statue I had made of him.

Mrs Bothwell breezed into our ruminations, took one look at the luce, which lay in a big oval tub by the front door, its tail hanging out one end, its head out the other, and trilled, 'Splendid! Bubby, we'll bake it tomorrow night for the big celebration.'

We looked up at her, all still in search of our tongues. She was in city clothes and freshly made up. She wore a dopey smile, one stray incisor hooked over her lower lip, a bit of drool at the corner of her mouth. She had been drinking. This was a smile that always made me feel desolate because it hadn't the faintest connection to what I knew as happiness.

'For the big celebration,' she repeated. Her eyes were brilliant.

'What occasion, Queenie?'

She replied in meticulous, liquid syllables, 'Georgie and I have taken out our papers! Now we're *all* Canadians!'

FOUR

Mrs Bothwell had ordained a feast. She had cajoled my father into asking

Amos and Regina. Amos said they might come, but they didn't, and only Mrs Bothwell was surprised (*Well, at the very least, they could have sent us their regrets, it doesn't take half a minute …*). She cajoled me into inviting 'little Butch', but his status around our house was *persona non grata* since his treatment of Amos the previous day. So I lied to Mrs B and said that Butch was having an operation. She cajoled Bubby into helping her and a new maid in the kitchen, and began dropping things, forgetting other things, weeping, then spending a good deal of time in her bedroom changing outfits and looking in the mirror. Bubby took over in the kitchen while Mr Hook read and reread aloud to her an old recipe for luce. Between bouts of depression, Mrs Bothwell bullied Mr Bothwell into driving all the way back to Edmonton to pick up a case of gin, some claret, and things we weren't familiar with, such as mace, winter savoury, pickled oysters, caviar and anchovies.

My mother made dessert, several saskatoon pies, and sent them over with me. I did not want to run into Mr Hook all by myself, so I got Hank to help me.

The Bothwell kitchen was a sight. Bubby and their bartender were ramming a spear-length spit into Adolph's mouth and out his tail. Old Mr Hook, still in his nightgown, sat in his chair in the corner reading out phrases like, *These being thus mixt with a blade or two of mace …* The maid, a smiling Scottish woman named Totty, picked up a handful of sharp sticks, and Guinevere lay puffing and slobbering beneath the kitchen table. Bubby was bossing everyone. Mrs Bothwell strolled through the kitchen with that smile of hers that stopped at the eyes, immaculate in a flowered silk blouse and neckerchief, sandals and a brown skirt. More than once she told us that Miranda was still in France. Several times she murmured, 'Oh, if only Randy could be here with us … if only.' Bubby gave her mother a sarcastic look.

When we returned home our own cottage was quiet. Hank and I knew that Mother and Father had been talking gravely, late at night, about Life of course. Something terrible was floating between them, certain looks – my father's was blanched with futility, my mother's coloured with doubts. So Hank and I stayed outside, shuffled around in our bathing suits and didn't say much.

Apropos of nothing, Hank said, 'You should try out for football this year.' Perhaps this was his way of commenting on the flab and the slackness of my body. Hank was a perfectionist in all things.

'I don't wanna play football.'

'You'd like high school if you made the team.'

'Yeah, well, I wouldn't make the team, so let's all stop dreaming.'

'If Bubby Bothwell can play football with us at the beach, you can surely –'

'Bubby Bothwell.'

'What's eating you?'

'She's as bossy as her mother.'

'She is not.'

'Rich bitch. She thinks she's sitting on the Todge-ma Hall.'

Hank advised me that I could shut my yap at any time.

Were the old patterns reasserting themselves? My adventure was scarcely thirty-six hours old and he was treating me like a younger brother again. We maintained an all but visible antipathy all the way up to the rec hall. At our beach, if the kids weren't down at the water in the daytime, they were at the rec hall, where they could play ping-pong and buy pop, ice-cream cones, cigarettes and magazines. It was constructed entirely of varnished logs, its patio enclosed by a log fence. Slumped on one of the logs, holding forth to a knot of cottage kids about our age, was Freddy Bullmer. I hadn't seen him much in three years. He had lost some front teeth and his lips looked sucked-in to accommodate this loss; he was the same Freddy Bullmer, more like his father now, lots of swagger and bluff, but somehow brought down a peg or two.

'What's up, bub?' he said to Hank.

Hank would have nodded, smiled. They would be sizing each other up, though not in any antagonistic way. Hank was being approved of by an old warrior. As I remember it, Freddy turned to me, and I knew everyone was watching.

'Little Edmond! Where d'fuck's my handline, eh?' He brought around a slow-motion haymaker, clubbing me on the shoulder. I realized he was making a joke with me, so I grinned and probably blushed. 'Hey! Dis is d'kid saved my baby brother. Whadya know, eh? Who'd ever think?' He gave me a gummy smile, and like a true student of brother Hank's taciturnity, I shrugged. Up close to Freddy I could smell what might have been the residue of last night's boozing, or perhaps something he'd drunk that morning, and something else, a smell of decay. On Freddy's finger was the same heavy silver ring I had delivered to Miranda three summers ago. Like Freddy, it seemed battleworn, scuffed, but still brilliant. 'You like my ring? Eh?'

I was taken off guard and mumbled, 'I was just remembering ... like ...'

'You like my ring? Eh, messenger boy?' He took it from the ringfinger of his left hand, the knuckles swollen and callused, and tossed it to me. The ring in my hand felt heavy beyond its size. 'It's yours,' he said.

I don't remember how I replied. This was one of those joyful agonies in which one sputters something like *Golly, thanks,* and wishes one could die or fly away to hide the embarrassment and cherish the moment in privacy. Some of the kids were looking at me. They knew, of course, something of what happened, but it was Freddy Bullmer who put the seal of heroism on it. For the first time in my life, I became aware, turning the ring over in my hand, that I was being approved of, and I thought maybe I'd try out for the football team after all.

'What's happened to Randy?' Freddy asked my brother. 'She around?' Hank shook his head, muttering something I couldn't hear.

'I'll tell you, man, she really had me goin.' He nodded with a gravity that went beyond locker-room bravado, and made me see him in a sad light. 'She was one fuckofa woman.'

It seemed to me from the way he spoke, from the desolation in his eyes and his broken old man's mouth, that under the web woven by eros and moonlight on the night I played messenger boy for Freddy and Miranda, after all the accounts were in, Miranda had kissed like the spider and Freddy had danced like the moth.

The whole beach had been invited, or so it seemed. Along with the usual married couples we knew at Lake Windigo, Aubrey the dentist came with his *companion,* as my mother referred to him. Along with these two gentlemen came an attractive widow, perhaps in her fifties, named Mrs Fairfax. She brought a ukulele and sang songs like 'On Moonlight Bay' and 'Love's Old Sweet Song'. At my request, Mrs Bothwell sang 'Teddy Bears' Picnic', and Hank slugged me on the shoulder because he knew that I knew how much he hated the song. My mother, Mrs Fairfax and Mrs B cleared a space on the living-room floor and danced a Charleston. Aubrey's companion told a joke about a lion named Herbert who kept eating his owner's friends and relatives. Bubby and Mr Bothwell did a skit from a music hall show, and every time Mr Bothwell missed a line, Bubby would hit him with a spatula. Mr Hook sat by the enormous stone fireplace in an old smoking jacket and baggy grey trousers, turning the spit, and Adolph, grinning at what seemed his own joke, went slowly around and around in the flames. Butter and drippings sputtered in a huge pan beneath him. Everyone drank punch, even Hank and I had a glass or two, and Bubby and her mother became quite sozzled. My father sang 'In the Blue Canadian Rockies' because wasn't it written by a Canadian, and after all fitting for the occasion?

In one of the surviving photographs that found its way to our place is a big oak buffet set up with a bar. At one end is the punch bowl, hissing and foaming with rosé and chopped citrus. On the other end are silver pitchers of water and bowls of ice, silver siphons of soda water, regiments of bottled stout, ale, Canadian Pilsner, and a large tray of gin and whisky bottles. The bartender was a red-faced fellow who, we were told, had come all the way from Edmonton with Totty. He arrived shaking, got pretty tight, and stayed drunk all night long and never spilled a drop. With every thrum of Mrs Fairfax's ukulele he seemed to sway but his face remained very solemn with concentration. Mrs Bothwell gave my father a passionate kiss which left a red spot on his mouth, and said, 'Bertie, I think you're wonderful.' My father looked perplexed, since his name was Douglas. My mother taught Mrs Fairfax and Bubby how to do ballin' the jack, and sang in a most unladylike fashion. Aubrey's companion leaned over to her and said, 'You naughty thing, you.' Aubrey helped Totty pass out *hors d'oeuvres*, which were swallowed up before they reached halfway into the living-room. Hank tried some of Aubrey's caviar on a cracker and spat it into the fire. 'I'm wounded!' Aubrey boomed. 'I'm wounded!'

Finally it was time for Adolph to be served and out came a cartful of steaming dishes with Adolph on a plank in the middle. Here is the ancient recipe read to Bubby by Mr Hook, complete with lapses in spelling and punctuation. (I got it from Bubby and her husband this morning.)

First open your Pike at the gills, and if need be, cut also a little slit towards the belly; out of these, take his guts, and keep his liver, which you are to shred very small with Time, Sweet-Marjoram, and a little Winter-savoury; to these put some pickled Oysters, and some Anchovies, two or three, both of these last whole (for the Anchovies will melt, and the Oyster should not) to these you must adde also a pound of sweet butter, which you are to mix with the herbs that are shred, and let them all be well salted (if the Pike be more than a yard long, then you may put into these herbs more than a pound, or if he be less, then less Butter will suffice:) these being thus mixt with a blade or two of Mace, must be put into the Pikes belly, and then his belly so sowed up, as to keep all the Butter in his belly if it is possible, if not, then as much of it as you possibly can, but take not off the scales; then you are to thrust the spit through his mouth, out at his tail. And then take four or five or six split sticks, or very thin lathes, and a convenient quantity of Tape or filleting, these lathes are to be tyed round about the Pikes body from his head to his tail, and the Tape tyed somewhat thick to prevent his breaking or falling off from the spit; let him be roasted very leasurely and often basted with Claret wine, and Anchovyes, and butter mixt together, and also with what moisture falls from him into the pan: when you have rosted him sufficiently you are to hold under him, (when you unwind or cut the Tape that ties him) such a dish as you purpose to eat him out of; and let him fall into it with the sauce that is roasted in his belly, and by this means the Pike will be kept unbroken and compleat: then, to the sawce which was within, and also that sawce in the pan, you are to add a fit quantity of the best Butter, and to squeeze the juyce of three or four Oranges: Lastly, you may either put into the Pike, with Oysters, two cloves of Garlick, and take it whole out, when the Pike is cut off the spit, or, to give the sawce a hogo, let the dish (into which you let the Pike fall) be rubbed with it: the using or not using of this Garlick is left to your descretion.

I might have been the only one there who didn't enjoy eating Adolph. I kept wondering about the many creatures he, in turn, had eaten. Most guests, however, had second and third helpings and congratulated Mrs Bothwell profusely. Since she'd had nothing to do with the cooking, she assumed she was being congratulated on having become a Canadian citizen, and said things like, 'Well, we studied away, you know, but we only had to answer a few questions, and in fact everybody was perfectly charming to us.'

When Adolph had been gobbled down to the last bone and his muddy aftertaste laid to rest with goblets of wine, and women were groaning and men lighting cigars or belching by the fireplace, Mr Bothwell climbed on top of an oak sideboard and tinkled his spoon on a champagne glass. He reached down for Bubby's hand and hauled her up on the table, clasped her around the waist, and said, 'I wish to congwatuate my daughter Wobin on a smashing performance in the kitchen. What do you all say? Shall we waise our gwasses?' People roared approval, clinked their glasses, and to everyone's delight, Aubrey's friend raised his spectacles. 'And my beautiful wife for keeping us all up to the mark,' he cried, extending his hand to Mrs Bothwell, who now smiled as though she really was happy and knew all along that life was sweet. She tottered a bit to the applause around her. 'And I'd wike to extend a special vote of thanks to young Dwew Edmond over there stuffing his face with pie, whom we all know as Henwy's wittle bwother.' Everybody cheered and Hank clapped me soundly on the back. 'This lad helped to beard the dwagon in his lair and haul him home to us. He is our own wittle Saint George.' Again, clapping, cheering, and a round of toasts. Mr Bothwell raised his hand. 'But Dwew,' he said, addressing me in a mildly admonitory tone, 'I think your choice of using Butch Bullmer as bait was a vewy bad show indeed.' This brought the house down, and Mr Bothwell down, and Bubby, who gave me a squeeze and a little peck on the cheek. Then Mrs Bothwell came over, grabbed me, and planted a great wet smacker right on my mouth that left me gasping.

She was holding a book and waving it in the air for silence. 'In honour of little Henry here' (Bubby corrected her but she didn't hear), 'I'm going to read a little something.' Her words came very slowly, measured, as though our minds worked at the speed of teddy bear minds. 'It's a little poem and it has for its setting this great northern land of ours,' she intoned, slurring her consonants and beckoning with unfurled arm to her lake-view window, which faced south. 'This is our way of saying' ... she paused, stricken, yet still smiling dreamily, tears rolling down her cheeks ... 'of saying how dearly we love our Canada.' Her book slipped from her fingers and I picked it up for her. 'Thank you, Henry,' she said, and stood by the fire, clearing her throat.

Everyone was silent. There was a distant roll of thunder. The last thing I remember seeing before she began was my father, his arm around my mother, squinting, as was his habit, at the top of a champagne bottle and lining it up with something else, perhaps the cuckoo clock on the shelf over the fireplace. They were swaying together, Mother and Father, like lovers, when Mrs Bothwell's nursery voice began to trill over the sound of the first raindrops on the window-panes.

> There are strange things done in the midnight sun
>> By the men who moil for gold:
> The Arctic trails have their secret tales
>> That would make your blood run cold;
> The northern lights have seen queer sights,
>> But the queerest they ever did see
> Was that night on the marge of Lake Lebarge
>> I cremated Sam McGee.

Mrs Fairfax was mouthing the words along with Mrs B, and looking fondly at Aubrey's companion, who was also mouthing the words (someone said Aubrey's friend was actually Mrs Fairfax's son). Hank and Bubby held hands, which made me wonder about the power in the ring I was wearing. Was it good luck or bad? Many others were looking very solemn. I could hear the Bothwells' cuckoo clock ticking and Totty walking around in the kitchen.

> Now Sam McGee was from Tennessee, where the
>   Cotton blooms and blows.
> Why he left his home in the south to roam round
>   the Pole God only knows.
> He was always cold, but the land of gold seemed
>   to hold him like a spell;
> Though he'd often say in his homely way that
>   He'd 'sooner live in hell'.

Mrs Bothwell was gathering her breath for the third stanza when Mr Hook kicked over a chair and hobbled through the crowd and past his daughter. 'By your leave, mum, I'll pay me respects to the old D.V.' His exit was both grumpy and histrionic and his face twisted so that you could see his teeth. He looked tormented, the way he had looked at my window in the moonlight. 'Good night, Daddy,' said Mrs Bothwell, and I'd like to think that there was more lightning and a nice dramatic clap of thunder.

> On a Christmas Day we were mushing our way
>   Over the Dawson Trail.
> Talk of your cold! through the parka's fold ...

My father had stopped swaying. He looked perplexed, and I thought perhaps he was concerned for old Mr Hook's wellbeing. Mother gave him a motherly look of concern.

> He turned to me, and, 'Cap,' says he, 'I'll cash
>   in this trip, I guess;
> And if I do, I'm asking that you won't refuse my
>   last request.'

My father's face went all stony and he wouldn't return my mother's glance. I heard a crick on the floor behind me and saw Hank and Bubby stealing out the back door. At first I assumed that they were checking to see that Mr Hook was all right. Then I surmised, by the stealth of their retreat, that they were going out to smooch, as we called it back then. They would find someone's car, tear each other's clothes off, and rut like animals. A wave of disgust went through me. I was the hero, after all, the wearer of the silver ring. I was the one who got the girl, and if I got her, I wouldn't degrade her by bouncing around with her in someone's back seat.

> There wasn't a breath in that land of death, and
> I hurried, horror driven,
> With a corpse half-hid that I couldn't get rid ...

Mrs Bothwell read on, sometimes so slowly that one wasn't sure if she would be able to finish the line, sometimes in a more animated voice appropriate for children. There was a flash outside and a great roll of thunder. A clear line of saliva issued from the corner of her mouth which seemed to have gone slack from drinking, and a half-smile remained frozen to her face as though she were somewhere else and wasn't sure where.

> ... on I went, though the dogs were spent and
> the grub was getting low;
> The trail was bad, and I felt half mad, but I swore
> I would not give in;
> And I'd often sing to the hateful thing, and it
> hearkened with a grin.

The grin of the corpse struck me as a fine touch. It reminded me not only of how Mr Hook would appear under similar circumstances, but oddly of Freddy Bullmer with his toothless old man's grin. Indeed, it reminded me of Butch and all the Bullmers, and even the grisly head of Adolph, which lay, still grinning, on a greasy plank just behind me. Mrs Bothwell's smile also came into the picture, a fact that at the time I ascribed to the effects of the punch. And Amos's. And Father's way of seeming to smile, wincingly, when he held his pipe in his teeth. How would he look when *he* was dead....

Some planks I tore from the cabin floor, and I lit
  the boiler fire;
Some coal I found that was lying around, and I
  heaped the fuel higher:
The flames just soared, and the furnace roared –
  Such a blaze you seldom see;
And I burrowed a hole in the glowing coal, and I
  stuffed in Sam McGee.
Then I made a hike, for I didn't like to hear him
  sizzle so ...

There was a flash of lightning, and something caught my eye. My father. He was hunched over, touching his temples as though in the grip of a bad headache, and my mother, looking very upset, led him by the arm through the crowd. I didn't run after them. I sensed that they would have wanted me to stay put.

It was icy cold, but the hot sweat rolled down my
  cheeks, and I don't know why;
And the greasy smoke in an inky cloak went
  streaking down the sky.

And then something more ominous than adolescence or thunder boomed in the cavity of my chest, an answer from Hell, palpable as a corpse. It struck me so hard, a straggle of forgotten words from Butch's mouth – *Walmsley. And he's dead. Fresh meat, for God's sake* – that I stopped breathing.

I was sick with dread, but I bravely said: 'I'll
  just take a peep inside.
I guess he's cooked, and it's time I looked,' ...
  then the door I opened wide.

Call it what you will, a memory gone berserk in the room, an imprisoned spirit. His name was nothing to me. Walmsley. He'd been a pilot once, and he liked to work among the native people in the North. And he died after a plane crash, and once dead, I now knew, had saved the lives of two more men. And one of them, my father, he had driven from the room in a plangent roll of thunder from the past. Bones from the past began to rattle and reassemble in my mind. I could now begin to understand that look exchanged by Amos and my father once Butch had been plucked from the pier: in his half-drowned state, it was as if he'd wanted to join the thing in the water, soar away with it: reminding them – is that it? – of something they both knew from long before. *Windigo,* I thought, and only once, afraid I might invoke it: the hunger that curls back the lips of dogs and bears and men, the thing that gets in you because you've been hungry for too long, the last thing Mrs Bothwell's brother must have seen coming at him with horrible jaws from the bottom of the Atlantic Ocean. I remember standing defenceless somewhere outside the circle of revellers, bombarded by visions of werewolf hunger: the look on Mr Hook's face, his plea to all the pretty children. *Untwist me,* he seemed to say. *I'm not really a monster.* The look of Freddy Bullmer yearning for a perfect love on the non-squalid side of the tracks, that desperation in his bony face; the look of Butch Bullmer when he said, *That there thousand bucks is mine;* the wincing, squinting look of my father lining up his sights, plumb-line or .22 rifle, taking deadly aim – and did he fire a shot to end the man's agony, little thinking this was a prelude, a necessary killing before that last supper in the far North? I would never know, and by this time my horror had run away with me. What I *did* know was already too much, though the visions kept coming. The way Hank's jutting teeth had looked that night we played the spy game and he murdered Bubby, and how he came for me, how he had played his assassin's role too convincingly, as if remembering something in the blood ... how I danced that night on the raft so exultantly over the convulsing body of my first jackfish, how I kept braining it till it stopped flopping around....

I found myself outside in the rain, looking for no one, stumbling away from people and their egregious hunger, and heard first Bubby, then Hank, calling for Mr Hook. Perhaps, after all, they had gone out to see if the old man was all right. He was not to be found in the old D.V., and apparently wasn't in his little summerhouse either. 'Granddad!' cried Bubby, and 'Hey, Mr Hook!' cried Hank, and some worried sounds I couldn't make out as I leaned against a tree, soaking up the rain.

Was *that* the night when Regina was conceived? What could be more fitting? A passion, she referred to herself, a passion that could not be prevented. Unplanned parenthood: Mother holding Father back from a plunge into his own black hole in the universe, and succeeding not only in that, but in getting pregnant, and afterward naming it Regina after Amos's wife, because up there Regina was all Amos and Father could think of when there was nothing else to hope for, while outside in the woods beyond the cottage Bubby cried into the storm, 'Granddad! Granddad, where *are* you?'

* * *

It's past 2 a.m. I'm writing this in the room Father called his study and Mother called her sewing room. A few hours ago, for old time's sake, I read the girls 'The Cremation of Sam McGee'.

They're both asleep now. So is Rachel, on the couch in the front room. I get the bedroom where Regina's life began. I'm glad Rachel is here, even in a provisional role, if that's what it is.

A while ago I heard one of the girls calling out. I felt my way through the dark to their room – my old room. I fumbled and shuffled up to the door and listened. From Jessica's side came a rattling of phlegm. She's fighting a cold, the one she always seems to get the week school starts. From Sally's side, whispered sobs from some nightmare. I eased the door open. The room smelled sweetly of my daughters in slumber and the musty smell I remember from when I slept there, the smell they will remember if ever they return. I tiptoed through the door into the room and Sally screamed.

'Shhh! It's me. Your dad, remember?' I picked her up and sat on the bed, rocking her slowly on my knees.

'You scared me,' she sobbed.

'Who did you think I was, the Big Bad Wolf?'

'I thought you were Sam McGee.'

Apparently her sadistic sister had told her that every year around this time Sam McGee would *come back from the furnace*. I could see Jessica face down in her bed, hear her congested breathing. Having told her tale, she had abandoned Sally to the demons of night.

'And what does Sam do?'

Sally answered in a grumpy, sleepy voice, 'He eats people.'

I nearly dropped her on the floor.

Assuming, perhaps, that I didn't believe her, she looked up at me. 'He was at the window.'

'How do you know he was at the window?'

'Jessica said.'

I swallowed down my shock and waited till my breath returned. 'For an older sister Jessica sure is dumb.'

'Yeah, she sure is dumb.'

'Anyone knows that Sam McGee only comes in wintertime. And then all he does is light the fire and sit on the stove.'

'Does he ever burn his bum?'

I had to stifle a laugh, and by the way my diaphragm was shaking, Sally knew that she'd got off a good one. Soon she was yawning, so I lifted her into bed. After a minute or so, she was breathing her way back to sleep.

When I tiptoed past the couch in the front room, Rachel jerked awake. I told her about Sally's nightmare. She blamed me, said I should have toned down my Boris Karloff number when I read the poem. 'Sally's not ready for scary stories. She's only five.'

'Most of their stories are scary. "The Three Little Pigs", "Little Red Riding Hood".'

'Those are your stories. And you *make* them scary, you get carried away. It never occurs to you to make the wolf funny.'

'The wolf at the door is never funny,' I said. I was trying to joke around.

'Oy! I ask him not to terrorize our youngest, I get pronouncements about life. You know what I think? I think this memoir you're writing is getting to you. I really do.'

'Rachel, you're acting like a she-bear, you're overprotective.'

'You should talk. You're beginning to see disaster and peril in everything. Bubby's husband takes the girls for a spin in the boat, you think automatically they're going to drown. She told me that. A black van's cruising up and down the road by the tracks, you follow it and take down the licence number. Lately you've been manufacturing fear and mistrust.'

'*You* should talk. What about this new life you've been leading?'

'New life? You mean like swinging singles and stuff like that?'

'Oh, never mind.' I shrugged.

'I've been *thinking things over.*'

'Do you intend to sleep on the couch for the next thirty years or what?'

'I'll sleep in our bed when I can feel right about it.'

'What if you never feel right about it?'

'Why do you assume I'll never feel right about it? Look, I *told* you already, I'm working on it,' she said, throwing up her hands in the dark.

'You've got to have some faith, Drew. That's your biggest problem, y'know?'

I am back in the study/sewing room, what I now call my stewing room, doing the graveyard shift, guarding my sleeping gals. In search of a book I thought I'd put there, in the pocket of my jacket I found a small piece of paper, part of an envelope. Scrawled in my hand are the words, *Butch Bullmer, 1953*. I needed a gesture of release, I needed to let go of this thing, so I crept into the kitchen, and from a height of several feet, dropped the scrap of paper into the stove and watched it flare up at me in a small tongue of flame. From Rachel's point of view it would have looked like a piece of paper burning in the coals. But to me it seemed like someone down in the old D.V. was saying goodbye.

☆ This Shot

The photographer had assembled his equipment in a neat pile on the front veranda. He straightened his jacket, touched the brim of his boater, swallowed the last residue of his peppermint, and knocked. A young lady opened the door. She was tall, striking, about eighteen. She leaned out from the door frame looking down on him and then past him.

'Is that your tin Lizzie?' she said.

'Yes,' he said.

His Model T was parked on the street in front of the house. It had *A. J. Twill Photographer* in gold letters on the door. He had bought the car in 1923 from his uncle, and it still looked brand new.

The young lady reversed her grip on the door frame and swung backwards into the house. She yelled, 'Mah-ther?'

Mr Twill thanked her and smiled, for after all wasn't it a beautiful morning, and didn't he have the most wonderful business in all of Saskatoon?

'You may as well come in,' she said, neither surly nor encouraging. 'My mum takes half her lifetime to get dressed in the morning.'

When Mr Twill (his friends called him Arthur) had brought his equipment into the front hall, the young lady was gone. He took off his boater, popped another peppermint into his mouth, and waited there in the dim light. Presently he spied another young lady backing her way out of the kitchen. She was dragging her little brother by the arms. She lugged him over to Mr Twill and planted him there before him. And my, what a winsome creature she was.

'Hi,' she said. 'I'm Jennie and this is Burt.'

'Arthur Twill,' he tried to say, but his peppermint popped out of his mouth and bounced along the hardwood floor. Jennie's little brother seemed to think that this was hilarious, and he let fly with a laugh that seemed, to Mr Twill, excessively loud.

'Give me your hanky, Burt,' said his sister.

'Blewaugh,' said Burt, but after a small scene, he gave Jennie his hanky, which was probably dirty anyway. Jennie stooped down, plucked the peppermint off the floor, and told little Burt just to settle down. At least one of the (he pulled a work order from his pants pocket and glanced at the name) Mullens, yes, at least one of the Mullens had good manners.

The older sister reappeared with a sweater thrown over her shoulders. She gave young Jennie a look of appraisal and made a snuffling sound with her nose that sounded to Arthur like disapproval. Then the older sister looked up at the ceiling, baring her throat almost brazenly to the feeble light from the lamp in the hallway, and again yelled, 'Mah-ther!'

'This is Caddy,' young Jennie said, and she maintained a grip on little Burt's shoulders while Burt stared down at the photographer's shoes.

'Who said you could wear my scarf?' said Caddy.

'Burt,' said Jennie, 'you go get Dad. He's in the basement. And come right back, okay? Promise?'

Burt shook his head.

'And if you let that dog in here again, I will have your head. Do you hear me?'

Again little Burt shook his head. Jennie sighed for Mr Twill's benefit and released the boy.

'Besides,' Caddy purred, 'it doesn't go with that blouse.'

Jennie stuck out her tongue in Caddy's direction, crossed her arms, and leaned beside a large Canada goose, one of two mounted on the newel posts like soldiers at the foot of the stairway. Neither of the sisters spoke. Caddy sat on the stairs and began to arrange her skirt with such care that Mr Twill seemed to have been forgotten.

'Well, well,' he said, 'it certainly is a fine day for taking pictures.'

'I think we should take them all in the morgue,' said Caddy.

'The morgue?' said Arthur Twill.

'She means the parlour,' said Jennie. 'She thinks dead animals are just swell.'

'Dead animals in your parlour?' said the photographer. 'May I see?' But before Mr Twill could follow Caddy out of the front hall, her mother came to the head of the stairs.

'You must be the photographer,' she cried. 'Mercy me, why didn't anyone call me?'

'Your daughter was about to show me some –'

'Not in the morgue. Please, Caddy,' said Florence Mullen, 'and that's final.' She turned to Jennie with a fearful little smile. 'Where do you suppose your father has gotten to?'

'In the basement banging on things.'

'And where is Burt? Jennie?'

'Fetching Dad.'

As if on cue, Burt banged through the door from the kitchen. 'Dad says he never knew nothin about no phodo graphy today.'

'Never knew *anything*,' said Jennie.

'Jennie, would you kindly inform your father he is wanted up here?' said Mrs Mullen. 'I'm afraid Mr Twill will think badly of us. Lord help us, he might think we're this poorly organized all the time.'

'Certainly not,' said Mr Twill with a winning smile. 'Why, young Jennie was just intro intro introd –'

A large black dog had waddled into the hall, and he came straight for Mr Twill. He stuck his nose into Mr Twill's crotch, did some snuffling thereabouts, and licked him on the thigh. It all happened so fast poor Mr Twill had scarcely any time to defend himself or his equipment. 'Oh dear,' he said dropping his hat on the floor. Now the animal was licking the leather on his camera and little Burt started laughing again.

Jennie appeared at the door. 'Teck!' she cried, and the big dog slunk to her side. She grabbed the dog by the scruff of his neck and hustled him out the door. Fortunately there was no damage done.

'Teck? My, that's an unusual name for a dog,' said Mr Twill.

'He got his name from the school,' said little Burt.

'From the school?' said Mr Twill.

'Yeah,' said Burt. 'Teck.'

'The technical school down the bridge,' said Caddy. 'The Tech?'

'Teck,' said little Burt. 'Like Teck? Dontcha get it?'

'I get it,' said Mr Twill.

By and by Mr Mullen sauntered in. He seemed a bit lost at first, and stopped at the door to clean his spectacles. He smiled at Mr Twill and shook his hand. 'It's nice to meet a fellow Arthur,' Mr Mullen said. 'We're a small select fraternity here in Saskatoon.'

Mr Twill heartily agreed. He complimented Mr Mullen on his many fine hides and trophy heads. 'I do my hunting with this,' he said, pointing to his camera.

'At least you bring em back alive,' said Mr Mullen, and the men chuckled.

'Artie,' said Mrs Mullen, 'I hope you do not intend on having your picture taken in that old cardigan.'

'What?'

'Your cardigan. Your *cardigan.*'

'What's wrong with my cardigan?' said Mr Mullen.

'What's wrong with it? Just look at it. There's holes in the elbows and you've lost a button there. People will think I can't even sew.'

'Ethel, I don't intend to pose for no picture with my elbows showing.'

'Artie,' said Mrs Mullen, 'I *really wish* you would change out of that sweater.'

'Know what?' said Burt. He was standing so close to Mr Twill he had to look straight up. 'I know somethin, I know a pome?'

'That's very nice, Burt,' said Mr Twill.

'Wanna hear? It's got a Arthur in it.'

'All right,' said Mr Twill, 'let's hear your poem.'

'Burt,' said Jennie, pointing her finger at him.

'This is just a pome I learnt at school,' he said. In a very loud voice he began to recite. 'Gene Gene made a machine, Joe Joe made it go, Art Art blew a fart and blew the bloody thing apart. Hahahahahahaha! Hahahahaha!'

Squealing like a pig, little Burt was led by his ear from the living room. 'Jennie, you're hurting him,' said Caddy. She was smiling for the first time since Mr Twill's arrival.

At last Mr Twill had set up his equipment, Mrs Mullen had prevailed upon her husband to change his clothes, and little Burt was allowed to return to the living room. Jennie held him in a firm grip. He shoved out his lower lip like a second tongue and stared at the floor. By now Jennie was flushed from her exertions with the dog and with little Burt and all.

'I think we'll sit here,' said Mrs Mullen. She acted as though she were hosting a grand party. 'Burt? Jennie? Caddy? Where's Caddy? Arthur?' she called to her husband, who was still out of the room. 'You bring that girl downstairs, do you hear?'

At last the five Mullens assembled in the living room by the fireplace beneath the head of what had been a very large moose. Mr Mullen thought it might be a good idea to include the moose in the pictures, but his wife thought otherwise. So the three young people sat on the sofa with little Burt flanked by his sisters, and Mr and Mrs Mullen stood behind them. On the first take, little Burt was startled by the flash of the powder.

'I wisht I could have one of them things,' he said to his father.

'One of *those* things,' said Jennie.

'What does that boy want?' said Mr Mullen to Caddy.

'He wants a flash,' said Caddy.

'A what?'

'He said he wants a *flash,*' Caddy said again.

'Well, why doesn't he just say so?' said Mr Mullen.

Young Burt was so fascinated with the flash powder that he behaved himself and didn't sulk for the rest of the session. Mr and Mrs Mullen both smiled brightly, and Jennie of course, but nothing in the world, not even Mr Twill's little dicky bird, would make Caddy smile. Such a shame it was, and such a pretty face!

When it was all over, young Jennie saw Mr Twill to the door. She walked him out to his car and helped him put his equipment in the rumble seat. He wanted to express his appreciation to her for being so helpful, but he couldn't think of anything to say. Just as he was about to drive off, she called to him that he had forgotten his sample album. And when he had taken the album from her, placed it on the seat and taken the wheel again, she called once more because he had also forgotten his boater. She handed him the hat with a lovely smile.

'Why don't you wear your hat in the car?' she asked him, for he had placed the boater on top of the album.

'Oh,' he said to Jennie. 'Sometimes I do and sometimes I don't.'

I was born fifteen years after this session. The above scene is of course partly my own invention, but as they say in the news business, I have some hard facts. I am Jennie's son and the nephew of Caddy and little Burt. I have the only photo that survived the above session. Its date is May 2, 1925. This shot is the only one I have ever found of my mother's family all together. The five Mullens of Saskatoon.

Aunt Caddy claims to remember the session in all of its salient details. For one thing, she insists that Mr Twill became so infatuated with my mother, then only fifteen, that he urged her to come down to his studio so that he could shoot her alone. Apparently she turned down these and other offers. My mother claims not to remember this subplot.

And no, Mr Twill did not become my father. According to the Saskatoon *Henderson's Directory,* Mr Twill left town only two years later, in 1927. It seems he succeeded in doing what the Mullens have always tried to do: disappear. Almost all of the family photos and memorabilia went up in the flames of my grandmother's stove some time in the late 1940s.

My Uncle Burt remembers the above session in much less detail. When I asked him why he looked so chipper, he says, 'Beats me.' Was it his discovery of the wonders of flash powder, as Caddy always claims? 'No,' says Burt, as though this theory is too absurd for serious consideration.

My mother scarcely remembers anything about the picture. She hardly ever talks about those early years. She fields questions about her family from a certain distance; a careful reserve creeps into her voice, as though life among the Mullens was not the stuff of blissful memories. Her father was a bad provider and deaf to all conversation that was not about hunting and fishing. Her mother was too neurotic for motherhood or marriage. Her sister Caddy had what people in those days called a reputation. Her brother Burt was too young to be a kindred spirit.

The Mullens could rise to certain occasions and put on a cheerful united front, like throwing a party or sitting for photographs. But before and after the shot, where life is really lived, they endured family life like a judgement upon them.

Aunt Caddy is the only one in her family to have preserved any photos, and I've inherited most of them. Five or six of these are of young Caddy with Teck or with other beloved pets. The rest were taken when she was between the ages of about twenty-five and forty-five. Unlike Florence, her mother, whose smile was her umbrella, her rod and her staff, Caddy would sooner die than smile for a photograph. And so in all of them she stares right at the camera with candour and world weariness, sometimes frowning but more often with a look of indulgent boredom as though, for her, the next moment is going to be a lot more interesting than this one. The older she gets in these shots, the more she comes to resemble the actress Joan Crawford.

More than once I mentioned this resemblance to Uncle Burt, and he used to frown with contempt at the very suggestion. Caddy's odyssey to Hollywood was always a sore point with the family.

I used to visit Uncle Burt in a care home out in the Saskatoon suburbs. In his final years he was suffering from Alzheimer's. At first he could shuffle all the way to the river with me. Sometimes we would walk along the path above the riverbank and gaze at the pelicans and Canada geese that gather there in the summer. He grew up by this river and hunted geese like these with his father in the thirties and forties. I used to imagine walking with him all the way upstream, six or seven miles along the South Saskatchewan, and right into town. We would march up to the house where my mother, Aunt Caddy and Burt grew up. This house is only two blocks from the river. The street is lined with elm trees so big the branches reach out over the roadway and meet in the middle. The only dangers I ever heard of in that neighbourhood were the Steinbrecker boys and their unruly dogs, and since the boys were rebels at heart, my Aunt Caddy was their friend as often as their enemy.

The house is still there, a bulky two-storey wood frame with a big front veranda. This veranda is where, as teenagers, the two sisters would greet the boys who dropped in on them. There were many of these, even my mother will admit. At the front door the young men would take off their caps (later, fedoras and boaters) and spin them like horseshoes onto the antlers that sprouted from the walls of the front hall and the living room. Others would aim for the big Canada geese that were mounted on the newel posts at the foot of the staircase. If my mother ever had any use for the past she might write a memoir of this lively time. And if she did, the front cover might feature a stuffed goose wearing a cloth cap.

The piano stood beneath a huge moosehead in the living room. I wonder if it looked out of place there, surrounded by all the evidence of the hunt: the game birds, the bear hide and the deer and elk peering glassy-eyed from their mountings. This is where the young people would gather to sing with Florence Mullen at the keyboard. Caddy's favourite was 'I'll Take You Home Again, Kathleen', because that was her real name. My mother and Caddy learned to Charleston in that same living room, and when things really got going, the dancers would spill out into the hall and dance around the kitchen. My mother preferred the dancing to anything else in those days, and her father always said her brains were in her feet.

When I was a little boy, our family inherited Florence's piano, a modest upright little Everett with a crazed finish. I am sorry to report that no one in our house ever did that piano much justice.

My mother's old house is now dwarfed by highrise apartments and office buildings on the fringe of downtown Saskatoon. It looks besieged. Any day now the house could fall to the wrecker's ball. This bothers me. Sometimes I imagine going inside with no one around. I would spend my time snooping for clues. Perhaps I would find some animal hair, or a pheasant's tailfeather in the basement, or the crushed skeleton of a chinchilla in the back yard. Perhaps I would hear my mother's long-dead mother playing the piano and singing, 'I'll take you home again, Kathleen, across the ocean wild and wide'.

When I was a boy our family visited Saskatoon and the Mullen house several times. I have a memory of feeble light from the street, darkish oak trim in the rooms downstairs, and everywhere the threadbare signs of a former gentility that must have been their style in long-ago Ontario. I remember Granddad Mullen's big high hunting boots next to Granny Mullen's delicate suede snowboots. Bert's deflated football made of pigskin. And guns: shotguns, hunting rifles with walnut stocks, the same brown as the oak door frames. Old camping gear stowed here and there, fishing rods, blackened pots, binoculars. All of this piled on sleeping bags and canvas, as though the men are always just back from a camping trip or just about to leave.

My mother remembers the house in terms of the critters they kept. To hear her and Aunt Caddy tell it, they had more animals than Noah's ark. Just a preliminary list would include Teck, their Labrador, and the exotic fowl and pedigreed hens Grandfather Mullen would buy from time to time to win ribbons with or perhaps make a fortune. These Artie lodged in the garage. My mother was sickly as a child, and for years they kept a Jersey cow tethered in the back yard. I used to ask why. More than once I was told it was because, as a child, my mother needed the cream. But surely they could have had their cream delivered by the milkman like anyone else in Saskatoon. Once my mother turned to me and said, 'A cow in our *back yard*? Whatever for?'

But Caddy remembers the cow, and Mum's uncertain health is a part of family lore that she never denies. She must have had good powers of recuperation, because according to all sources, she grappled with and defeated the fatal flu of 1918, and a year or two later, polio. More than once I have asked her how her own mother coped with all these maladies. And more than once she has told me that she didn't really have a mother. 'I had to be my own mother,' she says.

Her mother, my Granny Mullen, née Florence Sloan, was born into money. She was sent off to a finishing school where she studied piano, needlepoint, elocution and other such ladylike skills, and where she was to remain until she was of marriageable age. Under no circumstances was she to work. At anything. *No girlie ever needed money,* her father told her. In this picture of the five Mullens she smiles bravely.

Her husband smiles mischievously. My hunting grandfather. Like

Granny Mullen, he was Ontario Irish, a lapsed Catholic and reluctant Protestant. Artie Mullen loved dogs, boats, guns, fishing gear, anything that kept him in or near the water. Artie and Florence met on a beach near Lindsay, Ontario, where she was making her social debut. The first time he saw her, he was standing barelegged in the water doing repairs on a canoe. She stood on the wharf nearby. In the course of their conversation she informed him that she was giving a piano recital at the Literary that night. As the story is told, it was the first time Artie Mullen had ever come willingly out of the water. He put on his best suit and attended her recital, and promptly fell in love.

Florence's father refused to attend the wedding. Florence's dowry was her piano and clothes. Artie brought his tools, his guns, his fishing rods and boat, his skinning knives and meat saws. Everything but the smokehouse, they used to say. For some reason they decided to go west. Some say Artie had notions of being a gentleman farmer, some say he wanted to escape the long and disapproving shadow of Florence's father, and some say Artie simply wanted to go where the hunting and fishing were better. No one seems to know where Florence stood in all of this, but I can guess.

In spite of her father's angry dismissal of her, in spite of the financial embarrassment she had to endure in Saskatchewan, she remained devoted to her father long after he died. The farther away in space and time, the more she revered him. When she was an old woman and I was her little confidant, she told me *I never should have left him.*

According to Caddy, her mother wept a long stream the night of her wedding and wept rivers all through the honeymoon because she missed her father so. Both daughters agree that Florence hated intimacy of any kind, and rarely did a sign of tenderness pass between Florence and Artie. She should never have married, Caddy would say. She should have gone with her piano onto the concert stage. My mother claims to remember none of this, but several times I have caught her wondering out loud how her parents ever managed to have three children.

No girlie ever needed money, her father would repeat, but the old patriarch was probably not thinking of Artie Mullen. Nor, I suspect, was he thinking very clearly about his own daughter. To Florence, keeping track of domestic accounts was a bother. Artie was worse. He was a life-long devotee of get-rich-quick schemes. He gave away thousands to grubstake prospectors on promises of a quick strike. When he gave up on farming he turned to insurance and formed a small company in Saskatoon. But he was better at minding the lakes and woods than minding his own shop, and through the years one of his partners managed to siphon off enough funds to bankrupt the firm. By the time my mother was eighteen or nineteen, the family was penniless. Artie Mullen was not destined to be a breadwinner.

Perhaps old Moneybags Sloan did what he could to keep the family afloat. There must have been a partial reconciliation of some sort, because he came west on occasion to see how his daughter was faring. He was a hit with little Burt, and my mother and Caddy found him amusing, if only for his stately, well-bred Irish accent and his lordly bearing at the supper table. If one of the children misbehaved he would intone, *The black pig is on your back.*

Caddy is no more reticent about recounting the past than she was about any other form of pleasure. She is my main source for all of this, a writer's dream come true: black sheep and irrepressible gossip. Caddy was the oldest and the rebel in the family. She saw domestic rules and table manners as mere challenges to her own independence. When Caddy misbehaved at the supper table, Old Man Sloan consigned her to the parlour where she had to sit facing a corner in the darkened room. Thus, the parlour and the black pig became Caddy's.

Along the walls of the parlour where other houses would display bookshelves or knick-knacks, Artie Mullen displayed his guns, including an old Colt .45 that Caddy had somehow learned to load during her disconsolate hours with the pig. Perhaps Caddy dreamed of saving her family from robbers, or scaring the Steinbrecker boys and their nasty dogs. The parlour shelves lining three sides of the room were also crowded with glass cases of mounted game birds, rodents, pets and varmints shot and skinned by Artie and little Burt.

It was Granny Mullen who christened their parlour the morgue. Her only defence in a household given over to the pleasures of the sporting life was for two decades to feign sickness. Whenever any crisis arose (a fight with Caddy or a bill collector or the first appearance of a daughter's menstrual blood), Florence would take to her bed. She was available to play the piano at the drop of a hat, but whenever reality began to impinge, *Mother is not herself today.* And so my mother became her own mother and everyone else's too, a self-appointed Cinderella in a house as feckless and song-filled and eccentric as a talking movie. And sister Caddy became something else entirely. She never learned to cook, she never married, she took as many lovers as she pleased, and, frequently intent upon her own misery, she never smiled for a camera.

When she was a teenager she would duck out of her chores, so my mother had to get supper and wash the dishes and take care of little Burt. Sometimes at night Caddy would wait till the house was quiet and slip out of bed. My mother would wake up and see her climbing out the window. Caddy would swear her to secrecy and my mother would have to endure the tension that gathered in her stomach, which was always the preliminary to another scene between Caddy and Florence. To my mother's dread, Caddy would slide from the second storey window onto the back porch roof, then drop to the ground to meet one of the local pariahs with a bottle of home brew and a bad reputation.

In the spring of 1924, a year before Mr Twill came along with his boater and his camera, when Caddy was sixteen, the black pig must have become a permanent fixture on her back. I am referring here to her involvement with the chinchillas, one of my grandfather's many ill-fated get-rich schemes. Sometimes it was prospectors, sometimes it was gadgets Artie would invent and try to sell, and sometimes it involved breeding animals in the garage at the back of their lot. In the spring of 1924, it was chinchillas. Artie had a plan to raise thousands of these rodents, slaughter them, skin them, and sell the little hides for what furriers in those days called Chinese mink. Perhaps my grandfather envisioned bevies of fashionable but purse-conscious ladies wearing coats from his own garage.

As usual, he enlisted the help of his daughters – unwisely, because Caddy fell in love with the unfortunate animals. Never known to be patient with children, Caddy was a sucker where animals were concerned. The chinchillas were not smelly rodents to her; they were especially small, short-eared rabbits and therefore even cuter than rabbits. They were squealy and cuddly and completely dependent upon their captors for food. Artie Mullen's chinchillas were the ultimate underdog, and underdogs of all description were Aunt Caddy's bailiwick.

On that warm spring morning, Caddy awoke to a sudden burst of squealing. It sounded to her like crying from a ward of aroused newborn infants. She leapt out of bed. She raced down the stairs and grabbed the Colt .45 from the wall of the parlour. She dashed outside in her nightie and bare feet and threw open the garage door.

The Steinbrecker dogs looked up from their carnage. Not one

chinchilla had survived the attack. These were big dogs, though I don't know what kind, and there must have been several. They looked at Caddy, perhaps wondering, as dogs must, what she had in mind.

She opened up on them. She claims to have missed every one, but I have my doubts. The dogs vaulted out of the garage and down the lane with Caddy not far behind and still shooting until she found herself with an empty revolver swearing a blue streak in front of the Steinbreckers' home.

She looked down the street and saw a group of men with lunch pails on their way to work. The men had come to a sudden halt. Caddy adjusted her nightie, flung her hair over her shoulder, and strode back into the house.

Right now my Aunt Caddy lies in a hospital bed suffering from fibroids in her lungs and a recent stroke. She can't return to her apartment in the old heart of Winnipeg. She must lie on her back and wait until a room in a nursing home becomes available, and I dare say she is visiting the past that my mother has no use for a great deal these days. Whenever I can, I come to Winnipeg to see her, but Winnipeg is a long way from Saskatoon.

My mother swears she doesn't remember the story about the routing of the Steinbreckers' dogs, that it's just another of her sister's wild fabrications. But once on a walk with Uncle Burt, the Alzheimer haze seemed to lift from his pale blue eyes, and he said, 'That Caddy. She sure drove those dogs out. She showed em. She couldn't shoot worth a hoot, but by the Jesus she must of nicked one or two.' And then, as though to verify his brief return to my world, he pointed at me and smiled and said my name. 'Dave.'

The smile is Granny Mullen's. As I mentioned, she was particularly big on smiles. They were exacted like tithes whenever her daddy visited the house in Saskatoon. Perhaps Florence believed that smiles could hide any number of hideous uncertainties that reality imposes on a family, but Caddy, with her self-inflicted Joan Crawford complex, would always be there to counter her mother's relentless innocence with a worldly frown. And now, as Caddy lies in a bed in the Misericordia Hospital while the life of Winnipeg drives off without her, and with the dull fibroid pain upon her lungs, she might indeed wonder if the black pig hasn't returned to sit on her back.

I'm writing this memoir as a charm or a prayer for my prodigal aunt and my eighty-three-year-old mother, the last of the Mullens. Before their picture was taken by Mr Twill, they moved through their days in Saskatoon as I do now. And after Mr Twill had taken his shot and driven away with the immortal credo that still brings a smile to Mum and Caddy's lips, *Sometimes I do and sometimes I don't,* the five Mullens carried on their secret lives unwitnessed and soon to be forgotten. Even their house is about to be forgotten.

A good memoir is worth a thousand photographs; it struggles to release the captives in the picture frame. But I wasn't there much to witness the lives of the Mullens before they suffered the fate of so many chinchillas. So here I am now, seven decades later, taking my best shot. Sometimes when I walk past the old house on a summer night I can almost hear my grandfather telling stories of terrible blizzards, problem bears, deer hunts and monster pike; or hear my grandmother singing *I'll take you home again Kathleen* … Sometimes I think I can write the black pig off Caddy's back. Sometimes I think I can give my mother a memory, or at least a reason for remembering.

Sometimes I do and sometimes I don't.

Acknowledgements

In the writing of 'Luce', I was assisted in my understanding of the Windigo pathology and the Windigo myths by reading John Robert Colombo (ed.), *Windigo: An Anthology of Fact and Fantastic Fiction*, published by Western Producer Prairie Books. Lines from 'Teddy Bears' Picnic', reproduced on page 177, c1907, 1947 Warner Bros. Inc. Copyrights renewed. All rights reserved. Used by permission. The excerpt on page 181 is reprinted with permission from Scott and Crossman, *Freshwater Fishes of Canada*, Bulletin 184, Fisheries Research Board of Canada, 1973. The excerpt on page 195 is from Milton's *Paradise Lost*, Book One. The excerpt on pages 220 and 221 is from Izaak Walton, Charles Cotton, *The Compleat Angler*. Lines from 'The Cremation of Sam McGee', reproduced on pages 222 to 225 are from *Songs of a Sourdough* (Toronto: Ryerson Press, 1907, reprinted 1956), pp. 57–61. Used by permission of the Estate of Robert W. Service.

About the Author

David Carpenter lives in Saskatoon. He is the author of a series of novellas, long stories, essays and novels. His novel, *Banjo Lessons,* was awarded the City of Edmonton Book Prize and 'The Ketzer' won Descant's Canadian Novella Contest. His most recent novel is *Niceman Cometh.* He spends time willingly in canoes.